Pearls
from Carol

CAROL RUGGIERO

BALBOA.PRESS
A DIVISION OF HAY HOUSE

Balboa Press books may be ordered through booksellers or by contacting:

Balboa Press
A Division of Hay House
1663 Liberty Drive
Bloomington, IN 47403
www.balboapress.com
844-682-1282

Because of the dynamic nature of the Internet, any web addresses or links contained in this book may have changed since publication and may no longer be valid. The views expressed in this work are solely those of the author and do not necessarily reflect the views of the publisher, and the publisher hereby disclaims any responsibility for them.

The author of this book does not dispense medical advice or prescribe the use of any technique as a form of treatment for physical, emotional, or medical problems without the advice of a physician, either directly or indirectly. The intent of the author is only to offer information of a general nature to help you in your quest for emotional and spiritual well-being. In the event you use any of the information in this book for yourself, which is your constitutional right, the author and the publisher assume no responsibility for your actions.

Any people depicted in stock imagery provided by Getty Images are models, and such images are being used for illustrative purposes only. Certain stock imagery © Getty Images.

Print information available on the last page.

ISBN: 978-1-9822-5609-8 (sc)
ISBN: 978-1-9822-5608-1 (hc)
ISBN: 978-1-9822-5646-3 (e)

Library of Congress Control Number: 2020920073

Balboa Press rev. date: 10/14/2020

This little volume has been both written by and is dedicated to my late wife, Carol Ann Ruggiero

For twenty years she lovingly attended and wrote
For a writing group known as "Writers Unlimited."

These are her words, her thoughts, her humorous outlooks on life.

This book is meant to be enjoyed by anyone of any age or social background. It is real and utterly without pretense. The author possessed no hidden agenda nor did she ever aspire to be anything but what she which was a genuine lady.

Her life experiences endowed her with a healthy respect for humanity along with a large dose of common sense and humor.

This book can be read cover to cover but it also can be read and savored in small dosses over a long period of time. Each story centers on one brief moment. Each story is a tiny world of its own.

Early on, Carol was taught to "show" not just tell. This lesson well learned, is the key to understanding and enjoying "Pearls from Carol"

It is my firm hope that you the reader will both enjoy and pass on these pages for the enjoyment of many. This is a timeless gem.

In our troubled, complex and anxiety ridden society this book will provide many a smile and no small amount of comfort.

Albert J. Ruggiero

CONTENTS

THE EMOTIONAL TEA PARTY

They have been with me throughout my life. Never invited, always controlling and mightier than myself.

This is the first time I will see them together. I will be able to observe their interactions. Some have never seen each other. Others go hand-in-hand, visiting me when they please and leaving only when they decide their visit is over. And me, knowing, always knowing, they will visit again.

The tea table is lavishly set with silver tea service, china cups, lacey linens, fragrant flowers, trays of sprinkled cookies and little cakes with pastel icing. I have changed the seating arrangement several times. The only placecard not moved is my own, at the head of the table where I will pour and try to be polite to those I wish were not here.

"Who will be the first to arrive?" I wonder. My question is quickly answered as I see Greed coming up the garden path. Of course! Who else? She must always be first. She doesn't frighten me at all. She is the one who visits me the least and I am grateful for that. Behind her comes Confusion, not knowing which way to go but always wanting to do the right thing. I watch her as she trips and falls becoming disoriented as she tries to follow the path. Next, come the twins dressed in their bright green outfits accenting their glazing green eyes. Yes, they are Jealousy and Envy. They look so much alike and yet there is a slight difference in their appearance. They will watch the others closely and never find satisfaction in who they are or what they have, only and always wanting what is not theirs to have.

Love comes unexpectedly, next. Her starry eyes, moist with tears will be seated between Happiness and Sadness. She is much stronger than most of the guests but at the same time, very tender and easily hurt.

Hate is next, dragging Rage and Anger, chained to her scarlet garment. She comes when outrageous injustice has been done. She comes when demons laugh and get their way and leave me beaten, hopeless and in despair.

Many, many more fill the chairs around the enormous tea table. Only two are empty now. One, to my immediate right as close to me as possible. The other the farthest away, as I dread her coming. She is Grief. She is the strongest of all. I watch her now coming up the path dragging her crippled legs, pulling her deformed body inch by inch as I feel Fear reaching out for me. Her party dress is grey and her complexion is ashen, as she looks at me with yellowish eyes and remembers the sounds of wretched wailing and weeping. She rejoices as she tries to take my mind, my body and my inner soul. Stay away Grief! Drink your tea, eat your cake and go!

The last guest, dressed in brilliant white is my intimate friend. Her name is Peace. She is the most beautiful. She pops in and out of my life. She is the one I need the most. She and only she is the one I want with me through eternity. She is the only one I embrace and beg to stay with me long after this emotional tea party has ended.

AUTOBIOGRAPHICAL

Beaver Town

It was Saturday and I was glad there was no school. The weatherman promised a sunny day. I was anxious to go out and play but remembered a homework assignment I had to work on first. My third grade teacher listed famous explorers on the blackboard instructing the class to choose and write a report. I chose Meriwether Lewis and William Clark only because I hoped the name "Meriwether" belonged to a girl. I believed girls would have made great explorers. So why weren't there any?

I flipped through the encyclopedia until I came to a picture of Lewis and Clark, disappointed to see that Meriwether was not a girl. I studied the picture of two men wearing buckskin jackets and thick beaver fur hats. I turned the page. My eyes widened when I saw Sacajawea. Traveling with Lewis and Clark, the young Indian squaw acted as interpreter and guide, stopping only to give birth half way through the expedition. "Let's see Meriwether top that one." I thought. I finished the report and now wanted to be Sacajawea.

I pulled on high boots and searched for a feather. Plucking one from Mom's new hat I stuck it in my hair. I would put it back after the expedition. I continued preparing for the journey, squeezing peanut butter sandwiches into a brown paper bag. I traveled west, toward the woods. The path I followed disappeared and the ground became soggy. Curling my toes inside my boots I stood on a narrow riverbank looking at domes of piled sticks. I had discovered "Beaver Town" (the name I gave the community of eager rodents.)

I never saw a beaver close up but recognized the animal from the Ipana toothpaste commercials.

The largest smacked his wide tail on top of the water warning his friends that Sacajawea was watching. All dove under except the one who seemed to be the mayor. He swam closer. I saw his large, yellow teeth. I sang "brush-a-brush-a brush-a". He must have liked the tune because he was almost out of the water now. "Shall I run?" I thought. "What would Sacajawea do?"

I reached into the bag and flung a peanut butter sandwich. The mayor sniffed, grabbed and pulled it under a pile of twigs. Others now popped their heads above the water. It seemed Sacajawea had made new friends. I thought of the picture of her papoose wrapped in beaver fur. "Did the cute little beavers unzip their coats and offer them to the Indian squaw?" I thought. When reality hit me I shook my head and cried, "oh, no. Not Sacajawea." Mom's feather fell from my hair and floated downstream.

I returned home featherless but determined to find a new explorer to admire. I reached once again for the encyclopedia. A picture of Amelia Earhart filled the page.

On my next visit to Beaver Town, I flew in - arms stretched, a bag of peanut butter sandwiches dangling from my left wing as I got an aerial view.

Beaver Town no longer exists. The land was cleared in the early 50s for housing. I will always remember the peaceful stream and the beavers.

Mr. Leonard's Quotes

From my bedroom window I could see him walking up the steep hill coming home from work. I barely gave him time to wash and have dinner before I was at his door.

Mr. Leonard was not only my neighbor. He was my good friend. We enjoyed each other's company despite our age difference, I nine, he an old fifty-two.

"Come in my friend," he greeted. "You are just in time for tea. I will ask my wife to serve our tea in the fine china cups this evening. This is to be a special night. I will read to you 'Evangeline'."

Mrs. Leonard poured the tea handing her husband a little white pill. I felt my forehead wrinkle.

"It helps my heart," he said. "Nothing to worry about."

He asked his wife to join us but she said she had unfinished business in the kitchen. Before leaving she reached into her apron pocket, handed me a yellow M&M and said, "For your heart, my dear."

Mr. Leonard in his rocker and I crossed-legged on the floor began. "This is the forest primeval..."

Weeks later we closed the book. He threw his head back and laughed. "Now we will close our eyes and listen to 'Pagliacci'."

As summer days grew longer, I would find him under the large weeping willow with his easel and bright colors or his sketchpad and charcoal. I parted the wispy branches as he said, "hello my friend. You are just in time for a frosty glass of tea. Would you like to learn to draw?"

Looking at the magenta and purple palette I said, "I would rather paint."

"Do not be in such a hurry. You must first learn to draw. Remember to draw what you see. Draw what is, not what should be. Soon I will introduce you to the easel."

I agreed. "My first picture will be of you."

He laughed. "If you paint me without the scars and wrinkles I will not pay you a shilling."

Years later, I discovered this to be a quote from Oliver Cromwell to an artist about to paint his portrait in the year 1650.

Mr. Leonard studied my work, patted the top of my head and said, "I too am a painter." (A quote from Antonio Correggio on seeing Raphael's 'Saint Cecilia'.)

During the next few years we discussed life and oh yes, even death. One day he told me about the sinking of the Lusitania torpedoed by the Germans in 1915. He quoted Charles Frohman's last words, "Why fear death? It is the most beautiful adventure in life."

On a cold January night, from my bedroom window I waited for Mr. Leonard to come over the hill. It was sleeting and I wondered if he remembered to take his large black umbrella. It didn't matter. He did not come home that night. Mr. Leonard died of a massive heart attack while at work.

I was his friend, but I did not cry. Instead, I remembered he was on the most beautiful adventure in life.

I did not cry - until today.

Who Do You Look Like ?

As a child my mother always said I pouted like Shirley Temple but looked and acted more like Margaret O'Brien.

As a teenager, a neighbor told me I looked like Lana Turner. I did have blond hair, but trust me-I never looked like Lana Turner.

In the 60's my favorite aunt wrote to me saying, "I can never look at Jacqueline Kennedy without thinking of you."

My best friend recently said, "You remind me of Gena Roland."

I can not see that at all, but what a great compliment. Another friend said I resemble Jane Seymour. I only hope she meant the actress and not Henry VIII wife.

I always thought I looked like Nancy Walker who you may remember from the Bounty Towels commercials. She also played the housekeeper on MacMillan and Wife.

Today when I look into the mirror I say, "Poor Uncle Wiggly" because I know I look like that decrepit old rabbit.

As a child, I always enjoyed visiting my grandmother. She wore bright colorful dresses and sparkely clips in her hair. She also loved music.

In the center of her parlor stood a Victrola. On the inside lid was a picture of a dog. The label read, "His master's voice." I loved the dog and the music that came out of the horn when my grandmother turned the crank.

She rolled up the rug and we danced together. She laughed as my hair fell across my eyes each time she twirled me. She reached into her hair and pulled out a glittery hair pin and clipped my hair back.

That night I removed the treasured hair clip and put it in a box along with other barrettes. Through the years the barrettes have disappeared but I saved Grandmother's hair clip along with a wonderful memory.

A Holiday Amber Moment

Learning the words to "America the Beautiful" I asked Miss Norling, my third grade grade teacher, "What are 'amber' waves of grain?"

She answered, "Amber is a beautiful word used to describe the color yellow."

Years later, 'amber' lost its beauty as I discovered amber to be brownish-yellow, oozing, fossil resin.

Today, amber is merely the center color of a traffic light. I never know whether to brake or accelerate. I usually choose the latter and believe me, it is not an amber moment.

To capture my amber moment, I must return to Miss Norling's third grade classroom. We no longer sat alphabetically and Leonard Miller chose to sit next to me as we sang about the amber waves of grain.

Trying to impress me he said, "I have a cat with amber eyes." Without taking a breath he added, "Do you want to go steady?"

"Sure." I answered, not knowing what going steady meant. I thought it had something to do with the cat with the amber eyes.

Going steady took place on Tuesday and by Thursday we were engaged. Leonard slipped a piece of twisted leather on my finger and proudly announced he made it in cub scouts. The leather tightened and I sat with a blue finger while we rehearsed for our holiday pageant.

By dinnertime, I forgot about being engaged when my parents asked if anything exciting happened in school. "I was chosen to be the Christmas angel." I answered.

A different conversation was going on at Leonard's dinner table. Somewhere between the soup and the salad, he broke the news of our engagement.

The next day I took my place next to my fiancée. He told me his mother said I was a lovely girl but we could not marry because we were of different faiths. But we could be good friends forever. Relieved, I handed him the piece of leather and watched the color return to my finger.

Once again rehearsing, Leonard was hoping to sing what he called 'The Angel Song' while the angel was lowered by cable to the stage. At eight years old he had a wonderful voice and could hit notes higher than Janette MacDonald.

Since Miss Norling was combining Hanukka and Christmas celebrations Leonard was chosen to be the third candle on the menorah. On cue, the disappointed candle would step forward and explain to the audience what it represented. I was proud of the third candle when it spoke.

Strapping on my leather harness, I wondered why all this leather was coming into my life lately. The Magi, dressed in their father's bathrobes toyed with my wings until my cue.

The audience "oohed" as an amber colored spotlight followed the angel to the manger. I was not balancing well as in rehearsal. I heard tittering and realized the three wise guys had turned my wings upside down and I was having difficulty landing. Strange and embarrassing sounds were coming from the angel. It was then the third candle stepped forward with angelic voice and sang, "Hark the Carol Angel Sings!" It will always be my amber moment.

A Place That Gives Me The Creeps

I don't like being underground. Tunnels and subways give me the creeps.

One summer my husband and I visited Howe's Caverns in New York state. We boarded an elevator with a tour guide. The elevator descended one hundred and fifty six feet below the earth's surface. The doors opened to a prehistoric cavern 6 million years in the making.

The temperature remains at 56 degrees year round, yet it is uncomfortable because the humidity is about 75%.

As my eyes adjusted to the underworld sounds echoed from the walls. Stalagmites rose from the ground and long icicles dripped from the ceiling.

The tour guide turned off what little light we had to show us how the the cave was. In the darkness I thought of bats. The entire ordeal gave me the creeps. That's when I decided I will never go underground again. Well, almost never.

The Carpet Bag

My grandmother sailed from Italy to America carrying a suitcase called a carpet bag. It had black wooden handles and was made of thick maroon colored carpeting.

She clutched the bag tightly during her detainment at Ellis Island. It held all her worldly possessions – a hair brush, a pair of shoes, a prayer book and enough money to purchase a small plot of farmland in Connecticut where she raised chickens and sold eggs. During this time she also raised six children – the youngest, my mother.

When she was no longer able to manage the farm she moved in with my parents. My room was directly across the hall from hers and many times I watched her hold the empty carpet bag and run her hands over the worn fabric.

To her the bag was never empty – it was filled with memories.

AWAY IN THE MANGER
(A Christmas memory)

It was the year I received my first pair of single-bladed ice skates. Threaded through the laces silver and red bells jingled.

It was also the year the exclusive Brooklawn Country Club opened its gates to neighborhood children. Twinkling white lights surrounded a skating pond.

I sat on the icy bank struggling with my new skates. I wore two pair of socks but pulled the thick red pair off stuffing them into my pocket. The skates now slid on.

Pretending to be Sonja Henie gliding on the ice, I skated on my ankles looking more like Jerry Lewis.

The sun was going down and the temperature was dropping. When I could no longer feel my feet I knew it was time for the long walk home. I no longer wore skates but could still feel the cold blades against my painful feet. I threw the jingling skates over my shoulder and wondered how I would ever make it home.

About half way, Our Lady of Assumption Church appeared. I decided to go in hoping to find warm. The church was dark and cold except for a glowing nativity scene on the altar. The pain in my feet worsened as I looked at the baby Jesus swaddled in a blanket. His bare feet stuck out. My bottom lip quivered and I began softly singing 'Away In The Manger'. Tears streamed down my face. "Dear Jesus, please warm my feet so I can continue my journey home."

I looked at the Virgin Mary with Joseph beside her. The bare-foot child gazed toward them feeling safe and warm. I ached for my mother and father.

My skates echoed against the wooden pew as I picked them up and hobbled up the aisle and out the heavy church door.

One red sock fell from my pocket and stuck to the icy steps. Once again the pain in my feet brought tears and my nose was running, I made use of the odd red sock.

I found my mother making soup and Dad stoking the wood fire. They hardly noticed me until my skates fell hard and spoke.

Dad rushed me toward the fire and pulled off my frozen socks. Mother wrapped me in a warm blanket. Just like the baby Jesus-my feet stuck out. I hummed 'Away In The Manger' as I sipped hot soup and remembered to thank the holy family.

Merry Christmas Everyone

THE WRONG ROOM

Every summer my husband and I toured, traced and researched the Civil War.

Of course, this meant traveling hundreds of miles south. As I-95 became more brutal, we agreed it was time to travel by train.

Am-Track advertised their new "Luxury Train" promising an enjoyable and relaxing trip. Only round-trip tickets were sold with the understanding return dates were not to be changed.

A coachman ushered us to comfortable seats and handled our luggage. He told us of the dining car and game room. He also told us smoking was allowed in every car- fortunately or unfortunately, this was a big plus for me.

Dinner that evening was more than expected, white linen cloths, fine china, even a fresh rose. Most surprising, the water in the crystal stemware didn't move as the train wound its way along the tracks.

After dinner we played scrabble, card games and enjoyed the company of new friends, while viewing a panoramic countryside.

We got off the train in South Carolina commenting on the unpredicted rain. That was Monday and by Tuesday the rain carried high winds. Wednesday brought more rain and Thursday was worse.

Trudging knee-deep in red mud across battlefields I announced, I wanted to go home.

My husband joked, "Be a brave soldier. This is what is was like for the confederate army."

I began whistling Dixie but noticed I was the only rebel wearing a babuska white backsliding into a trench.

"That's it. We're going home." I said as my husband pulled me out of the crator.

"Let me remind you," he said, "We will have to sacrifice our round trip tickets. Also no dining car you know."

"I don't care. Call the station."

Holding the phone he said, "The next train out is at 2 o'clock."

"Good." I said. "We'll have lunch before we board."

I felt relieved until he said, "that's 2 a.m."

In some god-forsaken town in Georgia at 2 a.m. we boarded a broken down locomotive. Through the magnified sound of rain against the train I was certain I heard mooing a few cars away.

We dragged our luggage through narrow aisles and sat on torn upholstery. There was nothing to do except pick batting from our clothes and count the hours to New Haven. The only reading material was directly in front of me, "No smoking in this car."

The conductor punched the wet and wilted tickets as I asked, "Where can I smoke."

He snapped, "Four cars back."

"I'll be with the cows for awhile." I said to my husband and staggered down the aisle. Grabbing seats and falling against passengers I took three steps forward and two back while chanting, "Excuse me, pardon me, so sorry."

Climbing a grade, a door slid open. I saw overstuffed chairs and ashtrays bolted to the floor. I fell into the first chair and lit up. Leaning back I looked straight ahead at a lathered face staring back at me from a mirror. Another man came from behind a door fiddling with his zipper. I couldn't decide, nor did I care if it was half up or half down.

"What a ridiculous smoking car." I thought as a third man popped in and then out as if wearing springs on his shoes. He returned with the conductor.

Hands on hips he said, "Madam, one of us is in the wrong room."

I nonchalantly crushed the cigarette and graciously left.

COWBOYS

My early years were spent watching cowboys on T.V. The king of the cowboys was Roy Rogers. He sang "Happy Trails to You" along with Dale Eavans who wrote the song. Although Roy had a pleasant voice it was Gene Autry who was called the singing cowboy. Hopalong Cassidy was called "Hoppy" by all the kids. Hoppy was the reason we all ate wonder bread and carried metal lunch boxes with his picture on the lid.

But at this young age I wasn't interested in the cowboys - instead I fell in love with their horses.

Trigger, the most famous was a beautiful golden palamino. He was smart and liked to show off in front of the camera. Gene Autry sat in the saddle on champion, another beautiful horse – and who could forget Hoppy's white horse Topper?

The Lone Ranger who was not considered a cowboy yelled "Hi You Silver" as Silver reared on his hind legs.

As a teenager a T.V. program called "Bonanza" took over the screen. Rancher Ben Cartwright had three cowboy sons. When I saw his youngest son Little Joe, played by the handsome Michael Landon, I no longer cared about horses – I just wanted to ride off into the sunset with that cowboy!

PONDER A SUPERSTITION

He came into my life on Friday the thirteenth. It was obvious he was a stray and having a bad kittenhood. It could very well be, some superstitious individual dropped him off because of his jet-black color. He had large yellow eyes and at times resembled an owl. Animal lover that I am, I took him in. He was a pathetic sight and it was evident - he was starving. Of course, I didn't have any cat food, so I scrambled up some eggs and opened a can of tuna. He cleaned his plate and started to purr. "Your welcome." I said as he brushed up against me. I took him to the Vet. for all the necessary things. While he was being neutered, I shopped for his layette. I picked him up that evening at the animal hospital and carried a large bag full of cat stuff!

Together we decided on a name for him. I christened him "Friday." For the next seventeen years, "Friday" was my faithful friend. He was always there to greet me when I would get home from work. When I was sick he would somehow give me comfort. Once we moved and I was concerned as to how he would adjust to his new environment. "Home is where you are." He purred. How could one ever believe, when a black cat crosses your path.

EXCITE YOUR SENSES TODAY

It was not an exciting day for my senses until I reached for my favorite book of poems. I turned to Longfellow's "THE WRECK OF THE HESPERUS" and all those sleepy senses stood at attention. No one sets a story to poetry better than Henry Wadsworth Longfellow.

He begins -

IT WAS THE SCHOONER HESPERUS

THAT SAILED THE WINTRY SEA

AND THE SKIPPER HAD TAKEN HIS LITTLE DAUGHTER

TO BEAR HIM COMPANY.

You know, this guy is a jerk! He takes a young kid out on a cold wintery day on a boat knowing a storm is coming. He should begin to get a clue when the smoke from his pipe starts blowing, "Now west, now south." Even an old sailor tells him, "I fear a hurricane." But oh no, this skipper with the big ego tries to show his daughter what a terrific seaman he is. The poor kid is trembling in her boots (if she had boots), while he wraps her in his coat to keep her warm against the stinging winds. If that isn't bad enough, it starts to dawn on him that he bit of more than he can chew, so he ties the kid to the mast. She still trusts him at this point although questions the sounds of the bells and fog horns. Of course, fool that

"They Also Serve who only STAND AND WAIT"

My mother often told me stories of women working in defense plants during W.W.II. Women waiting for news from their sons and husbands. If one got a letter, she would bring it in to read while the others flocked around. They would hug each other and cry.

The women tried to entertain each other by telling stories and jokes during the long working hours. Laughter occupied their minds while the worrying continued.

The laughter would cease and the assembly line would shut down when they would see an Army official in the factory. Many women fainted if he seemed to walk toward them. The wretched wailing echoed through the plant as the officer would begin, "I regret to inform you..."

The assembly line would be one woman short the next day and the others would work harder to get the product out to the service men.

I think I would rather be serving in action duty than to wait and worry.

John Milton should have said, "They also serve who stand and wait." The word "only" makes it sounds like they <u>merely</u> wait.

THE MOST INFLUENTIAL BOOK

Working in a school library as a volunteer, there was never time for boredom. I would help Mrs. Wineberg, the librarian settle the young children down for story time. I loved to watch their eyes widen as Mrs. Wineburg read to them and accomplish her goal. They wanted to be able to read themselves. She would smile at me as the children would answer each other's questions about the story. When the older children quietly went to the shelves looking for books to help them with an assignment or book report, I found they were still confused as to how to use the Dewey Decimal System. It was my job to explain the system and to also remind them the importance of placing the book back I and it's proper place.

One morning I was repairing book spines as I glanced toward the biography section. It was easy to see if they were in order as they were listed alphabetically, according to the persons name. It was just about then, I decided that I would like to challenge myself to read every biography on the well stocked shelves. The first book was the story of Hank Aaron. I almost gave up the challenge because baseball didn't interest me at all. I did learn what a superior ballplayer Aaron was but I couldn't wait to finish the book and move on. I plowed through the biographies spending extra time with Amelia Earhart. Years later I named a pet bird "Amelia" in her honor.

"MOTTO"

"PLAN AHEAD" was always my motto. I mapped out every step of my life and tried to follow the steps in order. I always knew exactly what was suppose to happen. Never spontaneous behavior for me! The only problem was I only had "PLAN A" and that lead to many disappointments. I changed my motto to "BE PREPARED." I didn't think the boy scouts would mind since I would be taking their advice. I now developed "PLAN B". Still, things never went as planned. When I got up to "PLAN P" and things weren't going according to plan, I changed my motto. My new motto is "ONE DAY AT A TIME." This motto makes more sense, doesn't it? Yes, I still plan ahead but I don't get upset when plans fail. I figure, it wasn't meant to be. The Lord has other plans for me. I can't argue with that! I now realize my itinerary is His plan. He calls it "PLAN A". It works every time!

WRITE LETTER TO 10 YR. OLD SELF

Dear Carol,

Happy tenth birthday. It's hard to believe you will be going into the fifth grade. The red boots and matching umbrella were one of your favorite birthday gifts and because I know you so well, I know you will not want to get them wet. When it rains you will close the umbrella and keep it under your coat. The pristine boots will also stay dry as you walk home barefooted.

Everything must be perfect for you and I now know, you will not change. You will plan every step of your life and anxiety will make you move too fast. I must admit you are a responsible child and that will continue but unfortunately your perfect plans will crumble. The world is not a perfect place and you will all too soon realize this. Listen carefully to Mrs. Kaye, your new fifth grade teacher as she has her class recite "The Lord is My Shepard" everyday. The twenty-third psalm will make you understand that there <u>is</u> a perfect place.

Slow down Carol. Enjoy your unperfect life on earth and please little ten year old, stay with me always. You are so much fun.

With love,

from your adult self

always, Carol

GOOD FENCES MAKE GOOD NEIGHBORS

When I moved into my new home eighteen years ago, there was a lovely hedge on the property line dividing the back yards. This wonderful privacy was taken away when new backyard neighbors moved in and decided to remove the hedge. I was now looking at three children. That's nice. Two dogs. I like dogs. Three cats. Cats are cute. Two boats, oh dear. A tractor, oh my. A very large above ground pool complete with ladder and a high diving board. A car with no plates, another tractor, a large canvas tent next to a swing set and jungle gym, a bar-be-que area with lights on poles and an inground pond for frogs and other reptiles. Barnum and Bailey had arrived!

When I asked "Nancy" why she had taken down the hedge she said it made the yard look cluttered. "Are you putting up a fence?" I hopefully asked. "I'm not planning on it." She answered. "Well, I am" I said.

I wanted to put up a very high fence but zoning would not allow anything higher than six feet. So a hundred feet of six foot high fence was installed. Quite an expense but it would be worth it. The two dogs learned quickly to tunnel under the fence and visited me everyday. I couldn't blame them! Nancy would yell, "Could you send Samson and Delilah home please." I now bought a hundred feet of scalloped concrete blocks and ran them along the bottom of the fence. Another expense and back breaking work but it was worth it.

The fence weathered in a few years but was strong and sturdy and in good condition. Then Nancy's pool let go. Over ten thousand gallons of water came rushing toward me taking the fence, my prized azaleas, the top soil and red mulch. The force was so strong it took all the concrete blocks down stream as if they were made of cardboard. The three ring circus I had remembered had gotten even larger and there, was Samson and Deliah dog-paddling for dear life. I called Nancy. "Your pool let go and I have a lot of damage here." "Are Samson and Delilah over there?" She asked. "Yes they are." I smiled through clenched teeth.

My sane neighbor, to the left of me helped me carry all the blocks back and rake up the debris. My only thoughts were to put up another fence quickly. Another huge expense but it would be worth it. Nancy just told me they are getting a new pool. "Oh great, it will keep the fence company in business."

The neighbor who helped me clean up asked if he could have the old one. Don't ask me what he's going to do with it but I gave it to him saying, "Good fences make good neighbors!"

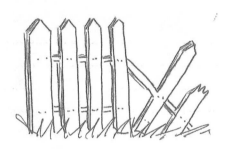

THIS IS
"FEATHERS"

POINT OF VIEW FROM MY PET

"Here she comes - here she comes. I can hear her slippered feet coming down the hall. I think I'll let out an ear piercing scream. That'll wake her up. I can't believe she's ignoring a beautiful parrot like me. She's just jealous. She looks like hell and I have my beautiful red and green suit on with the yellow lining under my wings. Now she's putting up the coffee. I'm glad I don't drink caffeine. That's why I'll live to be over a hundred years old." She finally says, "Good Morning feathers. Did you have nice bird dreams?" I run back and forth, back and forth on my perch and squawk as loudly as I can. Although I'm not a talking parrot I do have a three syllable sound that sounds like I'm saying, "Full of grease - full of grease." This sound is so loud it actually hurts her ears but that doesn't stop me. "Your such a bad egg." She tells me.

Now she's washing the kitchen floor. I wonder when she will wash my floor. I worked very hard getting it in this filthy condition. "You're next" she says. My seed cup gets washed and filled with fresh seed, a piece of apple and some carrot. My water cup is washed and filled with clean water and now my paper will be changed. She used to use newspaper and I would enjoy the comics but she decided I was getting black from the newspaper print. My reading is now limited to "Reynolds freezer paper, plastic coated." "O.K. you're nice and clean." She beams.

"I guess I'll take my bath now." I say, as the water goes flying everywhere and my cage is once again a complete mess. "Damn you Feathers." She says as she begins the process over again. "Change the water, change the paper." She yells.

"Oh come on, you can yell louder than that. Try this, "Full of grease, full of grease!"

FAVORITE TOY

Christmas was just a few days away when my father asked me what I was hoping Santa would bring me this year. Without hesitation I answered, "a sled!"

"Wouldn't you rather have an original John Nagy art set?" Every year Santa never failed to bring me paints, colored pencils and sketching paper. I usually ended up frustrated trying to draw like Norman Rockwell, even <u>with</u> John Nagy's easy instructions.

While Mom busied herself in the kitchen, Dad and I talked. "How are you doing with your Arithmetic?" I felt a quiz coming. He asked, "How old will you be in the year 2000?" I didn't know. I didn't even care. I couldn't comprehend 1950 was near. "You will see the new millennium" he said "but I will be gone." I wondered where he was going. I wanted to stop the arithmetic question so I changed the subject to, "Maybe I would like a John Nagy art set, but I really would rather have a sled."

Needless to say on Christmas morning a new sled was under the tree. I named him "Flyer" and he was my best friend. Being an only child I not only named everything, I also talked to everything. Flyer and I would go everywhere together for years to come. From sun up to sundown we slid down every hillside in the area. Each night I dried his runners. Then with waxed paper I would scrub on his blades. We would always be ready for any challenge. No one could beat us in a downhill race. "Go Flyer, go faster, faster." I would always congratulate him for winning - and we always won!

One day my father got the idea to burn my initials into Flyer. It was painful to watch and I hoped it wasn't hurting his oak body or his lacquered finish. When the wood burning tool was cool and Flyer's underbelly stopped smoldering, I gave him a trial run. He ran as well as ever and I was relieved.

The next morning was a sheet of ice. I had trouble standing up as

I pulled the sled up the steepest hill. We flew down the slope, Flyers runners on top of the ice. This was record breaking speed and I was becoming frightened as I saw the brick wall coming closer. I could no longer steer. Instinct made me turn my head as we crashed. I felt excruciating pain in my left ear. It hurt so much I could not cry. "Flyer where are you?" I said holding my ear. "I killed him." I thought when I saw him laying on his back, runners facing the sky. I pulled him home and talked to him all the way.

I never knew what had happened to Flyer after that. I only knew we had been through a lot together.

This year I received a Christmas card from my cousin and he wrote, "cleaning out fifty years of accumulation at my Mother's house. Your sled is in the basement. As I read I whispered, "Flyer, Flyer" and the memories came flooding back.

THEME SONG

My father's favorite Disney movie was "Pinochio" and of course he took me to see it. Jiminy Cricket gave me the creeps. He wasn't a cute little bunny or a fluffy gray kitten. He was a bug and I hated bugs! My father explained to me that the cricket was Pinochio's conscience. At the time I didn't know what a conscience was, but I was sure it couldn't be a bug. All the way home Dad sang, "When you wish upon a star." I just kept picturing that greenish colored insect.

Whenever I would ask for something extravagant or something impossible to attain, my dad would say, "Wish upon a star" and then he would add, "makes no difference who you are." So I started to wish upon a star, after looking at the night sky and selecting my favorite one.

That was the year my class went on a field trip to the planetarium and that is where I learned I had been wishing on Venus. When you wish upon a planet, your dreams do not come true!

"When you wish upon a star has been and always will be my theme song. I can still hear that darn cricket hitting that high note!

"KEEP YOUR EYE ON THE PRIZE"

As I approached my grandmother's front door I could hear the sound of the mandolin. This was the mandolin she carried from Italy and it was her prized possession. It was a beautiful looking instrument and it made the loveliest sound as she used the ivory pick on the strings. My grandmother would hear me at the door and squeal with delight. She would pinch my cheek and say something that sounded to me like "quan-a-si bella." "Come, I will play a song for you" she would say. She would explain the words to "O Sole Mio" as she played. This was long before Elvis had hit with the English version. When she played "Oh, Marie" and sang the words, it sounded like "Weigh Mahdu!" It was wonderful! I was fascinated watching her left hand run up and down the neck of the mandolin as her right hand picked the strings. It was like trying to rub your stomach and pat your head at the same time.

When I got to be about seven years old, (Yes, she was still pinching my checks) she decided it was time for me to learn to play. She positioned me and it was the first time I <u>felt</u> the prized mandolin. I stretched my little fingers as she showed me how to change chords. After many of grandma's lessons I learned to play.

"When I die, the mandolin will be yours."

THE MOST INFLUENTIAL BOOK

Working in a school library as a volunteer, there was never time for boredom. I would help Mrs. Wineberg, the librarian settle the young children down for story time. I loved to watch their eyes widen as Mrs. Wineburg read to them and accomplish her goal. They wanted to be able to read themselves. She would smile at me as the children would answer each other's questions about the story. When the older children quietly went to the shelves looking for books to help them with an assignment or book report, I found they were still confused as to how to use the Dewey Decimal System. It was my job to explain the system and to also remind them the importance of placing the book back I and it's proper place.

One morning I was repairing book spines as I glanced toward the biography section. It was easy to see if they were in order as they were listed alphabetically, according to the persons name. It was just about then, I decided that I would like to challenge myself to read every biography on the well stocked shelves. The first book was the story of Hank Aaron. I almost gave up the challenge because baseball didn't interest me at all. I did learn what a superior ballplayer Aaron was but I couldn't wait to finish the book and move on. I plowed through the biographies spending extra time with Amelia Earhart. Years later I named a pet bird "Amelia" in her honor. After many months I now reached for the large gray covered book. It's title read, "LEE, ROBERT E." Sure, I knew of Robert E. Lee - but did I really? This book led me to researching the civil war because I needed to learn more about the general. I went to all neighboring libraries and read everything I could get my hands on about this fine man. I was infatuated with him!

Years later I was able to travel, with my husband, visiting all the civil war battlefields. We spent time in Fredericksburg, Petersburg,

Richmond, Gettysburg, Charlottesville and so many more historic districts, too numerous to mention.

We ended our journey at Appomattox. I felt closer to Lee than ever as I walk down the same road he did as he led Traveller to the courthouse, where he surrendered to Grant.

As we walked I noticed a young boy eating a peach on the porch of a farm house. He was helping re-enact that famous day. He yelled to me, "Get off the road. Bobby Lee is coming." My great imagination allowed me to hear Traveller's hoofs plodding through the mud. I was overwhelmed. I could not turn around. What could I possibly say to the General? I did not want him to see the tears streaming down my face. Yes, it took a book in an elementary school for me to realize what a fine gentleman Robert E. Lee was and it inspired me to write the following poem.

TRAVELLER

ATOP OF ME SITS BOBBY LEE.
A FINER MAN WILL NEVER BE.
I'M SO PROUD HE'S CHOSEN ME
OF ALL IN HIS FINE CAVALRY.
BOTH OUR COATS CONFEDERATE GRAY,
WE SHARE The BATTLES DAY BY DAY.
HE TALKS TO ME, I HEAR HIM PRAY.
ON TO GETTYSBURG TODAY.
THE WAR IS DONE.
THE NORTH HAS WON.
THOUGH SAD, HE MOUNTS WITH PRIDE.
WE RODE TO APPOMATTOX
THE DAY THE GENERAL CRIED.
BEHIND THE CASKET MY GAIT NOW SLOW,
I HEAR HIS VOICE, I MISS HIM SO.
THERE IS A RESTING PLACE FOR ME.
I WILL SOON BE NEXT TO HE.
THAT IS WHERE I LONG TO STAY,
IN MY COAT CONFEDERATE GRAY,
WITH MY ROBERT E. LEE.

JOHNNIE TWO CORKS

His name was Jonathan Corks II but he was known to the world of gamblers as "Johnnie Two Corks." He carried two lucky corks in his vest pocket at all times.

He gambled with only the wealthiest of men (kings, rajahs, dukes, earls and barons) all, hoping to beat the famous Johnnie Two Corks. But the corks never failed and he carried home gold, silver and precious jewels from around the world.

While playing stud poker in the West Indies, his opponent wagered tons of saffron and rare spices. Johnnie raised the bet holding three queens. His opponent called the bet with a promissory note. It read, "One manservant named Otley."

Johnnie Two Corks turned over the fourth queen and Otley had a new master. Sadly but obediently, Otley followed Johnnie to his private plane destined for the Cork Estate.

At the mansion mornings began with Otley carrying Johnnie's breakfast on a silver tray. The first order was always the same. "Don't forget to put the corks in my pocket."

After years of investigation Jonathan Corks II was declared legally dead. His body never found and his disappearance remained a mystery. Although I did not remember him, he remembered me. Through his last will and testament I was traced proving to be his last living relative. I was now the owner of the Cork Estate.

Living in a small apartment, I didn't have much to pack, a few boxes for me and one for Fred my black and white Springer Spaniel. You did nothing for Master Cork. I took care of him for years and this property is rightly mine. Take your animal and leave."

"I am not leaving. It was my uncle's wish for me to own the Cork Estate. I'm sorry, I know you must have grown to love him but....."

"Love him? Love him? I hated him, he and his stupid corks. I wished him dead."

"You killed him didn't you?" I accused.

"Yes, but you will never be able to prove it. The case will not be reopened without a body and you will never find your uncle's remains."

Fred showed Otley his teeth as I shouted, "Get out of this house. Take only your personal belongings and remove yourself from the premises immediately."

Winter crept by and the estate was beginning to thaw. I saw the crocus popping up along the warmth of the stone well. Fred and I decided to get a closer look and trudged through the slush. On tiptoe I peered into the well. There was a thin film of ice across the top of the water. I heard the "plop-plop of something breaking through. I gasped when I saw the floating two corks.

To All The Dogs I Loved

The closest thing to a sibling I ever knew was Ginger, a mixed Pekinese. As an only child I shared my thoughts and secrets with her. We also shared a bed that carried us through measles and chicken pox. I loved her as much as a child could love a pet. It was a sad day when Ginger was struck and killed by a speeding car. At the age of nine, I realized life was unfair.

It wasn't until I was sixteen that I wanted another dog. That was Bambi-a black Chihuahua who thought he was a Great Dane. It was Bambi who greeted my first born and protected from visitors. If anyone reached to touch the child without clearing it with him, Bambi turned into the Tasmanian devil. When I moved to a place where pets were not allowed, Bambi was left with my mother not exactly an animal lover, but she grew to love Bambi. The devil spent his final days protecting my mom.

Many years later Albert came into my life. No, Albert was not a dog but he came with one-like a two for one deal. Blackie was a crazy French Poodle with an upsetting puppy-hood. He looked and acted like a little man in a poodle suit. When Blackie and I shook paws for the first time we immediately became friends. "Whacky-Blackie" loved everyone especially children. I was with him when he died and his stubby tail continued to wag to the end.

Albert wanted to get another dog and threatened to bring home a Dalmatian. I did not want such a large dog. Also I read that most Dalmatian's go deaf. I didn't need a spotted dog that couldn't hear me complain.

I visited the Milford Animal Shelter where I saw many straggly mutts all hoping to be adopted. I wished them luck as I headed toward the exit. It was then I saw an adorable young pug. He had bulging eyes, a slightly pushed in face and a tail that curled like a piglet. He sat up on his haunches and looked like a cookie jar.

The dog warden told me a witness reported a little dog was thrown out of a truck at the Milford dump. The warden said, "He is full of spunk. It took me all afternoon to catch him. Are you sure you want such an energetic dog?"

Albert named him Oliver after Oliver Hardy. As time went by he affectionately called him Ollie and at times Ollie-O.

Oliver was more than a handful but through the years he gave us so much pleasure. No dog will ever take his place.

OLD ENOUGH

My bedtime curfew was extended at the age of ten. At last, I was allowed to watch Ralph Edwards host a T. V. program called "This Is Your Life" sponsored by the Hazel Bishop Lipstick Company.

I didn't recognize many of the guests and waited patiently for the commercials. A model with long, blond hair and ruby lips held a jeweled lipstick case as the invisible audience "ooh and aahed." I desperately that lipstick.

I tried to get up enough courage as I looked toward my mother. The effort was wasted as the clairvoyant answered my unasked question. "I'm sorry, you're not old enough."

I resented needing consent. The answer was always, "I'm sorry, you're not old enough."

This thing called the aging process was taking forever as I listened to, "I'm sorry, you cannot drive until you are sixteen. I'm sorry, you cannot vote until you are eighteen. I'm sorry, you cannot marry without parental consent until you are twenty-one."

Time passes at a faster rate when one becomes the consenter. Too soon the automatic doors open at the Senior Center where I found myself applying for membership. I filled out the form, only hoping to hear, "I'm sorry, you're not old enough." Instead, the obliging bookkeeper handed me the official "joy of aging" card, smiled and said, "that's a lovely shade of lipstick you're wearing."

I fumble through my purse, pulled out the jeweled case and beamed, "It's Hazel Bishop and I'm old enough."

I LOVED SYLVIA

It was before the age of reason. The age when I believed all cats were girls and all dogs were boys.

My cousin Sylvia set me straight. Eyebrows tucked under her shiny black bangs, she snapped, "How the hell can all cats be girls and all dogs be boys?"

She was fourteen and I only half her age, idolized her. Sylvia in her pink angora sweater and Cleopatra hair looked down on me in my corduroy jodhpurs. I loved Sylvia.

Every Sunday my father and I visited his sister. My Aunt Mary would ask me the same three questions. "How are you? How's school? Do you like your teacher?"

After answering, I was free to roam the mansion and look for Sylvia. I always began in the living room, although I did not understand why they called it the living room. No one was ever there. I pulled the cord on the traverse rod opening the heavy drapes. I looked at the massive fireplace and the porcelain pieces displayed on the mantle. Above the mantle hung a huge oil painting of Sylvia dressed in an evening gown sitting at her piano. Sylvia's eyes followed me around the room. The other Sylvia entered.

"Close the drapes. Don't you know sunlight can fade paintings? My portrait is very expensive."

I ran to the window trying to block out the sun with my jodhpurs happy to satisfy Sylvia. As she left the room I noticed she was wearing her pink angora sweater. She looked beautiful. I loved Sylvia.

I popped into the room with all the wonderful books. Sylvia's library was complete with mahogany desk where Sylvia did her homework. A Tiffany lamp stood beside Sylvia's very own typewriter. One click and Sylvia appeared. "Leave my typewriter alone. I have the margins set." I loved Sylvia.

Hanging lights glowed over a green table in the billiard parlor. I picked up a cue stick and pretended to shoot pool. Sylvia's shiny black hair swung through the doorway. I was delighted to see her as she yelled,

"Put that damn stick down. You will tear the felt on my pool table." A little puff of pink angora floated to the floor. I picked it up, held it to my cheek and felt the softness.

A dartboard hung on the wall in the game room, but it was the ping-pong paddles and little celluloid balls that made Sylvia yell, "Don't touch my ping pong balls. They dent easily." She left the room leaving another wisp of pink angora.

The music room was filled with Sylvia's piano. I looked at the highly polished ivory and black keys. My little index finger could not resist reaching out, hitting a low C.

"Get away from my piano. I just had it tuned. Piano tuners are expensive."

I picked up angora and left the room trying to keep up with Sylvia. Maybe she was in the glass room. Sunshine streamed through crystal clear windows in the sun parlor. In the center of this room was a huge ball made entirely of tin foil, Saving tin foil had something to do with the war effort but the war had been over for years. I wondered how this ball had helped win the war. I also wondered how they were going to get it out of here. Then wondered why they would want to. "Stay away from my tin foil ball." My idol shouted.

Stuffing pink fuzz into the pocket of my jodhpurs, I backed out of the room. I found my father and aunt in the formal dining room. "Hello. How's school? Do you like your teacher?"

Before I could answer Sylvia screamed, "Leave the adults alone. They need their privacy."

Sylvia was so wise and wonderful. I loved Sylvia.

I padded along behind her only stopping to pick up angora, leading me to a jigsaw puzzle. I fiddled with the pieces while Sylvia shouted from across the room to leave her puzzle alone. She was sitting at a card table playing dominoes with her Uncle Mikey. Sylvia scowled when Mikey smiled at me. "Pull up a chair and watch me beat Sylvia." He winked.

Dominoes flew through the air mixed with pink angora.

It was before the age of reason. The age when all cats were girls and all dogs were boys. It was the age when I loved Sylvia.

My Name is Harrell Carrell

My name is Carol and you would think being an only child, my father could remember that. He also had trouble remembering my mother's name- Harriet. When he called one of us, it sounded like, "Harrell, Carrell, Carrell, Harrell."

One morning, reading the newspaper he announced, "The census taker will be going door-to-door this week in Fairfield."

I never heard the word 'census' before and decided to hide my piggy bank if this person was going to take my cents.

Days later, a lady holding a clipboard asked to speak with one of my parents.

I yelled, "Dad, the cents taker is here."

I stood behind my father and hung on to the back of his belt.

The lady asked a few boring questions before asking if there were any children under the age of eighteen. This was now about me and I perked up when my father answered, "Yes. One."

"Name?" she asked.

"Harrell, Carrell, Carrell, Harrell," he sputtered.

I lifted one finger from the belt and poked him.

The census taker frowned. "Pardon me?"

"Carol" he answered.

"Does she have a middle name?"

"Mary," he quickly answered trying to avoid another poke.

I pulled on his belt, interrupted, and peeked from around his left hip. "No, it's Ann. Mom's middle name is Mary, Dad. Mine is Ann."

His sheepish smile lead to his apology.

The census taker blew a strand of hair from her forehead and continued. "Age?"

"Six," he said reaching back to hold my wrist.

"Seven," I corrected.

Surprised he said, "Oh, you're seven now?"

The lady's eraser was getting smaller as she asked, "And what grade is...." She looked at her questionnaire, "...Carol Ann in?"

"She's in first grade."

The tug was meant to be painful this time as I shouted, "I'm in second grade."

I was glad when the census taker left. I'm sure she was too. I let go of my father's belt relieved that she didn't ask about my piggy bank. My father was also relieved. Through the years I still answered to Harrell Carrell. I miss that.

FATHERS GENUINE FIBERGLASS FISHING POLE

The phone rang and as usual Martha Ann yelled to her mother, "I've got it.

Hi dad. Where are you? What time will you be home? Are we going fishing tomorrow? Live bait or lures?"

Joe's answers were always the same. "I'm in Philadelphia. I'll be home early if the dispatcher doesn't send me on a "flyer" to Boston. Of course we're going fishing. Get the tackle box ready. Put your mother on now and I'll see you soon, Marty."

Today's call was somehow different. It began, "Hello Father. How are you? I won't be able to go fishing with you. I'm going with some friends for pizza and a movie. Mother is curling my hair. Here she is now. Goodbye Father."

He heard his wife's voice and asked, "What's with Marty? Yes, yes, I'm fine but what's with Marty? Are you twirling her hair too tight? I can't believe she would rather go with her friends than catch that big old bass we've been after for years. We're going to get him this time. I bought a new fishing pole. I've never seen anything like it. It's made of fiberglass. That old bass doesn't stand a chance. When Marty sees the new rod, she'll forget all about her friends and pizza."

"Joe, she doesn't want to be called Marty. She's a young lady now and wants to be called Martha Ann."

"Never," he said. "Fishermen are never called Martha Ann. She'll come to her senses when she sees the genuine fiberglass fishing pole and tell her to stop curling her hair. The fish like her straight hair just fine."

There was only one thing Joe liked better than fishing and that was driving a truck. Always hungry for adventure, driving fed his need. Behind the wheel he was a knight holding the reins of his silver steed. At the end of the week the knight entered his kingdom where homecoming kisses and love mingled with the smell of pot roast.

"Where's Marty?" he asked his wife.

"Martha Ann is in her room trying on her new pink blouse for the third time. Joe, will you please call her Martha Ann?"

"Never."

Martha Ann came down the stairs one at a time instead of her usual two or three. She was happy to see her father. Turning in circles with arms outstretched she modeled her new blouse.

"It's very pretty Marty but wait until I show you my new, genuine fiberglass fishing pole. It doesn't leave a shadow on the water to scare the fish."

"Oh, it's beautiful Father. It looks like an icicle. I can see right through it." She held the icicle flicking her wrist pretending to cast the line. "I'm sorry I can't go with you tomorrow but...."

Joe interrupted, "Marty, you have to go. While the other truck drivers were eating steak and mushrooms, I was eating chili and saltines saving up for this rod so we can outsmart that old bass."

Joe never had to bargain with her before but he found himself saying, "I'll let you use the new pole first."

Martha Ann felt her father's disappointment. She thought of the first sunfish he taught her to catch and how they laughed when they threw it back and watched it swim away. They never took a fish home. They caught it, held it, examined it and named the species. The prickly perch, the wide mouth bass, the slimy pickerel and the beautiful rainbow trout were grateful when released "We have to let them swim away and grow Marty, just like you," her father would say as she listened, respected and adored him.

Swallowing hard she said, "I'll call my friends to tell them I'm going with my father because he's letting me use his new, genuine fiber glass fishing pole."

"That's my Marty."

"Please Father, Martha Ann."

"Never," he smirked.

Arriving at the lake, Martha Ann said, "Remember, I get to use the pole first and don't put the plastic bobber on the line. I want to cast out far and go deep. Put the lead sinker on."

The line made a whirring sound until the sinker settled to the bottom. Instantly she felt a tug running through the clear fiberglass to her hands ready at the reel. "I got a bite," she said with amazement. Her father began to coach,

"Don't reel in too soon. Let him take the bait. Now, reel in and don't lose him Marty."

"Martha Ann," she whispered not wanting to scare the fish.

"Never," he whispered back.

When the glistening pole bent low she knew the heavy fish was ready to be seen. She pulled him out of the water and screamed, "Snake, snake, I caught a snake!"

At that moment she let go of the genuine fiberglass fishing pole. The shiny icicle skimmed like a streak of lightening across the top one lake. It stood straight up before taken under.

When the rippled rings calmed, Joe looked at his daughter in disbelief. "That wasn't a snake. It was an ordinary eel." He was feeling a burning in his chest and hoped it was only from all the chili he had consumed saving for the rod. "Why did you let go of my new, genuine fiberglass fishing pole? I never got to try it out. Pack up the tackle box."

"But Dad," the tear streaked face said, "can't we stay?"

"Please, call me Father. We're going home now, Martha Ann."

Olfactory Memory

My husbands favorite snack is popcorn. This is a good thing- no sugar-no calories. But for me, the aroma of kernels popping brings back a memory.

I was holding onto a bus seat traveling across the rickety wooden bridge leading to Pleasure Beach. The windows were opened and it was beginning to rain. I worried the amusement park would close. Although frightened, I was determined to ride the new ferris wheel that claimed to be the highest in the world. As we neared the amusement park I could smell the popcorn. Butterflies fluttered in my stomach when I saw the ferris wheel. It looked like a 400 foot erector set.

After waiting in line, I stretched on tip-toes to reach the height level and hoped the attendant would not notice. What a relief when he let me on and strapped me in.

A boy about my age hopped in next to me. The wind was kicking up and the rain was getting heavier. "Hi," I said. "I hope they don't close the ferris wheel down."

As the wheel ascended the boy noticed I was getting nervous. He laughed, "Maybe when we get to the top I'll push you out." Then he started to swing the seat until we reached the top. At this point the wheel stopped and the attendant yelled to us. "Hang on. It's just a shower. I'll start it up again when the rain lets up."

I was drenched and feeling faint. To make matters worse the idiot next to me was again swinging the seat back and forth. With every gust of wind the aroma of popcorn churned my sick stomach.

When my husband starts to pop his favorite snack I say, "Maybe when we reach the top, I'll push you out."

F is for Fig Tree

My grandmother's orchard hung heavy with peaches and pears. Apple trees were decorated with shiny red fruit. Nearby, green and purple grapes entwined an arbor.

Many summer days we sat under the shaded canopy as she told me about the fig trees in her native country.

She wrote to her cousin in Italy of how much she missed the fig trees.

One day a package arrived from Italy. Noticing her trembling hands, I helped her open it. Inside was a gnarled piece of root, she recognized as a fig tree. She treasured it.

She carefully planted the root on the south side of the grape arbor. Bricks were buried around the root to outsmart moles. She dug a trench around the base of the plant for drainage.

Her neighbors teased, "You'll never grow figs in Connecticut."

In the fall, she covered the small shoot with leaves. Then she covered the leaves with burlap and pegged the rough fabric into the ground.

In the spring she unwrapped her treasure. The twisted stem stretched its small limbs. Soon a few leaves sprouted. She laughed, "Adam and Eve have a new wardrobe."

Years later, on a summer afternoon while visiting my grandmother, she rushed me to the back yard.

My eyes widened. A plump, golden fig hung from her treasured tree. She plucked the luscious fruit and presented me with this great gift. I have never tasted anything as sweet.

The Mandolin

My grandmother lived in Bridgeport, Connecticut in the 1940's. The Italian neighborhood added beauty to the lovely "Park City." The fruit trees and arbors of green and purple grapes blended with the aroma of bread baking and tomato sauce "blub-blubbing" on the blacktop stove.

As I approached my grandmother's unlocked door I could hear her playing the mandolin. This was the mandolin she had carried from Italy. It was her prized possession and I never saw her without it. The mandolin seemed to have a voice of it's own as it harmonized to "O' Solo Mio" with it's high-pitched strings.

I would be in the kitchen before my grandmother sensed I was there. Pinching my cheeks and squealing with delight at the sight of me she would say, "Come, I'll play for you." I would watch her hand move up and down the neck of the instrument as she plucked the strings with her special ivory pick. She began teaching me to play when I was about seven years old, positioning my fingers and still pinching my cheeks as she stretched my left hand and showed my right hand how to vibrate the strings. It was like rubbing your stomach and patting your head at the same time! "When I die, the mandolin will be yours," she would say, "It is my prize to you."

Many years later, my grandmother called to ask how I was feeling. I was expecting her first great grandchild and she was getting anxious. "I'll play the mandolin for the baby while you listen," she said. I didn't want to interrupt her while she was playing but after what seemed to be hours, I thought it was time to tell her I was having labor pains and needed to get to the hospital. She lived about four blocks from Saint Vincent's Hospital and ran all the way in her slippers. Needless to say, she arrived before I did. As they wheeled me in she pinched my cheeks. It hurt more than the labor pains. I realized there was something different about my grandmother that day. She had forgotten the mandolin. It was the first time I ever saw her without it. She did remember the holy water, throwing it all over me as she pinched away!

Years passed as I watched my grandmother and her mandolin age.

The instrument was covered with tape and it's beautiful lacquered finish was worn but the sound was as beautiful as ever.

After her death, no one seemed to know the whereabouts of the mandolin. I have to assume she took "the prize" with her to play for the angels. Someday, I will claim that prize.

THE ROCKET

The odometer read seven miles when my father drove the 1949 "Rocket eighty-eight Oldsmobile" from the showroom in Bridgeport to our home in Fairfield, Connecticut. The men in the neighborhood were still at work but the women gathered to inspect "The Rocket" from its shiny chrome bumpers to its soft leather interior. In the center of the steering wheel was a gold rocket surrounded by stars against a royal blue background.

"Who wants the first ride?" my father asked, as the ladies squealed with delight, pulling off aprons and tidying wisps of hair before piling into the new car.

The very pregnant Mrs. Lanigan was allowed to sit in the front because the others decided she would take up too much room in back seat. For the next hour, my father toured the town with five ladies all singing, "Come away with me Lucille, in my merry Oldsmobile."

"We need gas," he said as the rocket coasted into the station. The attendant at the pump, wearing a large red Texaco star on his shirt looked like he was from the Milton Berle Show. The ladies continued singing about Lucille and the Oldsmobile. The Texaco man joined in as he wiped the windshield and admired the car.

Shortly after the gas station stop, Mrs. Lanigan confessed she had been having labor pains for the past hour. Since this was her sixth child the ladies agreed my father drive quickly to the Bridgeport Hospital only seven long miles away. By now, Mrs. Lanigan was letting out war whoops as the others tried to comfort her by saying, "Don't worry, the rocket will get you there."

An Angel's Amber Moment

Learning the words to "America the Beautiful" I asked Miss Norling, my third grade teacher, "What are 'amber' waves of grain?"

She answered, "Amber is a beautiful word used to describe the color yellow."

Years later, 'amber' lost its beauty as I discovered amber to be brownish-yellow, oozing, fossil resin.

Today, amber is merely the center color of a traffic light. I never know whether to brake or accelerate. I usually choose the latter and believe me, it is not an amber moment.

To capture my amber moment, I must return to Miss Norling's third grade classroom. We no longer sat alphabetically and Leonard Miller chose to sit next to me as we sang about the amber grain.

Trying to impress me he said, "I have a cat with amber eyes. Do you want to go steady Carol?"

"Sure." I answered, not knowing what going steady meant. I thought it had something to do with the cat with the amber eyes.

Going steady took place on Tuesday and by Thursday we were engaged. He slipped a piece of twisted Luther on my finger and proudly announced he made it in cub scouts. The leather tightened and I sat with a blue finger while we rehearsed for our holiday pageant.

MY FIRST LOVE

What was Dan Cupid thinking as he bent back his bow and aimed at my young heart? It was his fault I fell in love with this much older man and make matters worse he belonged to another. Her name was Elizabeth but he called her Bess. I could never understand what he saw in her. She always looked so stern and not pretty at all. It was years later when I realized what a beautiful person she was. She was his reason and his strength. He loved her dearly. Lucky Bess. Poor me!

I loved to listen to him speak and held onto his every word. His kindness and sensitivity made my heart melt. His determination and tough-guy attitude made me very proud. He acted a little like Jimmy Cagney but Mr. Cagney was acting and he was not. Once he had weighed his thoughts and made his final decision that was that! I could only dream of going for long walks with him or horseback rides or listening to his music. Was it love or admiration?

On December 26, 1972 I heard the sad news that he had passed away. I will always pray for his soul. I still love you Hany Truman. Thank you for being my first love.

Carol Ruggiero
22 Vermont Ave.
Milford, Ct. 06460

MRS. ELLINGTON'S BROOCH

by
Carol Ruggiero

Characters
Mrs. Ellington – mother
Edward – son
Maggie – maid

[Called by his frantic mother, Edward Ellington arrives at the manor.]

Edward: [Agitated.] What is it this time Mother? What has upset you at this ungodly time of the morning?

Mrs. Ellington: [Eyes glaring.] My ruby brooch is missing. I know she stole it. I had it pinned to my favorite smock and now it's gone.

Edward: The stones are not rubies, Mother. The brooch is made of red glass. You said yourself the catch was broken. You must have dropped it. It was worthless anyway.

Mrs. Ellington: Worthless? Your father gave me that brooch before you were born. He couldn't afford expensive jewelry at the time. It held sentimental value. It was mine and she took it.

Edward: You mean Maggie? Why would Maggie take your broken brooch?

Mrs. Ellington: They all take things. The ladies in my bridge club tell me about hired help.

Edward: Oh Mother, you're such a silly goose. Maggie wouldn't do that. She came with fine references.

Mrs. Ellington: I never wanted her here. You hired her now I demand you fire her.

Edward: Now, now Mother, you know you can no longer take care of yourself. Maggie takes good care of you. She cooks yeu nice meals for you. The house is spotless and she is a good companion.

Mrs. Ellington: [Pouting.] You should be talcing car e of me in my old age. I certainly took good care of you.

Edward: Yes, you did Mother but you know I have the business to run. What do you think pays for this elegant home and all your needs.

Mrs. Ellington: Don't ever forget it was your father who made the business successful before he passed it to you.

Edward: How can I forget? You remind me of it every day. I've kept the business running for over twenty years now Mother and it is still very successful. Are you having the ladies here to play bridge today?

Mrs. Ellington: Don't try and change the subject Edward. I want Maggie fired and that's that. I know she stole my precious brooch. She is always snooping through my things. I saw her going through the linens. I counted the napkins when she left. I hate it. Why does she snoop through my things?

Edward: Silly goose-she's just tidying up. That's not snooping. She knows how you like things neat and organized.

Mrs. Ellington: Here she comes. I hear her coming up the walk.

[The kitchen door opens and Maggie enters looking down.]

Maggie: I'm here Mrs. Ellington. I'll get you're breakfast in a jiffy. [Looking up.] Oh, Mr. Ellington. What brings you out this way so early?

Edward: We need to talk Maggie.

Maggie: Certainly Sir. Just let me hang up my coat. I'll be right back.

Mrs. Ellington: Be stem son. Get this over with fast.

Edward: I can't accuse her of something I have no proof of. But if you're sure Mother, I guess I have no choice. You will miss her Mother. She has a nice way with you.

Mrs. Ellington: Here she comes. Just do it.

Maggie: Excuse me Mr. Ellington, before we begin. I have a surprise for Mrs. Ellington. Day after day she complains about the broken catch on her ruby brooch. I took it to the jeweler. He cleaned it and repaired it in no time. He said it is a beautiful piece of costume jewelry and worth quite a bit of money now because of its age. Let me pin it on for you Mrs. Ellington.

Mrs. Ellington: It looks lovelier than ever Maggie.

Maggie: And so do you ma'am.

Edward: You're such a silly goose Mother.

Mrs. Ellington: You can leave now Edward. Don't you have a business to run?

TOU-TAYS

My grandmother called me Cad-o-lina. "What would you like me to cook for you, Cadolina?"

The answer was always the same - "Tou-tays."

She sighed, "Tou-tays are a lot of work - but if that's what you want I will make them."

I watched her spread an oil cloth across the metal kitchen table top. Then she dusted the cloth with flour. This prevented the dough from sticking. Her wooden rolling pin moved quickly until the dough was thin - but not too thin. She then cut out small squares and scooped a mixture of ricotta cheese and spinach onto each square. Another square of dough covered the mixture. She pinched the edges of the filled squares together and sang O' Solo Mio until she crimped the last tu-tay. The cute little pockets were now boiled in a large pot on the black top stove while she made a tomato sauce or my favorite, melted butter with parmesan cheese.

Wanting to learn to cook I asked, "How long do you boil the tu-tays, grandma?"

She answered, "Until they are done."

FUNICULI-FUNICULA

The lord is my shepherd – I shall not want. These words hold memories of Mrs. Kaye, my fourth grade teacher.

Each day she began class with the twenty-third psalm. "Pray children, pray."

I prayed I would somehow live through fourth grade and escape the cruelty of Mrs. Kaye.

She wore the same black dress everyday. It smelled like moth balls. When the scent became stronger I knew she was standing near ready to crack little hands with her wooden ruler.

When my classmate mispronounced a word, Mrs. Kaye pulled on my friend's new dress until it was torn beyond repair. When another student tried to comfort the crying, ragged child, Mrs. Kaye grabbed and twisted his hah' until his scalp bled. Then her weapon, the mighty wooden ruler came down like a guillotine. The lord is my shepherd.

Ten months of Mrs. Kaye was more than any child could bear. I was glad to be going into the fifth grade. But I soon discovered that Mrs. Kaye was also moved to the fifth grade. Another year with the evil Mrs. Kaye would surely kill me. Somehow I survived. The lord was indeed my shepherd.

It was sixth grade when I met the wonderful Mr. Reeves who brought joy and peace to all. The young black man always had a sparkle in his eye and a smile on his face. He greeted us every morning singing, "Life is but a dream – finiculi funicula."

We said the Our Father, pledged the flag and learned more in one week than we did in two years with Mrs. Kaye. Mr. Reeves had no wooden ruler.

Today Mr. Reeves, wherever you are, I thank you for turning a nightmare into a dream. Finiculi-finicula.

REMEMBER WHEN
By Carol Ruggiero

The day started with the milkman dressed in his white uniform, clinking glass bottles awakening every dog in the neighborhood.

Mother, an early riser, greeted him, "Good morning Sam. Do you have any butter and eggs on the truck today? How's the family? Is little Betsy over the chicken pox?"

We all knew the delivery men by their first names. Jack from J.D.F. Cleaners, brought the dry cleaning. Mother did all her own laundry but Jack cleaned the coats, suits, and her special dress.

One morning Jack arrived while she was soaking white organdy curtains. She asked him if he had seen the bleach man on his route because she needed star-water. Star-water? What a wonderful name for plain old bleach. I always expected the Milky Way to come streaming out. The bleach came in a clear glass gallon jug. Embossed on the cap was a blue star.

The Tip-Top man brought Hop-a-Long Cassidy's favorite bread and the fruit and vegetable man carried his harvest basket to the front porch.

At times, he gave me a soft over-ripe tomato and laughed as juice squirted all over my white blouse. He kept the star-wafer man in business.

Once a month, Mr. Veccharelli from the Prodential Insurance Company paid us a visit to collect $2.14. On the hottest of summer days, he wore his gray three piece suit; crisp white shirt and striped tie. The tie carried a metal clip representing the Rock of Gibraltar. We never called Mr. Veccharelli by his first name.

Mother kept the insurance premium with the little cardboard payment book in the cupboard, behind the cold water pipe. If we were not at home, Mr. Veccharelli knew where to find it. Our doors were never locked. The smell of Old Spice lingered and we knew he had collected the insurance payment. Mother checked the book, read the penciled word "paid" and felt secure for another month.

Today when I pick up the scent of Old Spice, I remember when.

The Pink Scarf

During the 1950's rock and roll music filled the lives of most teenagers. I was no exception.

Summers were spent at Pleasure Beach Amusement Park where rock and roll celebrities entertained.

I remember the night the Everly Brothers harmonized opening the show for Chuck Berry who had a new hit song called "Carol".

He came on stage with his guitar, struck a chord, and shouted to the audience, "Where you at Carol? Where you at?"

Carol was a common name in the 50's, so of course, there was always a Carol in the audience to answer.

"I'm here," I squealed with delight.

I was escorted to the stage and stood with Chuck Berry as he duck walked around me and sang "Carol".

Around my neck I wore a pink scarf. It was the style for teenage girls to wear pastel colored neckerchiefs - like Olivia Newton John and Stockard Channing in the musical "Grease". And let's not forget Natalie Wood in "Rebel Without A Cause". Her co-star, James Dean was my heart-throb. I must remind you, this was sixty years before Kevin Cosner. In the movie Jimmy wore his red jacket but it was Natalie who wore that pink scarf.

When Chuck Berry finished singing, he gave my scarf a little tug and thanked me for joining him on stage.

When I got home that night, I tucked the scarf away and kept its precious memory.

There will never be another Chuck Berry or another pink scarf.

HEAVEN IS MADE OF WARM BRICKS

My childhood home stands on the highest elevation in Fairfield, Connecticut. It is probably the closest I'll ever get to heaven.

My parents purchased the brick duplex in 1943 for nine-thousand dollars - a small price to pay for a heavenly kingdom.

As an only child I had my own room where I entertained favorite dolls while pouring Kool-Aid into pastel porcelain cups. Too soon the dolls were replaced with a mahogany desk and typewriter used for high school homework. A hi-fi stood in a corner. I now shared my bedroom with Fats Domino, Pat Boone and of course, Elvis.

Although I spent most of my time in my bedroom, my favorite room was the kitchen. On a black-top stove tomato sauce blub-blubbed and mingled with the love of family. Sausage and peppers sizzled while Mother conducted a symphony with her long wooden spoon.

Dad curbed his appetite working on a crossword puzzle while I set the table around him. He left me with his love for crosswords.

Mom lived alone in my childhood home for many years. Visits found me reminiscing in my bedroom where nothing had changed.

In 2008 I turned the key and locked the door for the last time. Fats Domino was singing 'Blueberry Hill', tomatoes blubbed and Mom's spoon thumped against the sauce pot.

I looked up at my bedroom window, placed my hand on the bricks and said good-bye to heaven.

FIRST DATE

The fragrance of apple blossoms filled the air. Soon I would be twelve years old.

I packed a lunch along with my Nancy Drew book and headed to the apple orchard where I climbed the highest tree and nestled myself among the the blossoms.

"This is what heaven must be like," I thought. Opening my book and munching on peanut butter sandwiches, two yellow bees joined me. While flicking them away I heard my friend Gordie calling.

"I'm up here Gordie."

He answered, "I thought I'd find you here. Do you want to go to the stream and catch salamanders?"

"Not today." I said. "I want to be alone."

Gordie climbed the tree and our eyes met between the branches. There was something different about him today. He seemed serious and grown up. Was it the arrival of spring that turned the boy into a young man?

With a slight stutter he asked, "Will you go on a date with me tomorrow?"

I didn't know if I was old enough to go on a date but did not want to disappoint Gordie. "Sure," I answered. "Where will we go?"

Gordie smiled his wonderful smile. "To the movies," he answered.

The next day I got ready for my first date. I don't remember what I wore but I remember covering it up with a pretty pink bolero jacket. It was the color of the apple blossoms.

We took the bus to the Lowes Polls theater in Bridgeport where we watched Doris Day and Gorden McRae paddling a canoe while singing 'On Moonlight Bay."

The movie was almost over when Gordie put his arm around my shoulder. I didn't like that - counted to five and threw it off.

We barely spoke on the long bus ride home.

The next morning I went back to the apple orchard and sat high in a tree. I had a lot of thinking to do.

Carol Ruggiero

The Metal Detector

My neighbor Tom bought his two young sons a used, thirty-dollar, metal detector.

His investment gave the boys a summer hobby. They enjoyed combing the beach hoping to find something of value.

I was pruning the lilac bushes when they arrived home after their first adventure. Sounding like chattering chipmunks, they opened their collection box. It contained a penny, two nickels and several rusted bottle caps.

"Wow" I said. "That's quite a haul."

Tom winked. "Someday they will find Captain Kidd's treasure."

The following summer there was no longer a need to share. Tom bought each boy his own $500 detector along with many new digging implements. The beach no longer held their interest. They now worked the detectors along riverbanks and wooded areas.

Years later, they spent weeks building a long, wooden contraption called a 'sifter'. As I pulled slivers from their hands, the young men explained it was what miners used to sift for gold. I noticed their latest detectors were more sophisticated. They were shipped in from South Carolina at the cost of $840 each. This was the same year they bought a jeep saying, "This jeep will pay for itself."

I thought, "Yes, if the dealership accepts bottle caps."

By nightfall, tired, dirty faces beamed showing me a diamond ring and a gold chain. Now a flat bed trailer was added to the jeep. Their excavations kept them away for days camping next to a crater until they unearthed the detected prize. Through the years they had learned to respect nature, always filling the dig before leaving the site.

The day finally came. They were going to Charles Island to find Captain Kidd's treasure.

That evening, mud-caked Levi's hung low, as they asked for advice. My heart swelled with concern when they told me they found a body wrapped in a blue and white quilt.

I said, "You must call the police and lead them to the grave site."

"We can't do that. It's against the law to dig at Charles Island. We'll get in trouble."

Haunted by their story, I couldn't sleep that night. I wished they hadn't told me. I ached for the chattering chipmunks and their bottle caps.

I needed to know more and asked, "Was it a man, woman or God forbid child?"

"We don't know. We hit something with the shovel. We kinda poked at it until we realized it was a body. Then we covered it up and left."

I said, "There is a possibility it is not a body. Why would the detector register something that has no metal? You must go back to be sure. Then please, call the police or I will have to do it for you."

They dug slowly until once again the blue and white quilt appeared. They lifted, struggled and knew, it was not a child. They opened the shroud to discover a St. Bernard still wearing his collar and metal dog tags.

ANGELS NEVER SLEEP

Years ago my husband and I were traveling to Canada on a tour bus looking forward to site seeing and relaxation.

After a stop for lunch the bus driver announced we would not be stopping for another four hours. When he started the engine, I found it amuzing that everyone immediately fell asleep - everyone except me that is. My fear of traveling allows no sleep. Instead, I spend my time listening to my husband snore and looking at the back of the drivers head which now fell foreward onto the steering wheel. I couldn't believe what I was seeing. At a high rate of speed, the bus was swerving over a bridge. I looked at the icy water below and knew we were all going to die. I thought of waking my husband but decided not to put him through the terror.

Thanks to some hard working angels we made it across the bridge. But once again the bus picked up speed crossing two lanes into oncoming traffic.

At this point everyone was screaming. Thankfully, two doctors were on board. The psychiatrist spoke softly to the driver while the medical doctor tried to calm passengers.

Suddenly the bus lifted and flew off the road into a ravine where the engine died. The angels were back - they never sleep.

A Friend Indeed

I was blessed with two good friends. Barbara and I grew up in the same neighborhood and continued our friendship, until sadly I lost her at the age of thirty-six to cancer. Forty years later, I am still missing my beautiful friend.

Years later, while attending a ceramic class I met Dorothy. It was Dorothy who led me to Writers Unlimited. She was a warm and wonderful lady and an outstanding writer. Through the years, it was Dorothy who was there for me – sharing laughter or drying my tears. And it was always Dorothy who ran to my side to hold my hand when I was in need. At the age of ninety three, she called from her hospital bed to tell me how much she cherished our friendship. I miss her so very much.

Today begins like everyday for me about 4 am. I sit at my desk breathing with a nebulizer to help my damaged lungs. I stare out the window into the darkness. The soft glow of the street light allows me to see my neighbor letting out the dog. Her name is Joey and she is a beautiful golden retriever. She never barks or leaves her yard. She sees me through the window and nods. Joey, indeed is my new friend.

GOOD-BYE SANDRA DEE

As a teenager in the 50's getting ready for a date was an ordeal. It meant getting out the umbrellas. Not that I feared rain- in fact I would never carry an umbrella on a date. It just wouldn't be "cool". Instead, I used the umbrellas to shape my horsehair crinolines.

Using a long wooden spoon I stirred sugar into hot water and soaked the crinolines in this mixture. Then I laid them over opened umbrellas. As they dried the sugar stiffened the fabric.

Getting dressed, I slipped a full circular skirt over the stiff crinolines. I tied my hair into a ponytail with a sheer pink scarf and giggled, "Well, look at me- I'm Sandra Dee." I was sure my date would be pleased.

The years passed, as did Sandra Dee. I no longer date because my husband may not approve.

Today, when I tie my hair into a ponytail, I frown and say, "Well, look at me- I'm Willie Nelson."

Writers Unlimited Assignment
What is unusual about your house?

My home on Vermont Avenue is called an oversized ranch. It is an ordinary house on an ordinary street. It is quiet during the day, almost too quiet-that is... until about three in the afternoon.

At this time something unusual happens. The house takes on animated life. The garage door opens its mouth and sings baritone. The shutters applaud and shout, "encore!" as the chimney gives standing ovation. The shrubbery dances as chickadees swoop in for a sing-a-long.

I am at the stove preparing dinner. Feathers', our pet parrot begins to stir and lets out an ear-piercing squawk. We both know my husband Albert has arrived home. I watch from the kitchen window.

He talks to Jim Crow first, then to Blue the jay bird. He asks them if they are having a good day as he freshens the birdbath. Keeping the beat, the woodpecker rat-a-tats a welcome on the metal down spout. Albert throws shelled nuts on the roof and asks, "Where's Johnnie Peanut?" his favorite squirrel. Two cooing doves waddle toward him followed by Johnnie and the rest of the squirrel family. The titmouse announces his late arrival with a high-pitched trill. He is a favorite because of his unique personality. Despite his size he stuffs two nuts into his tiny pink cheeks.

Albert tells his menagerie of friends he will be out later. Only then does he yell through the screen door, "I'm home."

I smile and say, "How did I know that?"

It is three o'clock, Albert is home and all is well at the unusual house on Vermont Avenue.

FRANKIE'S BUS

When I sit the past, I can hear Frankie's bus coming up the steep hill. Shifting into second gear, the grinding vehicle struggled to reach a village of duplex homes where children waited for Frankie's arrival.

It was said, the driver purchased the retired bus from the city updating transportation. He painted it blue and stenciled white lettering reading, "Frankie's Bus". Removing passenger seats, he installed shelves stocking them with dry goods. The bus was now a grocery store on wheels. Of course, there was no refrigeration. He sold sugar, cereal, boxed pasta and canned goods along with soap, shampoo and cotton balls. Best of all one shelf held penny candy.

The driver kept his money in a cigar box near the front of the bus where Frankie greeted shoppers as they boarded. He was always friendly unless someone got too close to the cigar box. Then he showed his teeth and growled.

Frankie was a wired hair terrier resembling Asta, the Thin Man's dog from a popular movie series.

I always gave Frankie a piece of candy before leaving. This made his stubby tail thump against the leather bus seat.

As food handling laws became stricter, Frankie's bus was forced out of business. But I will always remember the sound of the bus climbing the steep hill. Most of all, I will remember the sound of Frankie's happy tail.

Writers Unlimited
Halloween Assignment

At nine years old I was excited that it was Halloween. Tonight I would dress up and go trick or treating through the neighborhood.

Halloween fell on a Saturday that year. I enjoyed walking through the crisp leaves on my way to confession at Our Lady of Assumption Church. I wondered what outrageous sins I could confess this week. My sins were always so boring. I disobeyed my mother, seemed to be getting stale.

As I continued wading through the leaves I admired the magnificent white Baptist church across the street. It looked especially beautiful with its orange and red maple trees. On the lawn stood a sign reading, 'Halloween Party tonight- All welcome'. Did that mean Catholics too?

Returning home after confession and five Hail Mary's, I asked my mother if I could go to the Baptist Halloween party.

She answered," Absolutely not- Catholics don't go to a Baptist church."

"But who will know?" I thought. "I'll be in disguise."

I cut out some black felt to make a mask like the Lone Ranger wears, put on a white shirt and strapped my toy guns around my waist. "Hi-Yo Silver" The Baptists will love it.

The following Saturday, once again I walked to confession. "Bless me Father for I have sinned. I disobeyed my mother and won first prize at the Baptist Halloween party. For this I am sorry."

After ten Hail Mary's, I wondered if I was.

Carol Ruggiero

Oranges Are The Pits

During the summer months Mom always insisted I eat an orange before bedtime. She claimed it was a refreshing way to end the day and keep me cool during the night. I never liked oranges and rather have a fan. But Mom said oranges didn't run on electricity and until they did a fan was not in my near future.

On my fourth birthday I found Mom in the kitchen decorating a large sheet cake until she heard the trucks backing up to our front lawn. Somehow she got the Parks and Recreation Department to deliver picnic tables complete with benches. She directed the town workers to line the tables end to end. When they finished she tipped each worker with an orange. If oranges were money we were wealthy. It seemed she pulled them out of thin air.

Mom covered the tables with cloths and made party hats from newspaper. She placed an orange next to each hat. Then she hammered a large sign into the ground. I couldn't read but recognized my name. Mom pointed to the underlined words-Come To Carol's Birthday Party-No Gifts Please.

I scowled at the ungifted children gathering around the tables. Holding oranges they sang the birthday song and told me to blow out the candles and make a wish. I wished I never had to see an orange again.

That evening Mom asked what I wished for. I told her I wished I had one gift to open. She left the room and returned with something wrapped in a napkin and tied with butcher string. Although the gift was wrapped T instantly knew it was a wonderful rubber ball T could bounce and recite one-two-three O'Leary.

Of course it wasn't.

I found my freshman yearbook packed away with other "can not part with" items. The turquoise and white cover read, "The Flame".

In 1956 Andrew Warde High School opened its doors for the first time. As freshmen our class would be the first true graduates, completing four years.

As I flipped through the pages looking for a special someone to write about I could almost hear John Travolta and Olivia Newton John singing, "You're the one that I love". Many of my classmates actually looked like the cast from Grease.

The 50s' were great years to be a teenager; clothes, cars, drive-in movies, soda shops and rock and roll. Eisenhower was president but Elvis was king.

The yearbook slipped from my excited hands. It fell opened to a masculine looking woman with short hair and very large teeth smiling at me from the yellowed pages. She could have passed for a Phys-Ed teacher but Miss Emery was my English teacher.

It was Miss Emery who took my hand and gently led me through the world of Literature. Of course with Ernest Hemingway's "The Old Man and the Sea" it was more like a shove. I remember saying to her, "If Hemingway doesn't drown Santiago in the next chapter I will personally do it for him. Who cares if that old man catches a fish?"

When Miss Emery introduced us to Charles Dickens I braced for more boredom. I fell in love with Dickens' writing especially "A Tale of two Cities". Miss Emery's freshmen were assigned a character's part as we read the book, I wanted to be Madame DeFarge. She was cool, knitting her way through the storming of the Bastille. I wondered how Dickens knew what yam felt like in a knitter's hands. Instead, I was chosen to be Lucy Manette (Man-ay) never pronounced Manette (Man-ette).

My freshman year passed all too quickly. It was time to say good-bye to Miss Emery but did I ever say, "thank you Miss Emery-oh thank you so very much?"

Wherever you are today consider it done.

THE MAHOGANY BOOKCASE

In my childhood home, at the foot of the stairs stood a mahogany bookcase holding two sets of encyclopedias. It was my library.

When I reached Junior High School, homework assignments became more challenging and I found myself on a bus every Saturday traveling to the Burroughs Library located in Bridgeport Connecticut. This is where my first library card was issued.

Years later, I volunteered as an assistant librarian helping children select books to suit their interest. Dinosaurs were high on their list.

Moving to Milford, I was now able to often visit the Beinecke Library in New Haven where rare books are kept under glass at an appropriate temperature for protection. Beinecke has one of the only complete Gutenberg bibles in the world. Imagine that!

The Library of Congress in Washington D.C. Is the world's largest library, containing 128 million items including books. On my last visit to the Library of Congress, I was able to view my husband's book titled, 'Connecticut Newspapers, Party Politics and Reconstruction 1863 - 1870.'

I write assignment papers shorter than his title.

It saddens me that today's children click on the computer to research. They carry no card or wonderful memories of our fine libraries.

My childhood encyclopedias are gone now, but the mahogany bookcase proudly stands in my home holding precious books. It will always be my favorite library.

MARSHA'S AUNT
(A spring Memory)

As a child I knew spring had officially arrived when Owen Fish Park opened to the neighborhood. I never knew who Owen Fish was, but was grateful for the beautiful park named in his honor.

Across the street from the park lived my friend Marsha Tierney, a bit of a snob, but I liked her. We made plans to meet at the park that spring morning to watch the boys play ball.

I saw Marsha running toward me, jumping over a row of daffodils. I don't think I ever saw her run before and knew she was excited about something.

"I've got the biggest secret to tell you." She squealed, "Promise, oh promise, you won't tell anyone." I promised and she began. "My Aunt Gene is staying at our house. She's recovering from what Daddy calls a nervous breakdown. It's because of that movie she starred in called "Laura" and also the problems she's having with Uncle Oleg Cassini. Do you want to meet her?"

"Not really." I answered. "I'd rather try out the new swings in the park."

"You're just jealous that I have an aunt who's a movie star," she said with her nose in the air.

"I am not! How am I suppose to meet her if you're not suppose to tell anyone she's here.?"

Marsha smirked. "I have a plan. Sit on my back porch and pretend you're waiting for me. Aunt Gene will come out to have a cigarette. When she does, introduce yourself and ask if I'm ready to go to the park. She will tell you I've already left. At least you'll, get to see her in person. Believe me, someday you'll talk about this. Or write about it."

"I don't think so, but have it your way," I said, leaving Marsha at the park.

I walked into Marsha's backyard and saw Aunt Gene already on the porch, cigarette in hand. She was leaning on the railing and was startled when she turned and saw me.

"Hi, I'm Carol, Marsha's friend. Is she ready to go to the park?" I lied well and thought, "Who's the actress now?"

She snapped, "How would I know if she's ready? Did you know who she was?"

That was when I noticed her famous over-bite. I also noticed her tight brown slacks. Not many women wore slacks in those days and I wasn't sure if I liked the look. She wore no make-up and her hair was straight and pulled back with a piece of ribbon. The hand holding the cigarette was shaking. The other one directed me to sit down.

"I'm not good around kids," She said. "Kids make me nervous. Lately, everything makes me nervous." She inhaled deeply and asked, "Do you know Otto Preminger? Of course you do, kid. Everyone knows who Otto Preminger is. It's his fault I smoke. He insisted, if I ever wanted another part in one of his movies I would have to lower my voice. He made me smoke three packs a day. Now, my voice is lower but I can't break the habit. Don't ever smoke kid," she warned. "Do you go to school with my niece?"

She didn't wait for me to answer saying, "I went to Unquawa School. It was a private school and only the wealthy attended."

I now knew where Marsha had inherited her snobbery. She went on. "My father was very rich. After he broke my mother's heart with his infidelity, I never spoke to him again."

She lit another cigarette, both hands now shaking. "My mother passed away soon after that. I wished she could have seen my performance as Laura. Did you see me in that movie?" Again she did not wait for me to answer rambling on about Dana Andrews and Clifton Webb. "Do you think I'm pretty, kid?"

Nodding my head, I lied again.

"So where did it get me?" she asked. "Hiding out on a back porch across the street from Owen Fish Park."

The right side of her not so beautiful face twitched as she lit another cigarette and started talking again. I impolitely cut in. "I've got to go now. I'm sure Marsha is waiting for me at the park."

"Yeah, kid. It's a beautiful spring day. Go to the park," she ordered.

Gene Tierney died November 6th 1991 of emphysema. Darryl Zanuck was quoted, "She was the most beautiful woman in movie history."

To me she is a spring memory.

The Secret of William Tell and Annie Oakley

The voice on the phone said, "Hi. It's Pat."

Gruffly I answered. "Pat? I don't know any Pat."

"How could you forget your best friend from childhood?" she giggled.

"Patty? When did you start calling yourself Pat? I think of you often and always look forward to your Christmas card. You know, the one that says, "I'll call you soon." What made you call today?"

"I heard the William Tell overture on the radio this morning," she said. "Most would think of the Lone Ranger shouting "Hi Yo Silver," but not me. Do you remember our William Tell experience?"

"Of course I do. How could I forget? You made me swear not to tell anyone our secret. I vowed to take it to my grave. At times I hoped for early death."

My mind traveled back, visiting the summer of 1948. Patty and I were digging a hole, just deep enough to bury potatoes. We were sure the sun would bake them during the day and planned on returning in the evening to eat them-dirt and all.

We saw Patty's older sister Maureen coming toward us. She always hung out with the boys and today was no different. Petey Putnick was with her playing, 'William Tell'. She and Petey claimed to have made an exact replica of Tell's bow and arrow from a willow twig and a piece of kite string. When Maureen pulled the weapon, the string broke and the twig snapped in half.

Embarrassed she said, "Ah, boys don't know anything. Annie Oakley was a better marksman than William Tell."

Looking directly at me, Maureen said. "I know where my father hides his World War II rifle. I'll get it while you run home and get an apple."

We didn't have any apples but there was a bowl of oranges on the table waiting to be squeezed. "Mom would never miss one," I thought, selecting the largest.

Maureen ordered Petey to take ten paces and place the fruit on his head. He obeyed. The butt of the rifle was against Maureen's shoulder as she looked through the sight and aimed. The shot rang though air, orange rind flew and Petey fell to the ground.

Terrified, I screamed, "Maureen shot Petey! Maureen shot Petey!"

Patty shook her finger at her sister. "You're gonna get it when Dad gets home. You killed Petey. You'll be grounded for a month. And he'll ground me to."

Petey's "dead body" stirred. We ran to him.

He told us he heard the shot, felt the warm juice, thinking it blood, passed out cold. Somehow Maureen had hit the orange dead center.

We put the gun back in its hiding place and vowed never to tell anyone. Patty and I returned to the potato hole and silently dug. I still believe William Tell and Annie Oakley were digging with us for I know Maureen could not have hit that orange.

So Do I

As a child, Christmas was a magical time. A large decorated tree with a star on top twinkled and the scent of pine filled the air.

Best of all, Santa was on his way with his bag of toys for all good children. I was always a little worried about that deal.

Too excited to sleep, I called to the bedroom across the hall, "Ma, I hear Santa's reindeer on the roof."

"Go to sleep," she answered. "It's only ice cracking."

I wondered why she didn't believe me. With all my heart and soul I knew the reindeer were overhead. Why didn't she?

Christmas morning found me tangled in tinsel as I reached under the tree hugging a soft baby doll with blue glass eyes. I was also delighted to receive a little carpet sweeper, a dust mop and tiny tin pots and pans.

Now that I look back, I guess this was basic training for the years ahead.

As a teenager the magic of Christmas disappeared when my mother decided it would be chic to have a silver aluminum tree. It opened like an umbrella and smelled more like Reynolds Wrap than pine. Although she would not admit it, I think my mother hated that tree as much as I did because that night when I jokingly called to the room across the hall, "Ma, I hear reindeer on the roof."

She answered, "So do I."

The Genuine Fiberglass Fishing Pole

The phone rang and as usual Martha Ann yelled to her mother, "I've got it. Hi Dad. Where are you? What time will you be home? Are we going fishing tomorrow?"

Joe's answers were always the same. "I'm in Philadelphia. I'll be home early if the dispatcher doesn't send me on a "flier" to Boston. Of course we're going fishing. Get the tackle box ready. Put your mother on now and I'll see you soon, Marty."

Today's call was somehow different. It began, "Hello Father. How are you? I won't be able to go fishing with you. I'm going with some friends for pizza and a movie. Mother is curling my hair. Here she is now. Goodbye Father."

Joe heard his wife's voice and asked, "What's with Marty? Yes, yes, I'm fine but what's with Marty? Are you twirling her hair too tight? I can't believe she would rather go with her friends than catch that old bass we've been after for years. We're going to get him this time. I bought a new fishing pole. I've never seen anything like it. It's made of fiberglass. That old bass doesn't stand a chance now. When Marty sees the new rod, she'll forget all about her friends and pizza."

"Joe, she doesn't want to be called Marty. She's a young lady now and wants to be called Martha Ann.?"

"Never," he said. Fishermen are never called Martha Ann. She'll come to her senses when she sees the genuine fiberglass fishing pole and tell her to stop curling her hair. The fish like her straight hair just fine."

There was only one thing Joe liked better than fishing and that was driving a truck. Always hungry for adventure, driving fed his need. Behind the wheel he was a knight holding the reins of his silver steed. At the end of the week the knight would enter his kingdom where homecoming kisses and love mingled with the smell of pot roast.

"Where's Marty?" he asked his wife.

She answered, "Martha Ann is in her room trying on her new pink blouse for the third time. Joe, will you please call her Martha Ann?"

"Never," he said.

Martha Ann came down the stairs one at a time instead of her usual two or three. She was happy to see her father and modeled her blouse, turning in circles with arms outstretched.

"It's very pretty Marty, but wait until you see my new, genuine fiberglass fishing pole. It doesn't leave a shadow on the water to scare the fish."

"Oh, it's beautiful. It looks like an icicle. I can see right through it." She held the icicle flicking her wrist pretending to cast the line. "I'm sorry I can't go with you tomorrow Father but..."

Joe interrupted, "Marty, you just have to go. While the other truck drivers were eating steak and mushrooms, I was eating chili and saltines saving up for this rod so we can outsmart that old bass."

He never had to bargain with Marty before but found himself saying, "I'll let you use the new pole first."

Martha Ann felt her father's disappointment. She thought of the first sunfish he taught her to catch and how they threw it back and watched it swim away. They never took a fish home. They would catch it, hold it, examine it and name the species. The prickly perch, the wide mouth bass, the slimy pickerel and the beautiful rainbow trout were grateful when released.

"We have to let them swim away and grow Marty, just like you," her father would say as she listened, respected and adored him.

Swallowing hard she said, "I'll call my friends and tell them I'm going with my father because he's going to let me use his new, genuine fiberglass fishing pole."

Joe's eyebrows rose almost above his forehead. "That's my Marty."

"Please Father, Martha Ann."

"Never," he smirked.

When they arrived at the lake Martha Ann said, "Remember I get to use the pole first and don't put the plastic bobber on the line. I want to cast out far and go down deep. Put the lead sinker on."

The line made a whirring sound until the sinker settled to the bottom. Instantly she felt a tug running through the clear fiberglass to her hands ready at the reel.

"I got a bite," she said with amazement.

Her father started to coach, "Don't reel in too soon. Let him take the bait. Now, reel in and don't lose him Marty."

"Martha Ann," she whispered not wanting to scare the fish.

"Never," he whispered back.

When the glistening pole bent low she knew the heavy fish was ready to be seen. She pulled it out of the water and screamed, "Snake, snake, I caught a snake."

At that moment she let go of the genuine fiberglass fishing pole. The shiny icicle skimmed like a streak of lightening across the lake never to be seen again.

When the rippled rings calmed, Joe looked at his daughter in disbelief. "That was not a snake. It was just an ordinary eel." He was feeling a burning in his chest and hoped it was only from all the chili he had consumed saving for the rod.

"Why did you let go of my new, fiberglass fishing pole? I never got to try it out. Pack up the tackle box."

"But Daddy," the tear streaked face said, "can't we stay?"

"Please call me Father. We're going home now, Martha Ann."

Old Spice and Mr. Veccharelli

In 1946 our Connecticut mornings started with the milkman dressed in his white uniform, clinking glass bottles awakening every dog in the neighborhood.

Mother, an early riser, greeted him, "Good morning, Sam. Do you have any butter and eggs on the truck today? How's the family? Is little Betsy over the chicken pox?"

We knew all the deliverymen and called them by their first names. Jack from J.D.F. Cleaners brought the dry cleaning from Bridgeport to our home in Fairfield. Mother did all her own laundry but Jack cleaned the coats, suits and her special dress.

One morning Jack arrived while she was soaking white organdy curtains. She asked him if he had seen the bleach man on his route because she needed star-water to whiten the curtains. Star-water! What a wonderful name for plain old bleach. I always expected the Milky Way to come streaming out. The bleach came in a clear glass gallon jug. Embossed on the metal cap was a blue star.

The Tip-Top man brought Hop-a-long Cassidy's favorite bread and the fruit and vegetable man carried his harvest basket to the front porch. At times, he gave me a soft over ripe tomato and laughed as juice squirted all over my white blouse. He kept the star-water man in business.

Once a month, Mr. Veccharelli from the Prudential Insurance Company paid us a visit to collect $214. On the hottest of summer days, he wore his gray three-piece suit, crisp white shirt and striped tie. The tie carried a metal clip representing the Rock of Gibraltar. We never called Mr. Veccharelli by his first name.

Mother kept the insurance premium with a little cardboard payment book in the cupboard, behind the cold water pipe. If we were not at home, Mr. Veccharelli knew where to find it. Our door was never locked. The smell of Old Spice lingered and we knew he had collected the insurance payment. Mother checked the book, read the penciled word "paid" and felt secure for another month.

Today when I pick up the scent of Old Spice, I remember Mr. Veccharelli.

PENANCE

As a child I never knew what orange juice really tasted like. Every morning my mother used my orange juice to camouflage three drops of cod liver oil – or so she thought. The oil floated on top of the juice and smelled like a stagnant goldfish bowl. The taste was worse.

I held my nose and drank it down followed by sweetened oatmeal and buttered toast. This ritual went on until I was old enough to make my own breakfast. The oatmeal remained but I eliminated the cod liver oil by squeezing three drops into the sink. Now that I think of it, it was the only drain that never needed plunging.

Every day Mom reminded, "Don't forget your cod liver oil this morning. It's good for shiny hair, glowing skin and lubricates bones and joints."

I deceivingly answered. "I won't forget Mom. I just used three drops."

The feeling of guilt lingered day after day but at least the neighbor's cat no longer followed me to school.

I knew someday, somehow I would pay for my cod liver oil lies.

I managed to get through life with normal skin, semi-shiny hair and strong bones until recently. My arthritic bones ached and I felt tired and run down. I was sure my doctor had a pill for this lack of energy, I filled his prescription and returned home.

The bottle read – "Cod Liver Oil. Squeeze three drops into orange juice."

I'm sure it is my penance for lying to my mother.

BE IT EVER SO HUMBLE

Home is where the heart is. Home is family. Home is where seeds are planted and lifelong values take root.

I have lived in many houses through the years, but the brick house on Melville Drive was home. I was born there, took my first step, spoke my first word and I haven't shut up since.

Always the safe haven, the humble abode protected and filled my every need. When hungry, it was where I found Mom cooking. When cold, where Dad stoked the fire. If solitude was needed, I found my room at the top of the stairs. I could view the entire neighborhood from there. It was entertainment until our first T. V. was delivered. Just about all my "firsts" occurred in that home.

When I moved out I found no need to miss the house. No matter where I lived Melville Drive was home. It was where holidays were still celebrated with my parents. Things changed after Dad died. Mom now visited me, spending a few days at a time but always returning home.

I was devastated the day she entered the nursing home. How dare they call it home. Home was Melville Drive until it became obvious she would not return. I needed to sell the house. What value do you put on a lifelong friend you are about to abandon? When I closed the front door for the last time, I wept. No, I did more than weep. I wailed from my inner soul and then said good-bye to my beloved home.

I recently discussed the fact, with my husband, that our house is too large for me handle any longer. I asked what he thought about a smaller place - maybe a condo?

His answer filled the empty space in my heart. I stopped grieving for the home on Melville Drive as he said, "I don't care where I live. Home is wherever you are. Be it ever so humble."

The Easter Lie

Easter Sunday is the holiest of Christian celebrations. Christ has risen. It is also the anniversary of my first deliberate lie.

I was four years old and excited about the Easter bunny bringing a basket filled with candy. I hoped for a pink one with a large satin ribbon. Sure enough, Easter morning near the front door, sat a beautiful pink cellophane wrapped basket. I ran upstairs to tell my parents the Easter bunny had arrived.

At the breakfast table my father said, "I wonder what time the Easter bunny came? I was up until eleven and he wasn't here yet."

"Oh," I said," he came about midnight."

"Really? How do you know?" My father asked.

"I saw him!"

There it was-my first lie. Those three little words, "I saw him." This was not a child's imagination. It was a deliberate lie and I wondered if I could get away with it having been told that one lie leads to another.

My father looked above his glasses but it was my mother who spoke first. "What did he look like?"

I squinned in my chair. "He was big and all white with a pink nose."

"Anything else?" Mom asked.

"Yes he carried a huge basket filled with colored eggs. He said they were special eggs."

Amazed, Dad said, "Oh, so you also spoke with him?"

"Sure, he was a nice rabbit, Dad."

"Did he tell you why the eggs were so special?" Mom fattened my fib.

It seemed to be getting warm in the house. I blew a strand of hair from my forehead before continuing, "Well, you see if you gently tap the egg a strip of paper with writing will come out."

"Oh, like a Chinese fortune cookie?"

"Yes, exactly. Good one Mom."

"And what did the paper say?" She asked.

"Uh, it told me what I would be when I grow up."

My parents looked at one another in disbelief and laughed. I knew they were on to me.

"What did your egg say you would be?" Asked my smirking father.

I hung my head. "A liar!" I sobbed as tears streamed down my face.

"Now, now," Dad comforted. "Maybe more like a story teller."

A few short years later I discovered it was my parents who were lying. Life was

much easier without the Easter bunny from then on.

Christ has risen. Have a wonderful Easter everyone.

Be It Ever So Humble-Part Two

I attended Betsy Moore's birthday party. She was now seven- just like me, but she had it all.

Arriving home, I found my mother in the kitchen stuffing a chicken. "Hi" she said. "How was Betsy's party?"

"I hate this house. Betsy has an in-ground swimming pool, a balcony off her bedroom, marble floors and a crystal chandelier in the dining room. She said I'm poor because her father Dr. Moore, has a paneled library and my father only a wooden bookcase. I hate this house. I'm running away."

Mother seasoned the chicken holding it by its legs. "Don't forget your umbrella. It looks like rain." Then she began to hum.

My quivering bottom lip now covered my top lip. While her back was turned I crawled under the formica table.

"She'll never know I'm here. She'll think I ran far away. She'll be sorry."

Minutes passed and I wondered why she wasn't looking for me. Of course, she didn't care that I ran away. Just wait 'til Dad gets home. We'll have chandeliers in every room.

I was getting bored. I played a game with the distorted face living in the chrome table legs. I stuck my tongue out at her just about the same time she stuck hers out at me. She was also salivating from the aroma of roasting chicken.

I heard dad come in. "Chicken smells great. Carol's favorite. Where is she?"

"She ran away. Claims she hates this house. No chandeliers, you know."

What I couldn't see was her winking and pointing to the table.

"That's too bad." My father said.

I sighed. "Finally someone who cares."

"Guess I'll have to do the crossword puzzle alone from now on. Maybe we should get another little girl. One who will appreciate this lovely home and family. One good thing, I get both drumsticks tonight. Pass the salad please."

My stinging eyes no longer allowed me to see the face in the table legs. My feverish ears heard Mom say, "I baked a blueberry pie for dessert."

Struggling from the floor I banged my head. Rubbing the bump and taking my place at the table I said, "I'm back."

"And?" My father questioned.

"And I'm sorry. I love this house. We don't need a chandelier. Did you eat both drumsticks?"

Assignment: When was the last time you did anything for the first time?

THE CANOE

Friday had finally arrived and I was looking forward to spending the weekend with my husband Albert. He told me he had a surprise planned. I was amazed when he pulled into the driveway with a large canoe strapped to the roof of the car. He talked me into some pretty wild adventures in the past, but no way was I getting into that canoe.

"I'm not going canoing." I said. "I can't even swim, let alone paddle. I've never been in a canoe before."

Albert answered, "There's a first time for everything."

We headed upstate to Cornwall. The canoe hung over the windshield and looked like the beak of a large eagle. I began to see rental shops and wondered why Albert hadn't rented the canoe here instead of hauling "the eagle" all this distance. He explained he got a good bargain and couldn't pass it up.

We pulled into a station where two men unloaded the canoe and put it on an all- terrain vehicle.

The driver took us through a forest and then straight down a very steep embankment. I was sure this would be the most frightening part of the day.

At the shore, Albert told me to get in first. I couldn't understand why I was in front of the ship and where was the steering wheel? I also noticed the seat was missing and started to complain. Albert said, "So, the seat is missing. Sit on the floor and here's a paddle for you." The handle of the paddle was broken and jagged but Albert told me not to worry because he would be doing all the paddling and I would never need to use it anyway.

When my husband hopped into the canoe, my end came out of the water. "Shouldn't I be touching the water?" I asked.

"Stop worrying about every little detail." He answered.

The directions from the truck driver were to follow the stream for six miles and he would pick us up on the other end. Six miles didn't seem a great distance and should last about twenty minutes. All this way for twenty minutes of canoing tun. The water was calm and I started to relax tidying my clothes. I had worn a navy blue and white yachting outfit, cute little white shoes and of course I never went anywhere without wearing pantyhose.

Captain Albert began to give me the rules. "You have to sit Indian style. This helps balance the canoe. Most of all remember, never, never stand up no matter what happens because we will tip over."

My heart was pounding and it hurt sitting Indian style. No wonder indians were always on the war path.

"Here's a life jacket, just in case." Albert said, throwing me a bright orange thing with broken straps and buckles. It looked uncomfortable and didn't match my outfit. I tossed it aside.

As we approached the beautiful Cornwall covered bridge I heard loud rumbling. At this point the river bed suddenly dropped and we were in the angry white waters of the mighty Housatonic River.

I screamed, "Turn around, turn around. I'm not going through that. I can't swim. We'll never make it."

Trying to make me believe there was hope, Albert shouted above the roar, "Remember I got a merit badge in boy scouts for canoing. There is no way to turn around against this current. Hang on, I'll get us through."

I screamed, "Oh my God, we're going to die."

I unknotted my legs, slipped off my shoes and wondered what it was like to drown. What would my battered body look like when they drag me in by my soggy panty hose?

Huge rocks were scraping against the of the canoe making horrible, eerie noises. I closed my eyes as we crashed.

As we approached the beautiful Cornwall covered bridge I began to hear loud rumbling. At this point, the river bed suddenly dropped and we were in the angry, raging white waters of the mighty Housatonic River. I panicked, "Turn around, turn around. I'm not going through that. I can't swim. We'll never make it."

Trying to make me believe there was hope, Albert shouted, "Remember I got a merit badge in boy scouts for canoeing. There is no way to turn around against this current. Don't worry, I'll get us through."

I screamed, "Oh my God, we're going to die." I unknotted my legs and while slipping off my shoes I wondered what it was like to drown. What would my battered body look like when they drag me in by my saggy panty hose?

Huge rocks were scraping against the bottom of the canoe making horrible, eerie noises. I closed my eyes as we crashed. We had landed on top of a large, slippery rock pile in the middle of the river. Our troubles had worsened. I looked back to see if Albert was still on board. I didn't want to die alone. This was the first time I saw this man, who was never afraid of anything, look beaten. He shouted to me above the roar of the white water, "We're not going to make it. Carol, if I have ever done anything to hurt you in the past, I am sorry. Please forgive me." There was nothing to forgive. I screamed back, "Do you know what you can do with that merit badge? If we ever get out of this alive, I'm going to kill you." One way or another this was the end for that boy scout.

Our only hope was to get free from the rocks. The water was lifting and smashing us back down. I knew the Eagle couldn't take much more. To make matters worse, Albert was now saying the Hail Mary and he was standing! He pushed the paddle against the rock and the water lifted us.The canoe was now airborne. We splashed down into the mighty current as Albert yelled, "Paddle, Paddle, and stay clear of the rocks." I reached for the broken piece of wood and tried to imitate his motions.

About a mile later the water began to calm. I thought I must be hallucinating from the trauma as I saw a man wearing hip boots trout fishing. He was definitely standing. I jumped out of the canoe and pulled like a mule on the Erie Canal, until we reached the embankment. I continued to pull the canoe on dry land, up a steep hill with Albert still in it.

The driver had been searching for us and picked us up on the road. As he loaded the canoe onto the truck he asked, "How was it?" Neither one of us answered. I knew I was never going to speak to Albert again, but uncontrollable laughter set in. Tears streamed down my face as I said, "Look I've ruined my panty hose."

THE SNOW LADY

The sound of laughter breaks winter's gloomy silence and draws me to my front window.

Directly across the street, Maria and her grandchildren are building a snowman. I join the laughter, realizing their sculpture is not a man at all - rather a very curvaceous snow lady. On her head sits a flowered Easter bonnet giving hope for spring.

The snow lady melts into a memory as Maria prepares her flower beds, laying wheelbarrows of fresh mulch. Across the street, I am doing the same.

A blur of yellow forsythias wink at lilac buds. Soon the lilacs will bloom releasing a lavender fragrance throughout the neighborhood.

Summer finds me watering pale pink and fuchsia-colored impatients. Maria is tending her begonias. She waves and crosses the street to chat. I ask about her grandchildren who are grown now. I mention the snow lady they built many years ago. Through teary eyes we decide to talk about the flowers.

Red and orange leaves quickly turn to rust. Autumn will carpet the lawns and raking begins. Winter will soon arrive.

I am drawn to my front window where I reminisce to the sound of laughter and the snow lady wearing her Easter bonnet.

A Holiday Amber Moment

Learning the words to "America the Beautiful" I asked Miss Norling, my third grade grade teacher, "What are 'amber' waves of grain?"

She answered, "Amber is a beautiful word used to describe the color yellow."

Years later, 'amber' lost its beauty as I discovered amber to be brownish-yellow, oozing, fossil resin.

Today, amber is merely the center color of a traffic light. I never know whether to brake or accelerate, I usually choose the latter and believe me, it is not an amber moment.

To capture my amber moment, I must return to Miss Norling's third grade classroom. We no longer sat alphabetically and Leonard Miller chose to sit next to me as we sang about the amber waves of grain.

Trying to impress me he said, "I have a cat with amber eyes." Without talcing a breath he added, "Do you want to go steady?"

"Sure." I answered, not knowing what going steady meant. I thought it had something to do with the cat with the amber eyes.

Going steady took place on Tuesday and by Thursday we were engaged. Leonard slipped a piece of twisted leather on my finger and proudly announced he made it in cub scouts. The leather tightened and I sat with a blue finger while we rehearsed for our holiday pageant.

By dinnertime, I forgot about being engaged when my parents asked if anything exciting happened in school. "I was chosen to be the Christmas angel." I answered.

A different conversation was going on at Leonard's dinner table. Somewhere between the soup and the salad, he broke the news of our engagement.

The next day I took my place next to my fiancée. He told me his mother said I was a lovely girl but we could not marry because we were of different faiths. But we could be good friends forever. Relieved, I handed him the piece of leather and watched the color return to my finger.

Once again rehearsing, Leonard was hoping to sing what he called 'The Angel Song' while the angel was lowered by cable to the stage. At eight years old he had a wonderful voice and could hit notes higher than Janette MacDonald.

Since Miss Norling was combining Hanukka and Christmas celebrations Leonard was chosen to be the third candle on the menorah. On cue, the disappointed candle would step forward and explain to the audience what it represented. I was proud of the third candle when it spoke.

Strapping on my leather harness, I wondered why all this leather was coming into my life lately. The Magi, dressed in their father's bathrobes toyed with my wings until my cue.

The audience "oohed" as an amber colored spotlight followed the angel to the manger. I was not balancing well as in rehearsal. I heard tittering and realized the three wise guys had turned my wings upside down and I was having difficulty landing. Strange and embarrassing sounds were coming from the angel. It was then the third candle stepped forward with angelic voice and sang, "Hark the Carol Angel Sings!" It will always be my amber moment.

Who's O. Henry?

Pretending to be a deer, at four years olds I jumped over the wooden saddle that separated the kitchen from the living room. There, I found my father in his favorite chair reading.

"Hi, Dad. Do you want to play checkers?"

"Not now. I'm reading." he answered.

Seeking attention I asked, "What are you reading?"

Without looking up he answered, "O. Henry."

I thought that a funny name as my exaggerated laugh questioned, "Who's O. Henry?"

"A master of short stories," he answered.

The room seemed extra quiet now. He continued to read until I shouted, "how about dominos? Do you want to play dominos?"

He reached for a piece of paper. On the bottom he wrote my name, age and date. He handed me the pencil and said, "Here, practice writing your name. At eight o'clock we'll turn the radio on and listen to "The Shadow."

The shadow gave a young Orson Welles his first starring role in a radio series and introduced listeners to Lamont Cranston. I didn't like The Shadow because I knew when the program ended it was time for bed.

After printing my name many times, I ran out of room. I handed the paper to my father.

"Now what?" I asked.

"Very nice," he praised. "Give yourself a star."

I gave myself several stars until interrupted by the radio. "Who knows what evil lurks in the hearts of men."

I disguised my voice and deeply answered, "The Shadow knows."

Many years later, I inherited my father's complete set of O. Henry (copyright 1902). I promised myself to read the twelve volumes as I wiped each book and ruffled the pages before placing them into my bookcase. I thought it would be nice if a hundred dollar bill fell out. To my surprise something priceless fell did fall out. It read, "Carol Crocco. Age four. 1946." It was rated three stars.

FLYER

Christmas was just a few days away when my father asked me what I was hoping Santa would bring me this year. Without hesitation I answered, "A sled!"

"Wouldn't you rather have a magic set with all kinds of tricks?" he asked.

Every year Santa never failed to bring me a magic set with Houdini's picture on the box. I hated magic tricks. I usually ended up frustrated and in tears because I couldn't get the three metal rings apart and when I cut the piece of rope, it never went back together again.

While my mother busied herself in the kitchen, Dad and I talked about my schoolwork. "How are you doing in arithmetic?" he asked. I felt a quiz coming on, "How old will you be in the year 2002?" he tested. I didn't know. I didn't even care. I couldn't comprehend 1950 was near. "You will see the new millennium, but I will be gone." He said. I wondered where he was going. I wanted to stop the arithmetic questions. "Maybe I would like a magic set," I changed the subject, "but I really would rather have a sled."

Needless to say, on Christmas morning next to Houdini's box, was a new sled under the tree. I named the sled "Flyer." Being an only child, I not only named everything, I also talked to everything. Flyer became my best friend and we would go everywhere together. From sunup to sundown we slid down every hillside in the area. Each night I dried his runners. With waxed paper, I would scrub his blades. We would always be ready for any challenge. No one could beat us in a downhill race. "Go Flyer, go faster, faster." I would always congratulate him for winning and we always won!

One day, my father got the idea to bum my initials into Flyer. It was painful to watch and I hoped it wasn't hurting his oak body or his lacquered finish. When the wood burning tool was cool and Flyer's underbelly stopped smoldering, I gave him a trial run. He ran as well as ever and I was relieved.

The next morning was a sheet of ice. I had trouble standing up as I pulled Flyer up the steepest hill. We flew down the slope, Flyer's runners on top of the ice. This was record- breaking speed and I was becoming frightened as I saw the brick wall coming closer. I could no longer steer. Instinct made me turn my head as we crashed. The pain in my left ear hurt so much I could not cry. "Flyer, where are you?" I called while holding my ear. I saw him lying on his back, runners facing the sky. "I killed him." I thought as I ran to him. I pulled him home talking to him all the way.

I never knew what happened to Flyer after that. I only knew we had been through a lot together.

This year I received a Christmas card from my cousin and he wrote, "cleaning out fifty years of accumulation at my mother's house. Your initials are on an old sled in the basement." As I read I whispered, "Flyer, Flyer" and the memories came flooding back.

THE SILVER BICYCLE

I had just settled down for the evening with my book when I heard the low flying plane passing overhead. An eerie feeling came over me as I realized I was more aware of plane noises now. My thoughts once again went back to September 11th and then flashed to the silver bicycle and Michael. I saw his beautiful smile before me and remembered the first time he smiled at me.

"Hi, my name is Michael." He said, stopping the silver bilce on the front sidewalk.

"Welcome to the neighborhood."

I leaned the rake against a tree. "It's nice to meet you Michael. You're the first neighbor to speak to me." I said. "Which house do you live in?"

He pointed to a well-kept comer house with large oak trees and bird feeders. "My father and I feed all the wild birds. Bird-watching is our hobby. Would you like me to help you with the raking?"

"You're too late. I'm almost finished. I was just about to take a break. How about joining me with a coke?" I asked.

"Cool." He said, putting down the kickstand on the silver bike.

We sat on the porch while he talked about his dreams of finishing school and becoming a stockbroker and some day having an office in a tall building in New York. I was amused by the young boy's serious plan.

"Well, follow your dreams, Michael." I said, as he handed me the empty Coke bottle.

As the years passed, I saw Michael less. He did stop one day to show me he had traded in the silver bicycle for a silver Ford Mustang and told me he was going off to college soon. When he was home on break I would see him in the yard feeding the birds with his father. Michael graduated with high honors and was hired by Canter-Fitzgerald where he worked as a bond trader. In time he had earned the title of Vice President of the company located on the 106th floor of the World Trade Center.

He called his fiancée the morning of September 11th and said, "The building has been hit by something. We don't know what it was but we can't get out. There is no way up or down. I love you. Please call my parents and tell them I love them too."

Michael's body was never found buried beneath the rubble.

This Christmas the neighbors, as usual, decorated with bright lights pretending things normal for the children and themselves. The house with the bird feeders had only one bright light shining on a large American Flag. Looking out my window on Christmas morning I saw Michael's father feeding the birds and I remembered Michael and the silver bike.

INTUITION?

I am still not sure what occurred on that hot August night in 1995. Was it intuition, a premonition, or was my mind playing games with my reasonable self?

I had been asleep a couple of hours before the small dog at the foot of my bed decided he needed to go out. It was very unusual for him to wake me in the middle of the night. I reluctantly got up, pulled on my robe and said, "I guess when you gotta go, you gotta go."

I leashed the dog and walked him down the driveway. As he stood on three legs watering the oak tree, I glanced over at my neighbors home. How fortunate I was to have such wonderful neighbors and thought of them as family. I saw Tom's canoe in their driveway all packed, waiting for Tom and his teenage son Chris, to go fishing in the morning. I remember thinking how much they enjoy their fishing trips together. It was then I noticed a tall figure standing near the canoe. I was sure it was Chris and wondered why he was out in the middle of the night. I pulled the dog toward him. I realized, although Chris is over six feet tall, this figure was much taller and seemed to be wearing a cowl. It turned slowly to face me and seemed irritated that I was there. I felt an eerie chill and wanted to yell, "Who are you? Get away from that canoe." But I could not speak. I pulled the dog in the other direction and headed home. I felt a little safer reaching my own property and turned for one last look. Angry, sunken eyes looked back at me and vanished into the night air. I somehow knew, I had spoiled the creature's plans.

I returned to bed knowing I would not sleep. I listened to the little dog snore and wondered why he did not bark at the cloaked figure. "Of course," I thought, "because he didn't see it - because it wasn't there." But I knew what I saw and I knew it was "Death" standing near the canoe.

The next morning, my husband immediately sensed something was wrong. "What's the matter?" he asked.

"Nothing" I answered. "You wouldn't believe it. I'm still trying to sort it out. Will you take the dog out this morning?"

Returning he again asked, "What's wrong?"

Shaking, I told him the dreadful story. Knowing how my intuition has worked in the past he said, "You have to stop Tom from getting in that canoe."

"Don't be silly." I said. "Tom is the strongest man I know. He has big plans to move South and enjoy life when he retires. Nothing can happen to him. He could out-swim Buster Crabbe and so can Chris."

I did not convince myself and reached for the phone. Loud banging on the door ended my call. It was Chris. Tears streaming down his face he wept. "My father had a stroke. It doesn't look good. Pleasecome, he would want you there."

At the hospital I found Tom in intensive care, his left side paralyzed. The doctors had no hope,-but I knew better.

It has been almost nine years since my encounter with the cowled figure. Tom, although confined, sits near his pool in South Carolina with his family. I waited a long time before telling them my story. They never doubted and thanked me for scaring Death away on that hot August night.

Why Am I Saving This?

I opened the drawer. There it was again. I really should throw it away.

I looked at the yellow-creased handkerchief, felt the material and traced the flowers and leaves running along the boarder. I sat on the bed and ran my finger across the oversized letter "C" and remembered.

I would be starting kindergarten in September. Stratfield Elementary School was only two blocks away but I thrilled at the thought of walking there by myself. I had finally grown up.

The strict dress code for five year olds stated, "rubber soled shoes must be worn on the freshly waxed floors. Shirts and ties for boys and dresses for girls with a handkerchief pinned to the bodice."

Mother took me to Reads Department Store to select handkerchiefs at the lingerie counter. The saleslady was sliding her hand in a nylon stocking, spreading her fingers to show the sheemess and color.

"May I help you, madam?" she asked Mother.

"Yes." she answered." My daughter would like to look at some hankies."

The saleslady reached for the flat silvery boxes lined with white tissue paper.

The first handkerchiefs she showed me had Little Bo Peep looking for her sheep. On the reverse side were three little sheep. I shook my head. The next box held circus animals with the alphabet running around the hem.

"How juvenile." I thought. "Doesn't she know I'm in school now?"

I pointed to the pink box with four hankies displayed in pastel colors. I loved the blue one and Mother agreed.

"Shall I monogram them? I can have them ready in an hour."

"That will be fine." Mother said taking my hand firmly, leading me to the elevator.

On the top floor was a tearoom where we lunched on watercress sandwiches served on doilies. I sipped pink lemonade until it was time to pick up my monogrammed hankies.

I was disappointed to learn, Mother had to come to school with me the first day. I couldn't wait for her to leave. Only then would I feel grown up.

Her last order before introducing me to Miss Trotter was, "Don't forget to use your hankie."

The elderly Miss Trotter smiled at me saying, "My, what a lovely hankie."

It was difficult to hear her as most of the kids were lying on the floor screaming, crying and yelling for their mothers. I stepped over Peter Kaval who was wailing and turning blue. I knelt, bare knees against the waxed floor saying, "Don't cry Peter. We're grown up now." I unpinned my hankie and wiped away his tears.

That evening Mother asked, "Did you need to use your new hankie?"

I answered, "Yes, I did."

TWO HOUSES - ONE COAT

Pat and I entered junior high together. We were neighbors and best friends. Only a fieldstone path separated the two houses, just the right distance to run a piece of string with two tins cans attached between our upstairs bedrooms. Our stone-age cell phone was better than today's version, as we could also <u>see</u> each other as we talked. Through the string we plotted to get our mothers to buy us the coats we wanted. Only then would we be just like the "cool kids" at school. The coats were ankle length, navy blue wool, with large white mother of pearl buttons and a draping belt across the back. They called the creation Boy Coats. How cool can you get?

Pat was sure if we pleaded, our mothers would give in. I didn't have to plead long. My mother said, "No. Your winter coat is fine and a new coat would cost a weeks pay. You need to be warm, not cool." She added, the style reminded her of something Jean Harlow wore in a gangster movie.

In the morning Pat arrived wearing her new boy coat. I finally knew what envy felt like. Although I was happy for Pat, I desperately wanted her coat. I had to work extra hard on mother with hope of getting the coat by the big basketball game on Friday night. Pat would be wearing her new coat and probably sit with the cool kids leaving me alone. On second thought, I knew she wouldn't do that but I still wanted that coat.

I made promises to nty mother I knew I couldn't keep. In addition to shoveling the snow, I promised to shingle the roof, wallpaper the dining room and walk the dog every day, if we ever got a dog. By the end of the week she caved and bought me the coat.

"If anything happens to this expensive coat don't come home." She warned.

Somehow it happened. The last time I saw it, was on the bleachers at the basketball game. I waved to Coach Johnson and folded it neatly next to me. Now it was gone and I was in for it. I cried. "I can't go home. I'll run away to Alaska."

Pat tried to comfort me. "You can't go to Alaska. You have no coat. Maybe you should go to Mexico."

We walked home through the snow sharing Pat's coat. Five minutes for her and then my turn. Pat had an idea. "Wear my coat into the house, say hello to your mother and then go upstairs and throw it out the window for me to wear home."

It worked. The next morning I lowered the tin can string and Pat tied the coat on as I slowly hauled it into my bedroom. Wearing the coat I greeted Mom, grabbed a piece of toast and ran out the door where I found Pat, freezing waiting for her turn to wear the coat.

After watching the coat go up and down for two weeks my mother decided I had suffered enough and confronted me. She was holding my coat as I ran in the house wearing Pat's. "Coach Johnson found your coat under the bleachers and brought it here the night of the basketball game."

Ashamed I asked, "Do you want the dining room papered or the roof shingled first?"

THANK YOU EVERYONE - ESPECIALLY F.O.

by
Albert Ruggiero

"Come out and play." "I don't want to." An unusual thing for any nine years old to shout out the window to his cousin but I had my reasons. Cousin Butch was every inch a bully, braggart, trouble maker and sore loser. Yet, we had lived so very closely in our Chatham Street three family house it seemed we were just very different brothers of some sort. I much preferred my chemistry set to Butch by that time.

As I think back, I was part of two very distinct worlds. There was the neighborhood world; its throbbing heart was our little park. Here we played ball, roller-skated, looked for friends, ate our candy, chased the ice cream man ridding his bicycle (if we had a dime), met new kids from other parts of Fair Haven wondering in (some of whom enjoyed beating us up), threw snowballs at delivery trucks (and each other), and made snowmen and snow forts in the winter. Here we made plans for each day's activities, threw each other around playing "king of the mountain," and on occasion shared our dreams about the an unknown future.

Everyone knew everyone. The big kids, 13, 14, 15, even 16, years old would lead us into organized games like baseball. I was always the last to be picked, never hit or caught anything but always managed to get hit with a hard ball, ouch! No one could ever figure out why I really never got into sports. I didn't wonder at all.

Girls hung with girls, including my big sister Diane, but there were some like Kathy McDonald (later to have much to do with founding the Milford Senior Citizens Center) who had such strong personalities that they could round on the entire neighborhood – maybe twenty five kids, and with trumpeting- bugle, she would step boldly into the streets and stop traffic all the way as we paraded up to another park in Fair Haven Heights for an outing.

Mostly we boys messed with other boys; cousin butch hung with his own group, equally strange (how could a 12 year - old -Sally - have a full mustache?). We never, never crossed paths in the park - they did secretive things.

I remember how excited we all were as the 4th of July approached. Everyone was busy collected pieces of scrap wood for a neighborhood bomb fire. Oh such excitement! Some wild kids even managed to get hold of a few bottle rockets? Mostly we walked around with punks and sparklers – still, very cool. Weeks before, the town would build a stage for speakers to come and talk about the importance of the holiday. We kids just waited for the talking to stop then we mounted the stage and threw each other off into the dirt. What fun! We didn't come home until dark, and boy, was I dirty from head to foot!

How very different was that other world I belonged to; the world of family. We were card-carrying Italians in an Irish-German neighborhood. Our American roots ran up to Russell Street where my grandmother (Rose) presided over an entire city block, both sides of near and distant relations. My favorite was my uncle Mickey. He lived right next door to Grams.

It seemed to me that going to Russell Street was like going to the country with the added - curious - somehow comforting - realization that we (sister and I) were surrounded by aunts, uncles, cousins, third cousins, and their friends. There was big and little John, Uncle Joe, Aunt Jewel (a rather tough lady from the South), Aunt Francis, Aunt Rose, Uncle Charlie, lots of visiting in-laws whom I never really got to know and a most curious lady that went by the name of "Mugalod." She was kind of scary with wild hear, rags for clothes and no teeth to speak of. All I can tell you is that she and her house often came up in conversations when someone wanted to employ the superlative form of comparison. "You look like Mugalod." My house is getting just like Mugalod's."

You get the idea. From the road it looked like hoarders paradise. She took on the appearance of a wandering - raggedy gypsy - all part of the charm of Russell St.

Once in a great while I would sleep at my Grandmother's house. I can still remember the ultimate tactile sensation of climbing into bed -it was really high - and sinking - ever so gently into a mattress stuffed with down feathers. Oh boy! This was living! Never felt that way since.

I close this – already too wordy – (I know Carol) diatribe with a brief mention of my Maternal Grandfather. He died in 1955. I was all of nine years old. Yet, his presence, his accomplishments, his unique domination of the Onofrio clan and with it all of Russell St. and our home on Chatham Street was incredibly powerful. Arriving in America from a small town perched on a hill a few miles from Naples; F.O. never learned to read or write. He simply signed his name with the initials F.O. (Frank Onofrio). Yet, he formed business after business.

Starting in the 1930's with milk deliveries then moving into highway construction. Along the way he bought a thriving gas station and several apartment houses including our Chatham Street three- family. My uncle Mickey - returning stateside after the war lived on the third floor, we Ruggieros had the second, and my aunt Zoo-Zoo cowered the Melilos on the first floor.

We were very complete, as I tried to describe earlier, in our two-part world. There was no need for family get-to- gethers, excepting Christmas Eve which would take another paper to describe. We were ALWAYS TOGETHER! We were living in F.O.'s three family. My grandmother was the landlord; we laughed and fought, and were a secure in our memories as was the legacy of F.O.

POTPOURRI

Carol Ruggiero
2 of Hearts

The Person I Look Up To The Most

In 1961 the song 'Mother In law' was number one on the charts. The lyrics gave all mothers-in law a bad rap.

My mother-in law is my friend. She always understands and gives good advice. I respect her because I have learned she is wiser than I. Wisdom usually comes with age. She is almost ninety. She takes good care of my father-in law - he is ninety four.

She raised two devoted children (one my husband). She will admit she loves him more than any other on earth. For this reason, I love her. I take good care of her son and for that reason she loves me.

She calls to tell me I give her peace of mind knowing her son is loved and well taken care of. She trusts me and I trust her. Trust goes hand in hand with love.

I look up to my mother-in law and I don't care what that ridiculous song says.

C.A.R.

I took a friend to lunch one day or she took me. I don't know. I loss track of who took whom. I had some news and could not wait to tell her. We just sat down when I said, "Oh no, don't look now. Here he comes. I swear he smells you."

There is no nice way to put it. The old gent has the 'hots' for her. When he trips and falls on her I'm sure it's just a ruse to get a touch or two, if you know what I mean.

She is too kind to say, "Get the hell off of me." So I say it for her. No great loss.

He can't stand me nor I him. His ego makes him talk too much. He shows her his charge cards, all his cash and points out his new car through the glass. His name is Joe. I don't know his last name but I'm sure it must be Blow. He is so full of hot air.

I get up and leave with hope he will be gone when I get back. No such luck. His pant leg is pulled up to his knee as he shows her his scar from the war. I don't think he had to use his gun, he just talked our foes to death. I feel sick and ask for some ice. He, not glad to see me back, at last leaves. Now I can tell my news.

"Have you heard? There's a new group in town call 'The One Pulse Word Club.' I tried to join but had no luck. Dues in hand, they let me in but soon showed me the door. You see, I could not sign the sign in sheet. The rules state you must have a one pulse or one word name like Close."

Oh sure, my friend may join but I can't. She has all the luck. I know she did not plan it that way but to me it is not fair at all. She wed Jim who made her Close. At times she calls him James. See what I mean? She lucked out there too. Come to think of it, she had two one word last names in her life. She's such a pain. I had to go and say "I do" to Al with the long last name. What a mess. I guess it could have been worse. I could have wound up with Joe Blow and have to look at his damn leg each night.

I'll have to fake a name. No one checks my I.D. Let's see, I hear the name Bush in the news. Like "damn that Bush or God bless Bush. There were quite a few one pulse names in the White House - Polk, Grant, Hayes, Taft and Ford. I could steal one of their names but I don't care for any. Do you?

I want a name that will pop out at you when seen in print, just in case I write a great one pulse book. Pop! Now there's a good last name, but what will I do with my two pulse first name? I have been called Mom. That will do fine and I can keep my strong church name, which is Ann. I was named for my Aunt Ann. Now there was a strong gal, could lift a truck with one arm tied. Of course I fib but I need more one pulse words to please You-Know-Who in class.

So that's it. I have my new name. Good thing they're not too bright in that new club. I will sign in on the name line- Mom Ann Pop!

Light Bulbs?

Have you noticed light bulbs don't last the way they used to? Not only that- they seem to be in cahoots, all bum out at the same time.

Buying bulbs, a couple of packages at a time, was getting expensive. I decided to go to Home Depot, buy in quantity and stock up. I was overwhelmed by the size of the store and immediately tried to find help. I spotted a green apron and I'm sure it spotted me. As I walked forward, it turned picking up its pace. Somehow I outran it and breathlessly asked," Can you direct me to the bulbs?"

Without turning it answered. "At the end of aisle three, through the automatic doors."

"Which way is aisle three?" I asked.

The wooden paint stirrer sighed, pointed to the left and scooted away.

The doors flew open and sure enough- there were bulbs, displayed in large bins labeled, Tulips, Lilies, Crocus, etc.

To my surprise a green apron, dragging a water hose asked, "May I help you?"

"Yes, do hyacinths come in seventy-five watt?"

FOOTSTEPS

It seems at times, there are not enough hours during the day. For this reason I found myself grocery shopping much later than usual.

Alone, I felt uneasy in the dimly lit parking lot and to make matters worse, it was raining.

I felt anxious watching a young man slowly bag my groceries. Did I look so feeble that he was putting only one or two items into each bag? Noticing his nametag, I said, "Let me help you Andrew."

Andrew seemed a little upset with this idea. Did he feel I was after his job? I just wanted to get home and was losing patience with Andrew. I also lost patience with the confused cashier who was trying to make change. Why do they start with the higher denomination? That would confuse me too. I quickly grabbed the unwanted receipt and said, "Thank you" which is more than she did. Wheels flying, I headed toward the automatic doors.

The rain was heavier now. Nothing to cover my head, I condensed a bag of groceries, put the plastic bag over my head and tied the loop handles under my chin. With both hands I straightened my chapeau as the grocery cart took off over the curb. I chased rolling oranges through deep puddles while dodging splashing automobiles. When I realized the oranges were winning, I gave up and allowed them their freedom. I was exhausted and wet. I just wanted to get home.

While loading the groceries into the trunk I heard footsteps behind me. "Oh no." I said. "Not tonight. I'm in no mood to be mugged. Or worse, the mugger could push me into the car and tell me to drive. I decided he would have to kill me right there. No way was I chauffeuring a mugger on I-95.

I turned and saw a young male figure in a hooded jacket. I was trying to see his face when he said, "Your wallet."

My heart stood still. "It's true." I thought. "I'm going to die right here in a supennarket parking lot."

He repeated his words. "Your wallet."

"Take it." I stammered. Take the whole damn pocket book. Take my car."

I reached into a bag. "Here, take my chocolate covered Ring Dings too."

He pointed something at me and pulled his hood back. "Your wallet," he said. "You left it on the counter."

It was Andrew. I had forgotten my wallet in my rush to get home.

Carol Ruggiero
22 Vermont Ave.
Milford, Ct. 06460
Phone: 203-876-0308

The Dairy Farm

In the spring of 1947 my first grade teacher was teaching the class the importance of dairy products. Our health books pictured a boy and girl drinking milk and explained how dairy products are important for a healthy, balanced diet.

To our delight, Miss Becker announced we were going on a field trip to visit a dairy farm. A school bus was taking us six miles from the school in Fairfield Connecticut to the town of Easton. Many of us seven year olds had never been on a bus before as most of us walked to school.

Miss Becker handed out permission slips to be signed by our parents. The note requested we wear overalls and thick- soled shoes.

The trip began with us singing, "The farmer in the dell" until we saw the large red and white sign. It read "Snow's Dairy Farm."

Farmer Snow met the children at the bus and we followed him into the barn where he introduced us to the cows, each named after a flower.

"Say hello to the children, Rose," he said to the first cow as Violet "mooed" from the second stall. Pansy watched with her large brown eyes as two farm cats entered the bam. The farmer sat on a three legged stool and showed us how a cow was milked. The sound of the milk hitting the metal bucket made us all laugh. The cats stood on their hind legs and he squirted milk into their little pink mouths. "Express delivery," he laughed along with the children.

After the milking demonstration we gathered under a large apple tree and sat on the wet grass. The farmer's wife brought us little containers of milk and warm biscuits in a basket. She poured cream in a glass jar. Each child was asked to shake the jar twenty times and pass it on. When the jar reached the last child, it had turned to butter.

We spread our homemade butter on the biscuits. I have never tasted anything so wonderful.

Sadly, our adventure ended as farmer Snow walked us back to the bus. He was now certain we all wanted to be dairy farmers and asked Eddie, "What do you want to be when you grow up?"

"A pirate," Eddie answered without hesitation.

"I'm going to be a princess," Maryanne said.

The farmer laughed before asking me the same question.

"I want to live in the white house with Harry Truman and make him homemade butter!"

APRIL FOOL

After reading the poster on the school bulletin board, I spent the rest of the day avoiding Skippy. Not that I didn't like Skippy-I did. We grew up together. He was like a brother and I wanted to keep it that way. He had other plans.

I knew he was about to ask me to the April Fools dance and I just didn't want to go with Skippy. I had my eye on that dreamy new French exchange student and was trying to get up enough courage to introduce myself.

On the day we upperclassmen gave a luncheon for the freshman, I knew it was now or never. We wore name tags reading, "Hi, my name is...."

I saw the beret from across the cafeteria. I stuck my hand out like an eager politician as I read his name tag. "Hi, Jean Louis." I said, a little louder than anticipated.

His dark eyes sparkled. "It is pronounced Jean Louie, mademoiselle."

He bowed from the waist, took my hand and gently kissed it. It now hung from my wrist like tapioca. His accent sent me to Shangri-la and I was having difficulty continuing the conversation. "I hope to see you at the April Fools dance Jean Louis, along with your date, of course.

Again the accent spoke. "Since I am new here, I'm afraid I do not know anyone to ask."

"Well, you know me." I answered.

Grabbing a napkin from a place setting, I wrote my phone number and handed it to him. "If you get stuck, I'll be glad to do you the favor. I can easily rearrange my plans. All that meant, was saying no to Skippy.

I took the long way home looking back from time to time in case Skippy was following. I heard the phone ringing as I approached the front door and rushed to answer it. It had to be Jean Louis. It wasn't. It was Skippy.

"I saw you with Jean Louis today. I don't know what you see in him. What's he got that I don't?"

"Well Skip, besides the obvious, he has that romantic French accent."

Skippy snapped back. "I think he's putting it on. Anyone can fake a French accent."

"I gotta go Skip. I don't want to tie up the line."

"Wait," he said. "Will you go to the April Fools dance with me?"

"I'll talk to you later," I said. "And Skip, no one can fake that accent." Click.

That evening, I tumbled down the stairs when the phone rang. "It must be Jean Louis."

"Bon jour" the voice said. "I would be honored to take you to the dance, mademoiselle."

I wanted to yell, "Oui Oui, merci beau coup," but I kept my composure.

On the dark, rainy evening of April 1st, I admired myself in the full length mirror. The bodice of my gown glittered reminding me of Jean Louis' eyes.

When the doorbell finally rang, I counted to five. "Mustn't let him know I'm anxious."

I opened the door to see a tall silhouette dressed in a white dinner jacket. The beret added interest as I waited for him to speak first.

"April fool, mon ami."

It was then I realized. Skippy was standing under the beret.

THE PARTY

Harriet's thoughts began racing before her eyes flew open. She was sure he would come today. He had to come. It was her birthday and she planned for months to make it very special. She mailed herself seven birthday car ds tucked into pastel envelopes. She was careful to address them with different colored inks and wrote some with her left hand. Now she was sure he would come.

Mr. Sidney will arrive at one o'clock, give or take a few minutes. He will park the white truck on the hill and walk down the steep embankment to the front door where she will be waiting in her frilly party dress. "Lots of mail for you today ma'am," he will smile. That is when she will invite him in for pink lemonade and birthday cake she made herself. He will probably refuse at first, saying he has a schedule to keep but she will coax him with, "Please Mr. Sidney, it's my birthday."

She thought of birthdays past, the cottage full of laughter, music, good friends, Mother and Daddy. All were gone now. Her only friend was Theda and she seemed to be missing the last few days.

A noise at the back door startled her. "It couldn't be Mr. Sidney this early," she thought. "He would come to the front door as usual." She opened the squeaking screen door. It was Theda! "You tramp," she greeted. "Where have you been? Down at the lake with that Tom, I suppose. Look at your beautiful coat full of briar, thicket and thorn."

Theda's amber eyes widen to Harriet's shouting voice. The orange cat weaved her sleek body around Harriet's ankles and all was forgiven. "Theda the vamp, that's you," she laughed, bending to pet her friend. She was happy knowing Theda will be at her party.

Harriet's mind went back to planning the festivities. She placed Mother's silver candlestick in the center of the table. She had polished it until the silver shone blue. "It will be like having Mother here," she thought and looked toward Father's caned chair. On the chair she placed a coil of hemp. It was the same rope Father had used to tie the rowboat each night to the pier. "Father's spirit will be here for my party," she giggled. "Now, let's see, Mother, Father, Theda and of course Mr. Sidney.

What a wonderful birthday this will be." She checked the arrangements one more time. "Oh, the poetry book. I almost forgot the poetry book," she said, placing it on the table.

The clock chimed once as Mr. Sidney approached the front door. "Lots of mail for you today, ma'am," he smiled. Harriet smiled back batting her black mascara lashes. "Come in, Mr. Sidney. Please join me in a cold glass of lemonade and a piece of birthday cake."

"I would love to ma'am but I have a mail route to complete. I can't be late getting the truck back to the terminal."

Harriet's voice rose, "I won't take no for an answer today. It's my birthday." Her voice sweetened as she tried again. "Come, meet Theda and let me tell about Mother and Daddy. "Sorry ma'am, I have to go. Here's your mail."

"Step in and place it on the table." Her voice trembled.

The pastel colored envelopes flew into the air as she hit Mr. Sidney on the head with Mother's silver candlestick. Harriet tied Mr. Sidney with Father's rope as Theda arched her back and hissed.

Harriet reminded herself, "It's my birthday." She reached for the poetry book and began reciting to Mr. Sidney.

PATIENCE

If patience is a virtue - I am virtue-less. Anxiety drives while patience takes the back seat. Because of this I move too quickly. If its going to happen let it happen now - why wait? I soon realize patience delivers a reward while anxiety snaps its impatient fingers.

I only have patience with children and animals. A three year old finds the center of the alphabet difficult to recite. I am amuzed hearing "Lemon-Ello. Please." Patience and repetition soon correct L-M-N-O-P. Actually, I like the childs version better.

We have all seen a sad eyed dog balancing a milk bone across the bridge of his nose. He is salivating but waits for his master's voice before allowed the treat. The dog has shown patience - the virtue I lack.

Maybe someday I will learn to balance a milk bone on my nose before anxiety devours it.

Gretchen Lied To Save Her Friend

When the phone rang rang Gretchen knew it was Emily. They were friends since kindergarten and now at age twelve they attended junior high together. It was spring vacation and they planned on doing fun things during the week-but most of all they planned on avoiding Beverly Bennett.

"HiGretch." Emily began. "I need you to lie for me."

Gretchen answered, "Oh no, I hate lying. I'm not good at it. One lie always seems to lead to another."

Emily cut in. "The alternative is worse. Beverly called and said she wanted me to go to the movies with her. She is nothing but trouble. I don't like her and I know you feel the same. I had to think of an excuse fast so I told her you have the measles and I needed to sit with you while your mom goes to the store. So Gretch, after vacation when you see her in school, just stick to that story."

"Well, ok. I guess she'll never find out the truth." Gretchen said.

Gretchen hung up and the phone immediately rang. "I guess Em forgot to tell me something."

"Hi Gretchen. This is Beverly Bennett. I heard you are sick. I'm going to stop by to see you."

"Oh no-don't do that. You'll catch the chicken pox."

"Chicken pox? I thought you have the measles."

"Oh right-the measles. Yes, I have the measles." Gretchen lied.

"I've had the measles and can't get them again. I'm on my way." Beverly said.

Gretchen paced. "What am I going to do now. I knew lying would get me in trouble."

She reached into her drawer and pulled out a tube of red lipstick. She was saving it for the school dance but this was an emergency. She drew red spot all over her face and arms and hopped into bed.

The door flew open after one quick knock. "Oh, you poor thing."

Beverly said. "I thought you and Emily were lying to me. Where is Emily? She said she was coming over to sit with you."

Gretchen head began to ache. "She was here and then we discovered she has the measles too."

Beverly narrowed her eyes. "I guess I'll go visit her next."

When Beverly left, Gretchen called Emily. "Quick Em, start drawing red spots on your body- Beverly is on her way. And Em? Please let's never lie again."

Writers Unlimited
Assignment-Dialogue Two Characters
Carol Ruggiero

Carol   Books are like old friends to me. They are very hard to part with and some I have kept since I was a teenager. I know I will never read them again but it gives me comfort to know they are there.

              One day while dusting the bookshelves, I overheard a conversation between two of my favorite novels. I couldn't help eavesdropping.

Dorothy   "Mrs. Hanson, Mrs. Hanson, are you home?"

Carol   "I can hear you Mrs. Nolan. Where else would a fine, Norwegian mother of four be? Lars will be home soon and I am getting dinner ready. How are things in Brooklyn?"

Dorothy   "Not as wonderful as your life in San Francisco I'm afraid. I'm having a problem with Francie. She just stares out the window at a tree and is dreaming her life away while I scrub floors trying to make ends meet. My husband, Johnnie puts such foolish dreams in her head. She adores him and stiffens to me."

Carol   "Your alcoholic husband is no help. Singing in Irish taverns is no way to put money in the bank. Children need to feel secure. Lie to them. Tell them you have a bank account like I do. Teach them that they must never use this money so it will always be there for security. By the way Mrs. Nolan, why did you name your son that ridiculous name? I never heard the name, Nealy."

Dorothy	"Do you think Dagmar, Katrin and Nels are such great names? I can't even remember your other daughter's name because she is so insignificant to the story."
Carol	"Her name is Christina and she was named after my Uncle Chris who taught me to lie to my children if it would make them feel secure. Don't tell me you have an Uncle Nealy!"
Dorothy	"What is your first name Mrs. Hanson?"
Carol	"I really can't remember Mrs. Nolan. I've been called Mama for so long. I won't easily forget that name. I can remember Mama. Now, let's get back to your problem. I think your author should kill off your husband so you can marry that nice cop on the beat. Then you can have a baby and name her Annie Laurie. I know this is Johnnie's favorite song because I am placed so close to your novel on the shelf. I can't help hearing him stagger in after hours, singing Annie Laurie. I can almost smell his breath. Yes, Francie will miss him but you will be able to move out of the cold water flat with your children and new husband. By the way, I was sorry to hear they are taking down Francie's tree. I'm sure another one will grow in its place. I have to go now Mrs. Nolan. I hear Lars coming and I must get him his sweater and pipe. Maybe your author will write a sequel and call it Another Tree Grows In Brooklyn. Thank you for sharing the bookshelf with me."
Dorothy	"Goodbye Mama. I'll always remember you."

My family And Friends Love Me
But They Like Me Because...

I am always there to listen. If dealing with a problem I never say, "This too shall pass." It sounds like an uncaring cop-out.

If asked for advice I will only give it if I have experienced a similar problem. I never lie to family or friends. Whatis-is.

I always try to keep a sense of humor and hope I make humorous sense.

I care deeply about my friends and family. Best of all, they know it.

PAGE THIRTY-THREE

As usual I was at the kitchen stove when my husband came in from work.

"Did you have a good day Carol Ann?" He asked.

He playfully uses my middle name when he is excited about something. The "something" doesn't have to be much and today was no exception.

I shrugged pretending not to notice he was hiding something behind his back.

"I have something for you." He chuckled.

I decided to play the game and asked, "Where did you get it?" hoping the answer was "Tiffany's."

He held out a small beat up book. "Ta-da! I rescued it from the school's library dumpster. It's a three-act play called, "The Land Is Bright" written by your favorite author Edna Ferber. It takes place in New York City at the fifth Avenue home of the Kincaids."

Not wanting to touch the book I continued preparing dinner, forced a smile and said, "turn to page thirty-three and read me the first complete sentence."

Most would think this a strange request but my husband immediately ruffled through the pages and read, "Fashions in decorating have changed in the twenty-five years that have passed over the Kincaid's living room."

Hearing Edna Ferber's voice I thought of my grandmother's parlor with the Victrolla in the middle of the room. I remembered the day she plucked a laced doily from the overstaffed horsehair chair and placed it on my head as we danced around the room.

Someday I will write about that-but not today. Today I will thank my husband for the little book. I enjoyed it more than anything from Tiffany's.

I Am Saddest When...

Grief is the strongest of all emotions. It goes deeper than love or hate.

Sadness fills the emptiness that grief has left.

I am saddest when grief rears its ugly head. Sadness can be pushed aside but grief lives forever.

~~~

I Opened the Door of the Closet...

I opened the closet door and my husband's hat fell from the shelf. I picked it up and another fell and then another.

"How many hats does this guy need?" I said aloud. I was sure he had only one head.

I stood on a chair and began sorting dress hats-stacking the largest brim on the bottom. Stetsons, fedoras and a safari hat took another row. It was obvious he was ready for anything like a cattle drive or a raging bull elephant. Straw yard hats to protect his bald head were next. Woolen hats for snow folded easily. Baseball caps with logos completed the collection. Baseball caps? He doesn't know the Yankees from an ice hockey team but the visors are perfect for reading outdoors. I'm surprised I didn't come across at least one sombrero.

Satisfied, I hopped off the chair and closed the door. When my husband arrived home from work he opened the closet door removing his hat.

"Oh, wow, you organized all my hats. Where shall I put this one?"

I was about to tell him but instead decided to get dinner on the table.

Later I heard the mail truck and opened the closet door to get my coat. Hats tumbled to the floor. I accidentally stepped on one and then jumped on two. I wanted to set fire to the rest as I screamed, "How many hats do you need?"

He laughed. "I don't know. How many pocket books do you have?"

I picked up the hats and was grateful we weren't talking about shoes.

The Most Valuable Lesson I Learned Last Year

The most valuable lesson I leaned last year was never put your hand on a hot stove. Or was that kindergarten?

~~~

The Most Important Things In My Life

Like a book, life has many chapters. At different times different things are important.

My husband, family and friends are always important. This never changes.

Some things that seemed important at the time proved unimportant later in life.

The most important thing now is knowing what will remain forever important.

~~~

I Am Best Known For...

I am known for getting the job done. If I take on a task I do my best to complete it. I am organized and neat. I love a challenge and solving problems. I am obsessed until I conquer or know I have done all I can to the best of my ability.

I enjoy a gentle battle. If I have a theory, I like to prove it true. If I am wrong I have no problem apologizing. I'm getting good at that.

~~~

I Really Should Stop...

I really should stop worrying about trivial things- like how does one repair a bongo?

I began worrying in kindergarten. The teacher handed out musical instruments. I hoped to get the triangle but Tommy pushed ahead. The wooden sticks were my next favorite. I watched Maryanne smugly click them together. I began to worry that I would be left with the empty oatmeal box. The teacher convinced me it was a bongo drum.

I worried I wouldn't be able to keep the tempo. Anxiety kept me one beat ahead of the triangle and wooden sticks.

The one-step ahead beat took me through life. Worrying brought on anxiety and tension. Tension put a hole in my oatmeal box. So now you know.

POLICE BLOTTER

An auto theft was "thwarted." Now there's a word you don't hear everyday. In fact, you can bite your tongue off trying to say it. I think the word "foil" would have fit. Of course, I don't think that word would have caught my eye like "thwart" did. I wouldn't even be reading the police blotter if I hadn't drawn the Jack of Spades. Maybe the Jack of Spades was the thief who was thwarted. I'm starting to like that word.

Well anyway, the thwarted thief was out working at 3 A.M. in the snow - such ambition and stamina! Of course he did have his marijuana for company or whatever. It is obvious the thwarted thief never looked back or he would have seen his own footprints in the snow thwarting him every step of the way, leading the Auto Theft Task Force right to him. This task force must have a pretty easy job. It's like Blue's Clues, just follow the paw prints and thwart the thief.

Did you think this was a good story? I <u>THWART</u> so!!

I Celebrate Myself and Sing Myself.

If I were Walt Whitman I would be able to celebrate myself often. Everytime I wrote something I would applaud myself. My words would take my own breath away and the songs I would sing would release praise for myself.

Alas, I am not Walt Whitman. These words have quite a different meaning to me. I celebrate <u>by</u> myself and sing <u>to</u> myself. There have been times when I have accomplished very little and other times I have accomplished a great deal. The important thing is I <u>have</u> accomplished and I celebrate myself. I throw my hat into the air like Mary Tyler Moore and sing, "You're going to make it after all!"

CHECK HOROSCOPE - HOW DOES IT COMPARE...

CANCER (June 21-July 22)
★★★ Use the morning to achieve
your goals. A boss smiles upon you.

You see, I do have an excuse. My zodiac sign is Cancer the crab. People born under this sign are known to be moody and sensitive, so it's not my fault!

I cut out my horoscope as instructed and it read:

1. - <u>USE THE MORNING TO ACHIEVE YOUR GOALS</u>

Bingo! I am a morning person. I get up at 4 A.M every morning and start right in with chores. I break to read the morning paper and lately wrote in my Writers Unlimited assignment book. I am at the grocery store by 7:30 almost everyday. My horoscope seems to be right on target because if I'm to achieve any goals it will definitely be in the morning. My Ever-Ready battery runs down in the afternoon but this bunny keeps on going. I wonder what goal I will achieve today?

2.- <u>A BOSS SMILES UPON YOU</u>

I only have one boss and <u>He</u> is always smiling upon me. I only answer to Him in heaven above. I follow his orders and he trusts me to use common sense and good judgement. If I fail he forgives and gives me the opportunity to try again. I have a lot of seniority on the job. I will never quit and he will never fire me. When I reach retirement I will look forward to the gold watch he offers which will continue to run through eternity.

I think my horoscope is darn good today.

REVISE

I knew sooner or later I would draw the ten of hearts and following instruction, I would have to revise something I wrote.

I have a problem with revising. Maybe it's really not knowing how to revise or not wanting to revise. When I write a piece, I'm finished with it. I want to move on. I don't want to correct or change it. I don't want to amend it, update it or improve it.

As far as I'm concerned, I have filled my obligation to the ten of hearts. Sorry, but today is Washington's birthday and I cannot tell a lie!

"MOTTO"

"PLAN AHEAD" was always my motto. I mapped out every step of my life and tried to follow the steps in order. I always knew exactly what was suppose to happen. Never spontaneous behavior for me! The only problem was I only had "PLAN A" and that lead to many disappointments. I changed my motto to "BE PREPARED." I didn't think the boy scouts would mind since I would be taking their advice. I now developed "PLAN B". Still, things never went as planned. When I got up to "PLAN P" and things weren't going according to plan, I changed my motto. My new motto is "ONE DAY AT A TIME." This motto makes more sense, doesn't it? Yes, I still plan ahead but I don't get upset when plans fail. I figure, it wasn't meant to be. The Lord has other plans for me. I can't argue with that! I now realize my itinerary is His plan. He calls it "PLAN A". It works every time!

NO MAN IS AN ISLAND

I seem to remember a story about a United States Navy radio operator during W.W.II on the island of Guan. The Japanese invaded the island and he hid in the jungle for about three years with the help of some islanders.

The survival of a man seemed to have a spiritual message about faith and human kindness.

I'm sure there were times in my life I felt deserted on an island with nothing but surrounding water and maybe one lonely tree. At the top of the tree, there always seemed to be a bright yellow lemon. If I struggled and climbed high enough, I could pluck the lemon and with my only other asset being water, I could make lemonade.

THE CARVED HEART

Sara could see Joe waving from the park bench.

"There you are – I thought you stood me up," he teased.

"I would never stand you up. I always come when you call. I'm just a little slower these days."

Joe took Sara's hand and led her to the wooden bench where she slowly ran her fingers over the carved heart that read, 'Joe Loves Sara'.

"Do you think young people still carve their names on park benches, Joe?"

"Sadly, I think they're too sophisticated to commit vandalism. They must do it electronically."

Sara pointed at a dog heading their way. A handsome golden retriever seemed confused, cocking his head from side to side while his expressive eyebrows kept Sara amused. The dog quickly lost interest when a squirrel scampered up a nearby tree.

"Remember how we planned on getting a dog and a house with a white picket fence to keep him in?"

"I remember Sara, I remember."

"Oh Joe, look at the little boy walking with his mother. Isn't he cute? Remember how we talked of having children?"

The child tugged on his mother's skirt and asked, "Mommy, why is that lady on the bench talking to herself?"

Sara lowered her head and once again ran her hand across the carved heart.

CARTOON

Remember when you were able to hand your prescription to the pharmacist and his felt bad because you had to wait ten minutes? Today you need to have a prescription filled before you get sick. Your temperature is rising and the druggist tells you he doesn't have the medication but he is expecting it in on tomorrows truck. So now you pray that the teamster doesn't get in an accident on I-95!

You traipse back to the drug store the next day. "The truck isn't in yet. Come back later." The new pharmacist tells you. Finally your 'script is ready and a little brown plastic bottle in placed into a white bag. Upon arriving home, you open the bag, take out the plastic bottle and find it empty! Back at the drug store, the pharmacist looks at you as though you're lying. "Oh here it is." He says. Your blood pressure is soaring but you decide not to fill your prescription because the procedure will kill you!

Watch a Movie - Rewrite Ending.

Last night I watched "Twelve Angry Men," for the tenth time. It was an excellent story with incredible acting. Henry Fonda tries to convince the other eleven jurors, a shadow of a doubt may save a young boys life. Maybe he did commit the murder, but what if he didn't? That is the dilemma they are faced with while locked in the juror's room on a hot summer day. What better way to get to know each other? An old man is the first to side with Henry Fonda. The count stands 10-2. Eventually they all agree that there very well maybe, a shadow of a doubt.

The last scence shows them leaving the courthouse. The old man walks up to Henry Fonda, introduces himself and they look at each other with respect. Then they walk away in separate direction. Awesome!

I would have ended it a little differently. The old man would walk up to Henry Fonda and say, "He did it, didn't he?" Fonda would look into the old man's eyes and say, "I'm afraid so." Very Awesome!!

FAVORITE COLOR

When a child sees his first box of Crayola Crayons, he will reach for the red one. Not me! I reached for the <u>blue</u> crayon. I have never understood why blue means to feel sad. If I'm feeling blue, I'm feeling more like pea green or dark brown.

Hundreds of songs have the word "blue" in their title. Alice had her blue gown and Elvis, his blue suede shoes. You may be blue-blooded or order a blue plate special. It was such a thrill for me the day I won the blue ribbon at the ceramic show. As I looked at the fancy blue ribbon, I wondered, "why blue?" David Feldman gives credit to King Edward, in his "imponderables" book. In 1348 King Edward established the Order of the Garter, now considered one of the highest orders in the world. I have collected all of David Feldman's books. I knew they would come in handy someday! I also collect cobalt glass. I never tire of the pretty pieces or the deep blue color.

Today is Monday. The song "Blue Monday" helped make Fats Domino wealthy. I sure hope it's a blue Monday for me. I love blue!

"They Also Serve Who Only STAND AND WAIT"

My mother often told me stories of women working in defense plants during W.W.II. Women waiting for news from their sons and husbands. If one got a letter, she would bring it in to read while the others flocked around. They would hug each other and cry.

The women tried to entertain each other by telling stories and jokes during the long working hours. Laughter occupied their minds while the worrying continued.

The laughter would cease and the assembly line would shut down when they would see an Army official in the factory. Many women fainted if he seemed to walk toward them. The wretched wailing echoed through the plant as the officer would begin, "I regret to inform you..."

The assembly line would be one woman short the next day and the others would work harder to get the product out to the service men.

I think I would rather be serving in action duty than to wait and worry.

John Milton should have said, "They also serve who stand and wait." The word "only" makes it sounds like they merely wait.

March 3rd
3 of Hearts
5 P.M.

MAGAZINES

Unless I'm in the dentist's office, I very seldom read magazines. I have been going to the same dentist for eighteen years and the magazines have not changed. At my last appointment I was told, the doctor would be running about an hour late because of an emergency. There I was with "Field & Stream" to entertain me. After ten minutes of redecorating the office in my mind, I was <u>lured</u> into opening the fishing magazine. I now know the difference between a perch and a pickerel. That should come in handy somewhere down the <u>line</u>. Anglers must get full use from this subscription, after reading the articles they can use the pages to wrap up the fish guts. I would change the name of the article about the huge "rainbow trout" to "the one that got away." Most of the stories are about just that!

I thought it must be my lucky day when I noticed a yellowish, dog-earred copy of Good Housekeeping. A recipe for a "Special Birthday Cake" caught my eye. I wondered if one had to churn the butter and get the eggs at the hen house. Women raved that the cake was worth waiting 365 days for. As I continued to read the recipe it called for one box of Duncan Hines cake mix. I guess the magazine was printed in this century afterall! If I were Duncan Hines, I would change the name to "The Special Unbirthday Cake." I'm sure more people are having an unbirthday and wouldn't this boost sales? Another thing, we have all seen pictures of Betty Crocker, Aunt Jemima, Uncle Ben and even the Pillsbury doughboy, but who is Duncan Hines? I think he should merge with the ketchup people and call the company Hines & Heinz!

In The Heat Of October

by

Carol Ruggiero

The nakedness of winter surrounded us. My husband and I spent the month of October battening down our home. Twenty-two windows washed in and out with storms in place. Gardens cut back, hoses packed away, we fertilize and frost the autumn lawn with lime. Disheartened, our final project dismantles the bird bath where feathered friends visited throughout the summer. It is hard to say good-bye.

Indoors, I almost look forward to our annual disagreement. We rarely argue and it breaks the monotony. Holding my elbows and hugging my body I begin, "I'm cold. Turn on the heat."

My husband answers, "It's too early" as I reach for the thermostat feeling the forgotten plastic ridges indenting my fingertips.

The hibernating furnace stretches and coughs. A thumping drum roll begins beneath the floorboards as fuel pumps through its arteries. The first whiff of heat tickles and comforts my thawing nose.

"Ah, that's better" I smugly say, knowing I have as usual won the debate.

I direct a smile to my losing opponent. "We make a great team, don't you think? We got a lot accomplished today. Thanks for all your help."

He takes off his sweater and loosens his collar in silence feeling the heat of October.

As a child, I always enjoyed visiting my grandmother. She wore bright colorful dresses and sparkely clips in her hair. She also loved music.

In the center of her parlor stood a Victrola. On the inside lid was a picture of a dog. The label read, "His master's voice." I loved the dog and the music that came out of the horn when my grandmother turned the crank.

She rolled up the rug and we danced together. She laughed as my hair fell across my eyes each time she twirled me. She reached into her hair and pulled out a glittery hair pin and clipped my hair back.

That night I removed the treasured hair clip and put it in a box along with other barrettes. Through the years the barrettes have disappeared but I saved Grandmother's hair clip along with a wonderful memory.

Carol Ruggiero

D is for Dreams

I was disturbed by a recurring dream. A nun with outstretched arms seemed to be asking for my help. I could not make out her face and wondered who she was.

I hadn't seen any nuns lately. Not like years ago when they were everywhere. They traveled three abreast reminding me of a stack of Oreo cookies. I always stepped aside allowing the cookies enough space while nodding, "Good afternoon Sisters."

"Bless you child," they harmonized.

But what did the dream mean? I thought of my childhood friend, Sister Wilemina. She was young, full of energy and so much fun.

On Saturdays, while the other kids were strapping on roller skates I was walking two miles to the convent. Once there, I helped Sister Wilemina dust and hang laundry. It was the first time I realized nuns also wore underwear.

At the end of the day as usual, Sister walked me half way home. Many times we took the short cut through the golf course where the grounds keeper would turn his head pretending not to see us trespassing. When we reached the pussy willows, Sister and I parted. Except for the day I asked to see her hair. I expected to find Yul Bryner under the wimple. Ducking behind the pussy willow, she exposed her short, auburn hair.

"Not bad. "I giggled.

"Not bad at all." She agreed.

With that out of the way, I said, "Let's pick some pussy willows Sister.

"Oh no. We mustn't. The golf course is like the Garden of Eden and the pussy willows are forbidden fruit."

Then we picked the pussy willows. I carried them home, only because Sister had to once again pass the grounds keeper. She doubted he would be willing to turn his head from a pussy willow thief. I felt a special closeness to my friend that day. Was it her invading my dreams? If so, what was it she needed me to do?

Lunch was spent with my husband in a diner where I finally told him about my dream. In the booth behind him I noticed a mm sipping soup. I said nothing until we were in the car.

"Do you suppose the nun is traveling alone?" I asked.

My husband answered, "What nun?"

I was unusually quiet until we reached our next stop, the Christmas Tree Shop.

"I'll meet you up front when I'm finished shopping." I said as he went on his separate way.

I began filling my cart with absolutely, unnecessary stuff until I reached the candy aisle. A nun on her knees was sorting through Christmas candy, checking prices and putting it back. I was certain she thought the lower the shelf, the lower the prices.

I smiled and questioned, "For the children Sister?"

Slowly nodding her head she answered, "It's always for the children."

I reached into my purse, placed a hundred dollar bill into each hand and pulled her up. Her eyes widened. Then tightly closed.

"Bless you dear." She sighed as I scooted away.

I un-shopped. Who needs a singing snowman anyway?

On the way to the car my husband said, "I can't believe you didn't buy anything."

I asked, "Did you see the nun shopping for the children?"

"Yes. I did."

Relieved, I said, "Oh good."

I know Sister Wilemina is relieved too. I'm also certain the pussy willow incident is forgiven. The dreams have stopped.

Carol Ruggiero
Assignment

BUYER BEWARE

I was working in the yard when a man in a pick-up truck pulled up.

He had an overbite that caused a speech impediment.

"Hi, I'm Ernie and I'm a rather."

"What the heck is a rather?" I asked.

Pointing to the roof he answered, "A rather replaces ruths and your home needs a new one. I can thave you money because I won't have to remove the old rath. The fire Saw allows two."

I felt sony for Ernie when he told me he was a family man living in Milford and needed work. Also I found him to be quite charming.

He showed me a sample of high quality white shingle and claimed he would be using this product. He then quoted me a price of $6000. The price was a little high for the times but I liked and trusted Ernie to do the job.

The next day he covered the existing roof. I paid him, shook his hand and said, "You finished just in time. It's starting to rain."

As the rain got heavier I heard metallic noises running across the gutters. AU the nails had pulled up and were coming out the metal down spouts. The basement was now flooding because 'Charming Ernie the Ruther' did not flash around the chimney.

I called him. "You've got to come," I cried. I'm bailing water. It's running down the walls."

"I'm not coming," he answered.

I finished the conversation with, "If you don't get over here you will hear from my lawyer."

Since I didn't have a lawyer, I needed to find one. I did. In the meantime I also had to find a new roofer. This roofer showed me the shingles that Ernie used were made of corrugated cardboard and the nails were not much longer than thumb tacks. The entire job cost Ernie about $200 – the rest was pure profit. Two roofs now had to be ripped off for the cost of $9000.

I jumped when the judge slammed his gavel and ordered Ernie to pay $20,000 for damages including a new roof.

Ernie's charm failed when he told the judge that he had no money to pay. At this point for some unknown reason I once again felt sorry for Ernie.

The judge looked at me. "Do you want his track? He has nothing else in his name."

"No, your honor. I don't want his track or $20,000. I only want the original $6,000."

The gavel slammed and the judge spoke. "The court orders you to pay $10 a week for the next twenty years. Case closed."

Weeks went by and of course no $10 – not that I wanted it – but I still wanted justice. After all, Ernie was now ignoring a court order.

I called the judge. "What do you expect me to do madam? There are no debtor jails. My only advice to you is buyer beware."

Dear Margaret,

I have known and admired you all my life and feel close enough to call you by your first name. I hope you don't mind.

I have red and enjoyed everybook you have written. I treasure my copies of your memories of your parents. I also have wonderful memoried of them. Of course, I was on the outside loking in!

You have inspired me to write. I have recently joined a wonderful group of writers. I now have a captive audience to listem to what I have written. The "Writer's Unlimited" instructor's assignment to her class was to title a paper called "My First Love" and write about it. I did just that and have enclosed a copy for you to read. I hope it makes you smile.

I pray for your good health and thank you for all your good deeds. Most of all, thank you for sharing "MY First Love."

God Bless You Margaret,

Carol Ruggiero
22 Vermont Ave.
Milford, CT 0646

~~~

Jan. 3, 2001

Dear Mr. Chichak,

I have been trying to forward a letter to Margaret Truman Daniel. I think she may enjoy reading it. As her literary agent I hope you can help me.

It has been suggested by the deouty director of the Harry S. Truman Library to contact you.

Thank you for taking the time to read the following letters. The Truman family meant so very much to me and with your help I would like to make Margaret smile.

Sincerely,

Carol Ruggiero
22 Vermont Ave.
Milford, CT 0646

FULL MOON TONIGHT – WEREWOLF'S DELIGHT

Reoccuring nightmares of Vietnam leave Joe drenched and shaken. His buddy's voice echoes, "Take cover Joe, take cover - they're in the trees."

There is no place to take cover. A sniper's gun-fire knocks him to the ground destroying his optic nerve. His buddy throws himself on top of Joe and takes the next bullet. So long ago and yet like yesterday he carries the guilt.

Today a dog lays his head in Joe's lap trying to calm and give comfort. Now Joe's best buddy is a mixed shepherd and trained seeing eye dog named Charlie.

Joe's trembling hand pets Charlie's long snout. He gropes for Charlie's harness saying, "I need to go for a walk and get some air."

Charlie pulls back knowing there is a full moon tonight and rumors of a werewolf come from the residents of the retir ement village. But Joe insists and Charlie obeys.

As they walk down the path leading towards the woods the dog picks up the putrid scent of a hairy creature. Charlie's ears stand erect. He hears panting fr om behind an eerie oak. He nudges Joe away fr om the tr ee and gr owls showing his teeth.

Eyes glaring, a werewolf appears, fangs and claws ready for the kill.

At this moment I, the writer, leaves the grizzly scene. It is unbearable to continue.

Instead I recall a 1957 movie starring Michael Landon called "I Was A Teenage Werewolf". I also remember Lon Chaney Jr. growing fangs and fill'. I laugh hoping they have returned to help Joe and Charlie. I know I can't – until the next full moon.

Wrong Again

"Adam, I'm frightened. What was that loud noise?"

"What do you think it was Eve? It was the door to paradise slamming. We are now on the other side and it's all your fault. You listened to that evil serpent and ate the forbidden fruit."

Eve pleaded with Adam, "You need to find us shelter. I am so cold."

"Of course you're cold - we are standing here naked. Quickly sew together some fig leaves and cover us."

Eve obeyed, but then suggested they find a warm motel room to spend the night.

Adam angered. "We can't do that. How will we register? Mr. and Mrs. who? We don't even have a last name. Also I have no money to pay for a room. I have no money because I have no pockets to put it in."

"Well please, think of something Adam. I don't like this new world. There is no peace here."

Adam answered, "Maybe we can trick Saint Peter. He holds the keys to the kingdom. Flash your fig leaves and distract him while I snatch his keys. And if we do get in, don't you dare eat any fruit. And Eve, about the kids... have you noticed Cain and Abel aren't getting along well lately?

"Oh don't worry Adam – it's just a little sibling rivalry. I'll give them a nice shiny apple to share. They will make peace and so will our new world."

PETE

Although the calendar insisted spring was here, for me it is not official until Pete arrives.

This year he was behind schedule. I worried he would not show up to keep me company while I prepared the flower beds.

I began tidying up the beds without him, but quickly got off my knees when I heard his distinct voice.

He came as close to me as his comfort zone would allow.

I greeted him. "Welcome back, Pete."

"Pete-Pete," he answered with a sharp shrill – then cocked his tufted head with curiosity.

Pete is a tiny bird called a titmouse. What he lacks in size he makes up for with his personality.

It is Pete's job to keep insects off my plants.

Of course, he doesn't work for free. He knows I keep peanuts in my pocket and waits for me to toss some in his direction. He stuffs the nuts into his cheeks like a chipmunk.

Throughout the summer months, Pete will bring me joy and work hard keeping the mosquitoes away. The best part is – Pete works for peanuts.

A Comedy Of Errors

"Park in the fire zone and keep the motor running," I said to my husband. "I'll only be in the store a minute - so don't move - I'll be right out."

Of course, he never listens to me and why I thought that day would be any different was beyond me.

When I rushed out of the store and hopped back into the car I noticed crumpled papers and coffee cups on the floor and front seat.

I raised my voice and nagged, "Why is this car such a mess? It's not like you. Please clean it up right now."

It was then I looked over at the stranger sitting behind the steering wheel with his mouth hung open.

"Oh, excuse me sir. I'm so sorry. I got into the wrong car."

I fumbled with the door handle and struggled to get out. It was about that time his

wife came out of the store and ran toward me shaking her fist and calling me some pretty low down names.

I tried to reason with the enraged woman. "No, no, wait, it's not what you think. I mistakenly got in the wrong car."

She refused to listen and was now directing her fist at her innocent husband.

Thanks to me, this poor guy was having a really bad day.

As for my husband witnessing the entire comedy and laughing uncontrollably – well, let's just say he was also about to have a bad day.

At a young age I was drawn to the novel "A Tree Grows In Brooklyn" written by Betty Smith.

Writing instructors stress, the first sentence of a story must pull the reader in. Surely, I was not grabbed by, "Serene was a word you could put to Brooklyn, New York in the summer of 1912."

OK-I now knew where and when but was that enough? I continued to read page one. Francie Nolan, the main character, recites a poem she learned in school. "This is the forest primeval. The murmuring pines and the hemlocks bearded with moss." Bingo! I was hooked. I realized Francie and I were about the same age studying Evangeline.

The next three paragraphs described a tree. Today, my writing teacher would say this is poor and boring writing. Well, it certainly worked for Betty Smith. But I agree -I found myself saying, "OK, OK, I get it. It's a tree. Thankfully, I read on.

The next five hundred pages were a masterpiece. The author proved uncommon skill and natural talent. Because she showed all action with her words, every chapter was more like a scene from a movie.

I wished the story would never end. When it did, simplistic, artistic truth took a bow.

I wondered if a story of that nature would sell today? Of course it would-Frank McCourt proved it writing Angela's Ashes. Frankie like Francie comes to life. The reader identifies and relates to honesty.

Over fifty years ago I read "A Tree Grows In Brooklyn" for the first time. Last week I reread the story. The authors last words were simply, "Good-bye Francie."

I will never say good-bye.

JUST MOLLY AND ME

As I packed for vacation I talked to my butterscotch spaniel. "I rented a cottage at Pastel Paradise along the beach for us Molly. I'm told lots of guys go there. Maybe I'll finally meet Mr. Right." Molly agreed with a sneeze.

I continued packing, placing my bathing suit on top, along with a new romance novel.

"You're lucky Molly- you don't need a bathing suit. You look great just the way you are. In fact, I'm a bit jealous. You always seem to get more attention than I do. But you know Moll, I think this year will be different. I look pretty good with my 120lb. curvy little body."

Entering the powder blue cottage I noticed everything was in order. I put on my swimsuit, grabbed my romance novel and headed toward the beach with Molly eagerly running ahead.

I was on page four when I looked up and saw a handsome man heading my way.

"Hi, I'm Joe," he said. "I'm in the pink cabin next to yours." He bent to pet Molly.

"Oh, a dog lover," I thought. "How perfect. Joe could definitely be Mr. Right."

"Nice to meet you Joe," I smiled. "And don't worry, Molly doesn't bark at night. She won't keep you awake."

"No problem," Joe answered. "I have a dog too. I'll introduce you to Comet later. But watch out Molly, Comet has an eye for the ladies. I let him run the beach about 6 o'clock-hope to see you then."

Sure enough, at 6 o'clock a beautiful golden retriever ran along the shore stopping long enough for Molly to instantly fall in love. I watched the dogs run and play together until they were out of sight.

It was then I heard Joe calling for Comet. He was with an equally handsome man. Joe waved to me and said, "Don't worry-they'll come back. In the meantime, I'd like you to meet my partner Jeffery. My jaw dropped leaving my lower lip in need of a coaster.

My romance novel entertained me through the rest of my vacation.

As for Molly- her puppies are due any day now. I have promised the pick of the litter to Joe and Jeffery.

Next year I'm planning a trip to the mountains. I think I'll leave Molly at home.

A Lifetime Of Heroes

It has always been important to me to feel safe. Safe from what – I'm not sure. Maybe it goes back to air raid drills and crawling under school desks where children were told they would be safe from bombs.

As a child my father was my hero. He told me there would never be bombing in America. I always felt safe when my father was near.

It wasn't until the sixth grade that another hero came into my life. After surviving fourth and fifth grade with the deranged and cruel Mrs. Kay, Mr. Reeves brought joy into my life. He made learning fun and I finally felt safe from the evil Mrs. Kay.

As a high school freshman, Miss Emery was my new hero- or shall I say heroine? She was masculine looking and had very large teeth, but what she lacked in beauty she made up for with her unique teaching ability. It was Miss Emery who introduced me to Charles Dickens and The Tale of Two Cities. This amazing English teacher took my hand and together we stormed the Bastille.

As the years passed I met a priest from Saint Anthony's Church in New Haven, I knew him only by the name of Father Mario. He not only listened - he understood. I was blessed to have Father Mario in my life. He was indeed my hero.

Today I live with my good natured husband who makes me smile because of his sunny disposition. Although he wears no cape or big red "S" on his chest, I believe he can leap tall buildings in a single bound. I feel safe. He is my hero.

MRS. JACKSON AND THE MAYONNAISE JAR

Amanda was looking out her bedroom window. She could see Mrs. Jackson wearing her straw hat and gardening gloves as she tended and talked to her flowers.

This would be a good morning to tell Mrs. Jackson about the flower show held in the school gymnasium. A blue ribbon would be awarded to the best arrangement.

"Good morning, Mrs. Jackson." Amanda said. "Never mind me! Did you say good morning to the pansies? Their little faces are looking up at you. Black-eyed Susan is also looking your way. Did you comfort the bleeding heart as you walked by and did you notice Creeping Myrtle wandering toward you?"

Amanda took the time to say hello to all of them but she skirted around the snap dragons as she never did trust them. When she told Mrs. Jackson about the flower show, she asked, "Would you like to enter some of my flowers?" "I would love to Mrs. Jackson, but a second grader would never stand a chance against the fifth and sixth graders.

They will bring cut glass and crystal vases to display their flowers." Amanda had nothing to do Mrs. Jackson's flowers any justice.

"Wait here and we'll see what we can do." Mrs. Jackson said as Amanda became hopeful. When she returned, Mrs. Jackson was carrying an empty mayonnaise jar. Amanda's heart sank. When Mrs. Jackson filled the jar with cold water, Amanda had to admit it sparkled as the morning sun hit the clear glass.

The orange tiger lily was the first to be cut and placed in the jar. "Stay still and stop growling." She warned. "You are going to a wonderful flower show today." White daisies were next. Their yellow noses complimented the tiger lily. Purple pansies made a great clash along with yellow and orange marigolds. Around the rim and down the side of the jar she draped English Ivy, telling her to be on her best behavior in front of the judges. As Amanda thanked Mrs. Jackson and started to walk away, Mrs. Jackson said, "Wait" and tucked in some baby's breath. "Imagine," Amanda thought, "Capturing a baby's breath in a mayonnaise jar."

Amanda placed the flowers on the designated table in the gym. The colors were magnificent as were the wonderful fragrances. The mayonnaise jar was sparkling every sparkle it could sparkle as the overhead lights hit the glass.

The show went on for three days. The flowers were limp and most were gone. On the fourth day Amanda sadly carried home the empty mayonnaise jar to return it to Mrs. Jackson. "Why so sad?" she asked. "It's not empty at all. It is full of memories now. You keep the jar and oh, tuck the blue ribbon inside."

YOU CAN'T TEACH AN OLD
DOG NEW TRICKS

We began digging under the oak tree in late summer. We dug a little each day before the sun came up. This allowed time to tend the last of the crops and prepare the fields for spring.

I sat next to Jane on the bench seat of the tractor as we leveled the com stalks.

"How many times have we plowed this field Beau?" Jane knew exactly. She brought me home seventeen years ago and named me Beauregard but soon called me Beau.

Only when my clumsy paws stepped on baby pepper plants or worse, budding geraniums, did Jane call me Beauregaud.

"You can't teach an old dog new tricks" Jane said, "but you are young and I will teach you."

Jane loved the challenge and I loved Jane. I quickly learned to walk between the rows.

When the com stalks were cleared it was time to take down the scarecrow. Jane laughed remembering the first time I saw the straw man. I showed my teeth and growled, happy to see the crows circling overhead. I wagged my tail greeting the large black birds until Jane said, "Oh Beau, you are so young-you can't tell friend from foe. Crows are farmer's worst enemies."

The sun was going down as the tractor headed back to the farm house. I was lookdng forward to sprawling across the old blue quilt at the foot of Jane's bed. She helped me down from the tractor. I stood at the edge of the hole and looked in. "Why were we digging this hole?"

Morning came too quickly. We got up before the rooster crowed. Of course-this gave time to dig.

Jane helped me from the bed. I left her cooking breakfast and went outside. I hobbled to the oak tree. The hole wag still there.

I returned in time to watch Jane mix bacon drippings into my food. It helped my aching bones.

We returned to the hole. Jane loosen the dirt with the pointed shovel and said, "Dig-Beau-dig."

It hurt to dig but I didn't want to disappoint Jane. I seemed to be doing most of the work kicking the dirt away. After days of digging, Jane said the hole was deep enough. "Tomorrow we will cover it with a sheet of plywood."

"Why did we dig the hole Jane? Why?"

That night Jane patted my head and spoke softly. "My poor Beau. You are so tired. I doubt you will make it through the winter. We have prepared for this before the ground freezes."

My tail thumped twice against the quilt. I dreamed of running through the fields chasing rabbits. I dreamed of flying, snapping my teeth at the crows.

I woke to the sound of heavy rain hitting the windows. I thought about the hole filling with rainwater. I wanted to wake Jane and ask, "What have we prepared for?"

Shadows moved as lightening lit the room. Again I thought about the hole. It was then I realized what it was for. "Oh no-Jane taught this old dog to dig his own grave."

I growled at Jane and listened to the rain until the rooster crowed. I jumped from the bed not wanting her help. Although I was hungry I backed away from breakfast. "Maybe she poisoned it," I thought feeling betrayed.

"Suit yourself." Jane said reaching for her high rubber boots.

I watched her struggle, dragging a sheet of plywood through the mud. When she slipped I tried to control my happy tail.

"So you think that's funny do you?" she said playfully rubbing mud on my nose.

We looked into the hole. Raindrops hit the muddy water. I took two steps backward and stood behind Jane. It only took one hard nudge. I felt the back of Jane's raincoat against my head.

"Beauregaurd!" Jane screamed tumbling into the hole.

One last trick for an old dog.

SHOES

It seems the things we need most in life we cannot buy.

Wouldn't it be nice to push a button at an A.T.M. and out comes an over-stuffed envelope full of good health? Another button labeled "peace" blinks and a bucket of serenity spills over the brim onto your shoes.

Speaking of shoes, that is what I buy. Not that I need another pair of shoes. My shoe closet looks like a centipede lives there along with Imelda Marcos.

I know I should get rid of some but never the the straw wedgies with the hanging fruit. I always liked the way the cherries bobbled as I walked. Also I cannot part with the blue sling-backs purchased in Capri. I dance'my way around the Isle in those. I refuse to let go of the glittery, silver evening shoes. Their crisscross straps hold Cinderella memories. Then of course the parfait colors can't be throw away. You just never know when honeydew, muskmelon or shimmery peach will once again be considered chic. Then there are the brown ones- not just brown, every shade of brown from coffee to oatmeal to toast. I must have worn them during the working years whenever I skipped breakfast.

A managerie of snapping alligators and stubborn mules become upset as I favor my comfortable old black loafers. My choice always makes my bunny slippers hopping mad as the hush-puppies beg to be worn.

My mailbox overflows with shoe catalogs I cannot resist. I fill out the order blank, item number first, size five, medium width. I spend a little more time with quantity and color. "Let's see, one pair flamingo and oh what the heck, one pair rancid plum."

Why do I buy so many shoes? I guess when you can't buy the things in life you need, you buy what you can or go barefooted.

The Empty House

The house echoed as I deliberately prolonged each step down the staircase. The smell of roasted turkey, dressing and spices toyed with my imagination.

Silhouettes on ecru walls stung my eyes. A lonely cobweb where Mom once kept her "Gone With The Wind" lamp fluttered. My hollow heart ached at the sight of cardboard boxes reluctantly waiting for the Goodwill truck.

"'Tis the season for goodwill." I droned. "Fa-la-la-la-la."

On cue, the scent of pine filled the air. The dark room brightened as the child pulled gifts from beneath prickly boughs, tangling tinsel in her hair. Her amused father chuckled. How long since she heard his laughter? Twenty years? Longer? Does he know Mom is in a nursing home?

Sadness lifted when the child squealed with delight. The "magic skin" doll promised by Santa was hugged tightly, all other gifts ignored. I tiptoed around ribbon and tom wrapping paper. I decided not to tell her. Instead, I left her there safe, warm and happy. I closed the door quietly and knew the house was full, not empty.

We landed on top of a large rock pile in the center of the angry river. Our troubles had worsened. I looked back to see if Albert was still on board. I didn't want to die alone. This was the first time I saw this man, who was never afraid of anything, look beaten. "We're not going to make it Carol. If I have ever done anything to hurt you in the past, I am sorry. Please forgive me."

There was nothing to forgive but I screamed back, "Do you know what you can do with that merit badge? If we ever get out of this alive, I'm going to kill you." One way or the other this was the end for that boy scout.

Our only hope was to get free from the rocks. The water was lifting and smashing us back down. I knew the eagle could not take much more. To make matters worse, Albert was now saying the Hail Mary and he was standing! He pushed the paddle against the rocks and the water lifted us. We were now airborne. We splashed down into the mighty current as Albert yelled, "Paddle, paddle and stay clear of the rocks."

I reached for the broken piece of wood and tried to imitate his motions.

About a mile later the water began to calm. I thought I must be hallucinating from the trauma when I saw a man wearing hip boots trout fishing. I jumped out of the canoe and pulled like a mule on the Erie canal, until we reached the embankment. I continued to pull on dry land and up a steep hill with Albert still in the canoe.

The driver had been searching for us and picked us up on the road. As he loaded the canoe onto the truck he asked, "How was it?"

Neither of us answered. I knew I was never going to speak to Albert again, but uncontrollable laughter set in. Tears streamed down my face as I said, "Look, I've ruined my panty hose."

Dear Writers Unlimited Group,

I am writing to you from the Old Gate Prison located on Old Gate Lane in Milford. The building use to be the Jai-Alai fronton until the city took it over when the new adverb law went into effect. The prison is now being used for the overflow of adverb offenders.

Posted on the town's property lines are blue and white signs reading, "Welcome to Milford. Leave all adverbs before entering."

I read about the special task force used to control adverb abuse but I didn't believe this ridiculous law would be enforced until the morning I watched my neighbor, Mrs. Corbett being taken from her home in handcuffs. It seems she made the severe mistake of patting her little son on the head after seeing his report card. It wasn't the pat on the head that got her arrested. She told Christopher he did wonderfully well and she was extremely proud of him. Two adverbs in one sentence, the judge threw the book at her!

Mrs. Corbett will be paroled in May. That's nice, Christopher will have his Mom home for Mother's Day. I hope he doesn't lovingly hug her. Just a hug will have to do.

I wound up in the same cellblock with Mrs. Corbett. As they were hauling her off in the squad car she looked at me and pleaded, "Please call my husband."

"Don't worry," I cried back. "I'll call him quickly and we'll have you out promptly."

Always remember, adverbs weaken sentences. I'm getting out in July.

Sincerely yours,
Oh no, make that September!

While you were away:
Dan's assignment:
write something
without using adverbs
He was the biggest
offender!

WHIMSY

Poets and Hamsters

I try to avoid Dylan Thomas whenever possible but his 'Do not go gentle into that good night' follows me throughout life and pops up when least expected.

I'm almost certain if I have a few minutes to kill before my death, I will think of his poem. In fact, now I am sure.

If I could have peeked into the mind of Dylan Thomas, I believe I would have witnessed little inebriated hamsters dressed in dark cowls, running around on wheels searching for the exact word to fit an emotional scene. The scene must always come first and then the words-but oh, those words that only miniature hamsters and gigantic poets can unriddle, rhyme and finally reason.

I wonder if Dylan Thomas, along with a few hamsters, somehow got into the mind of William Shakespeare?

'Rage, rage against the dying of the light,' screams Dylan Thomas as the haunting scene of his father's deathbed reveals the power of death.

Yes, I try to avoid Dylan Thomas because he is the Prince of Darkness. Instead I enjoy heartwarming short stories like, 'A Child's Christmas in Wales' with pure, simple, well written words. The author writes, "One Christmas was so much like another. I never knew if it snowed for six days when I was twelve or twelve days when I was six." No gloomy hamsters here, just simple genius written by Dylan Thomas. You know, the Prince of Darkness.

Dear Mama,

Thank you so much for your thoughtful going away gift. I will begin writing in the handsome leather bound journal when I am settled in New York which will be soon as we are now approaching the coast of Massachusetts.

So you see Mama, all your worrying was for nothing. The ship has made its 100th crossing safely. After all, it was blessed by the Archbishop of Genoa. It is considered the safest ship built with a double hull, water tight compartments, plenty of life boats and best of all, it is equipped with sonar.

It is nearly 11 P.M but I am too excited to sleep. I wanted to go on deck but it is so foggy I decided to stay in my cabin.

I hope your fears are put to rest as I close this letter. I will tuck it away in my new journal until I can mail it to you from New York.

I miss you very much and thank you again for the gift. No need to worry any longer. I am safe aboard the Andrea Doria.

Your loving son,
Antonio

Where To Ma'am?

I was born in the wrong century. I would be quite content to ride a horse and use the word "whoa" instead of the brake pedal. But Henry Ford had other plans and produced an affordable automobile scaring skittish horses from cobbled streets.

Unlike other teenagers, I never wanted to drive. Approaching the age of sixteen, my parents offered to buy me a new 1958 Oldsmobile. I immediately declined because I never felt comfortable in a car- let alone driving one. I was satisfied to ride the city bus or walk.

At the age of twenty-seven, I found it necessary to apply for a drivers license. To this day I don't know how I passed the test. And oh yes, after all these years, I still hate driving.

When I saw a driverless car on the market I decided to check it out. This ugly robotic vehicle looked like a bread box with headlights- not at all like the classy chromed Oldsmobile from the 50's.

I programmed the brainless wonder to take me around the block for a test drive. I shouted, "You're going too fast. Watch out for the child on the sidewalk. Do you see the pedestrian on the comer? Use your signal light. Do you have signal lights?"

By the time the bread box pulled back into the showroom, I was a total wreck.

The car salesman beamed, "Well, what do you think? Shall I wrap it up?"

I snapped, "Call me a taxi."

I soon realized the courteous cab driver was all I needed when he asked, "Where to ma'am?"

A Favorite Short Poem

"The Wreck of the Hesperus" has always been my favorite poem, but Henry Wadsworth Longfellow never wrote a poem that would be considered snort. When Mr. Longfellow wrote, he wrote and wrote and wrote. I will not be able to read to you about the Hesperus because of its length but it brought to mind an earlier assignment. It was called, "Excite Your Senses Today." This is what I wrote.

It was not an exciting day for my senses until I reached for my favorite book of poems. I turned to Longfellow's "The Wreck of the Hesperus" and all those sleepy senses stood at attention. No one sets a story better to poetry than Henry Wadsworth Longfellow. He begins:

IT WAS THE SCHOONER HESPERUS

THAT SAILED THE WINTRY SEA

AND THE SKIPPER HAD TAKEN HIS LITTLE DAUGHTER

TO BEAR HIM COMPANY

You know, this guy is a real jerk! He takes a young kid out on a cold wintry day on a boat knowing a storm is coming. He should begin to get a clue when the smoke from his pipe blows "now west, now south." Even an old sailor tells him, "I fear a hurricane." But oh no, this skipper with the big ego tries to show his daughter what a terrific seaman he is. The poor kid is trembling in her boots [if she had boots], while he wraps her in his coat to keep her warm against the stinging winds. If that isn't bad enough, it starts to dawn on him that he is in big trouble so he ties the kid to the mast. She still trusts him at this point although questions the sounds of the bells and foghorns. Of course, fool that he is, he lies to her and heads for the open sea. A short time later, he turns into a frozen corpse. Witnessing this, the girl starts to pray. A little late for prayer I think. Longfellow goes on to tell all the gory details of the night, heading toward the "Reef of Norman's Woe." Wow, what a name. Norman's Woe!

The next morning a fisherman finds the girl lashed to a mast. Not only was the sea salt frozen to her breast, her tears had also frozen. Imagine!

Longfellow ends his poem:

SUCH WAS THE WRECK OF THE HESPERUS,

IN THE MIDNIGHT AND THE SNOW

CHRIST SAVE US ALL FROM A DEATH LIKE THIS,

ON THE REEF OF NORMANS WOE.

There was a time I challenged myself to visit every state in the U.S. My goal to spend at least one week per state – enough time to understand its history and enjoy whatever it had to offer.

Finished with New England, my husband and I traveled south by car. Every year distance grew and soon we traveled by train until finally air travel was the only way to go.

We covered thirty-seven states until my health no longer allowed me to travel distance. I sadly packed away the luggage but they certainly were full of great memories.

My favorite state is Virginia especially the colonial Willamsburg area. Through the years we always snuck in an extra trip to Virginia. I still hope to return some day but as times goes by it seems they will have to carry me back to old Virginy.

My least favorite state is Georgia with the exception of Savannah. The Carolinas are full of beauty. West Virginia held my interest with its history as did Tennessee and Kentucky. Florida is one big vacation land-not what we were looking for at all. I must admit I did enjoy Saint Augustine, the oldest settlement in America.

Several times we toured Canada just to go in a different direction for a while. We also visited France, Switzerland and Italy. Yes they all held a different beauty but there is no place as beautiful as America.

My one regret is that I never made it to Texas. I really wanted to visit San Antonio. I guess I'll just have to remember the Alamo through picture books.

I wish the state of Connecticut had more tourism. We are fortunate to be living in one of the most beautiful states in the U.S. Of course we will have to blindfold our visitors through Bridgeport, New Haven and Hartford.

WHAT ARE YOU WEARING TODAY

Today is Tuesday and that means I attend my ceramic class. The studio used to be a factory. It has cinder block walls, so it is always very cold. I wear layers of clothing and thick socks. My clothes have paint on them from the previous class. No matter how hard you scrub that paint won't come off. It is important to feel creative and the Bohemian look helps.

I wish it wasn't winter because I love to garden. My gardening clothes are even funnier than my ceramic get-ups. My old straw gardening hat tops off the ensemble. The creativity is helped along by Mother Nature. I'll bet she has a junky outfit too!

Tomorrow is Valentine Day. Maybe I'll wear red clothes, without any paint on them but I won't feel creative. I'll feel pretty – oh so pretty.

Mrs. Wellington's Boarding House

Mrs. Wellington's boarding house stood on the corner of North and Park Avenue in Bridgeport Connecticut.

During the early 1940's the dark green, two storied home trimmed with gingerbread displayed a sign in the front window – Rooms for rent - $12.00 weekly.

Because of the war, the city of Bridgeport was booming with industry. Men left the coal mines of Pennsylvania and surrounding states seeking work in defense plants. After settling, they would send for their families. Until then, some called Mrs. Wellington's boarding house – "home".

Each room was furnished with an iron bed, a small dresser and a standing lamp. With every breeze white sheer curtains blew in tangling around the lamp.

As families migrated to Bridgeport, the city found need for more school teachers. For this reason, young Marion Mason also moved to Bridgeport finding a room at Mrs. Wellington's where every evening a hot meal was served, complete with a tossed salad and one sweet roll.

Although occupied with school work Marion was lonesome and looked forward to dinner with the other boarders. Unfortunately, the elderly Mr. Kruzinski was hard of hearing and shouted across the dining table explaining he was a violinist until his arthritic hands could no longer hold the bow. For this reason, Mr. Kruzinski dropped his silverware opite often. Mrs. Wellington always felt obligated to replace it and called to Julia, her kitchen helper to bring another fork. In addition to cooking, Julia also helped with laundry, mopping floors and making beds. Julia never spoke unless spoken to. Marion wondered if there would ever be someone to talk to.

Tonight, when she entered the dining room, a handsome young man rose and waited for her to be seated. She was immediately attracted to him and felt herself blush.

He introduced himself as Charles Carter and was looking for work as an English teacher with the Bridgeport school system. Marion was sure she could help and continued the conversation with Mr. Carter while Mr. Kruzinski continued to drop his silverware.

As Julia poured coffee, Mrs. Wellington served rhubarb pie and reminded her boarders of her strict rule- no visitors in rooms.

Of course, They could entertain in the front parlor, complete with Victrola and love seat.

Many years later retired school teachers, Mr. and Mrs Charles Carter, stood on the corner of North and Park Avenue with their grandchildren watching a work crew with bulldozers level Mrs. Wellington's boarding house – but Marion's memories could never be demolished.

IMPORTANT THINGS

Things that mean a great deal to me at this stage of my life are different than in the past. Now that I'm all grown up, I seem to enjoy the little things life has to offer.

My husband is the most important <u>person</u> in my life. He is my best friend and I love him. He is my family. He is my home.

My mother is very important to me. I do not know a day without her. I still look to her for advice, approval and love. My husband's parents are important to me. I always need to know that they are safe and well taken care of.

The important things in my life seem to be <u>people</u>, although there are significant other things. Time is important to me. I never had time for myself. I never had time for fun. I think I took life too seriously. I now have the time to do things that please me.

I thank God more often. My mind visits the past but I do not dwell on past tragedies. There was a time I believed I had total control of my life only to find out God had other plans. I have learned to take my problems to him alone. I do not pretend to know what the future holds. I pray for strength and good health so I may enjoy each day the Lord has given me.

My ABC's

A is for Albert: Albert is every letter in my alphabet and he vacuums too. Because of this Albert is more than an "A". He is an A plus. He does not know this and I trust you will not tell him, as I am trying to teach him to iron his shirts for extra credit.

B is for Books: My home is full of books. Most belong to my husband, but I claim the Civil War collection. I also collect "First Lady" biographies. Limited shelves, allow each first lady one space. I keep only, what I feel is the most knowledgeable and best written. This is why my collection begins with Abigail Adams. I have not yet found a biography worthy of Martha Washington.

One of my favorite first ladies is Bess Truman. I really like her. I guess someone has to. My least favorite is Mary Todd Lincoln. I'm surprised I give her space at all. But after making room for Hillary, Mrs. Lincoln looks good.

I actually shed tears when I dust Pat Nixon. My heart weeps for this lovely lady. Trishan is my favorite white house child. What a great kid she was. Of course, although I adore her parents, Margaret Truman was my least favorite. I blame this on Harry. He spoiled her rotten. But Bess kept the princess's tiara from getting too big and she turned out well.

I hope I never find the perfect Martha Washington biography. This would mean, moving over 40 books to squeeze her in. But I guess 'Patsy' as George called her, deserves the honor.

C is for Child: It was the eighth day of heavy rain and I was beginning to pace. Feeling like a prisoner in my own home, I looked out the rain-streaked window. A child wearing a yellow slicker and rain hat was splashing through deep puddles on her way to school. Her hair poked out from beneath the water resistant hat. Her bangs were stuck to her forehead. For some reason, I found this funny.

She continued to amuse me as I noticed she was talking to herself. Then I realized she wasn't talking to herself – she was singing. Dgbbie

Reynolds could not have been more entertaining than this child singing in the rain. I wanted to join her and feel the rain as only a child could.

I watched until the yellow slicker disappear. It was then I thanked God for the rain and the child.

Love In A Parking Lot

I'm not sure if it was love at first sight or if it evolved through years of respect and admiration. I do know, the two men love each other more than brothers.

This week my friend and I witnessed our husbands hugging in a parking lot of a restaurant. Eyes sparkling, they run to each other almost forgetting we are there. Macho takes on a new meaning – a combination of marshmallow and sweet chocolate.

We trail behind the marshmallows entering the restaurant. My friend pokes me saying, "Look at that." The men are now holding hands. Then one slips his arm through the others. They are discussing books they have shared, history, politics and current events.

When we reach the booth, my husband slides in first. My eyebrows raise and he slides back out never loosing a beat of conversation. They read the menu to each other and order drinks. Whatever one has the other agrees.

My friend and I make small talk. We are talked out from our weekly phone calls. But the guys haven't seen one another for weeks and barely take breaths.

With lunch over, we are invited to their home to play cards. My husband drives faster than usual only to get lost. It doesn't matter. His friend is waiting patiently at the door.

The two go out onto the balcony where my husband is showered with candy, cigars and special pipe cleaners. When the time finally comes to play cards, choice of partners is not considered. The men sit across from each other and gloat, "Nice going. Great play. Good job." Somehow they lose the game but they are still complimenting their strategy.

We put away the cards. My friend opens a gift we brought. The new word game excites our friends and we play for hours. No longer a need for partners the boys continue to compliment each other on their word choices.

As we are leaving, one marshmallow says to the other, "When you get a day off, let's take a ride to the book bam in Bethany."

"Any time," the second marshmallow answers.

We watch them clasp hands and arms as they say good-bye.

I say to myself, "Parting is such sweet sorrow but this is ridiculous."

I begin to re-think, "Wouldn't it be a nicer world if all men put down their weapons and instead held hands in a parking lot. This I believe.

POSTHUMOUS

Isn't it sad that a person is honored posthumously? Is it guilt that leads his peers to finally applaud his work?

The cartoon strip B.C. Was created by Johnny Hart in 1958. The strip is set in prehistoric times and features cavemen and and stone age animals. And oh yes, cave women too.

Looking at the assignment cartoon, we see how simple the drawings are. But even in this simple drawing we are aware of the added detail that brings the strip to life-notice the daring cleavage, especially on the brunette beauty. The cave resembles an easily drawn igloo. The birds are simply little m's in the sky.

A cartoonist, in addition to drawing must be a clever writer. The drawing leads to his punchline. Johnny Hart was a master. Sadly, he died after suffering a stroke. Fortunately, his daughter and grandson have taken over the drawing and writing duties.

As far as I know, Johnny Hart never won an award. Maybe now he will.

The posthumous award should not stem from guilt-but from awareness and gratitude to a talented and great cartoonist.

GRANDMOTHER

I know nothing of my grandmother's childhood except she was born in Italy.

When she and my grandfather traveled to America they bought farmland in Connecticut. How they managed to scrape up that much lira is beyond me. Along with fruit and vegetables they raised chickens and sold eggs. From then grape arbors they made and sold wine.

When my grandfather died at an early age my grandmother was left the farm along with six children. The oldest had to quit school to help maintain the farm.

My mother, the youngest, milked the cow and collected eggs for marketing every morning before leaving for school.

My grandmother's best friend was Jack, a border collie. He was always by her side protecting her and the farm from any intruders. When Jack died a large stone was placed over his grave. Etched were the words, "Here Lies Jack- Never Forgotten". The stone is still there.

The farm was sold when my grandmother could no longer tend to it. Her six children now had families of their own.

For the last time, they gathered in the kitchen of the farmhouse to decide where my grandmother would now live. She sat at the head of the table and said, "One mother knew what to do with six children but six children can't seem to figure out what to do with one mother."

GOING DOWN?

After visiting a patient on the tenth floor of Saint Vincent's hospital, I felt uneasy entering the elevator. Descending turns my butterflies into ferocious bats.

I stepped to the rear, allowing room for a priest and a young intern dressed in green scrubs.

My anxious heart thumped as I watched the floor indicator move to nine - then eight I silently talked to myself, "Stay calm. Soon well be on the ground floor."

Between the sixth and seventh floor, a loud snap and a grinding screech jolted the elevator. When the car stopped the lights went out. It was quiet until I screamed- "Son of a bitch'"

When a dim auxiliary light blinked on I apologized, "Sony, Father."

"Oh, was that you? he answered. I thought it was me."

The intern laughed. "Don't worry – tills happens a. tot here. These elevators are almost as old as Elisha Otis. Good thing he was clever enough to invent an elevator that would immediately stop if a cable snapped."

He pushed the emergency button and activated the alarm. "A couple of guys from the firehouse will come and get us out of here."

The priest opened his prayer book. "Dear' Lord, please have mercy on Mrs. O'Reilly's soul. I think I'll be too late to administer the last rights."

I lowered my head. "Keep that page open, Father. I'm going to need it."

About an hour and a half later, I was thanking a firefighter and Ms crowbar as he escorted me to the next elevator.

The intern was on his assigned floor and I tearfully said good-bye and wished him luck with his medical career.

Not wanting to get in the elevator first I said, "After you, Father."

I pushed the ground floor button and counted down five-four - Snap- Grind- Screech."

"Son of a bitch!"

THAT DAMN NUTCRACKER

My name is Sugar Plum and in the land of fairies I'm right up there with Tinker Bell and Cinderella's godmother.

Like Cinderella, I too am waiting for Mr. Right – but for some reason that damn nutcracker thinks I belong to him and with a name like 'nutcracker' the other guys fear to date me.

Believe me – the stem upright nutcracker is not my type. I am usually attracted to bad boys. For this reason I was drawn to the hideous green Grinch. He stole my heart. Of course he did – he steals everything.

Fluttering my wings, I found the courage to tell the nutcracker I was inviting the Grinch for tea and fruit cake. I hate fruit cake. In fact, except for my friend Shirley Bilski, I don't know anyone who likes fruit cake.

After giving it some thought, I decided to also invite Shirley and the nutcracker – kind of a double date. She could slice the cake and distract the nutcracker while I moved in on the Grinch. But when the Grinch saw Shirley and the fruit cake it was over for me.

They left with the cake and each other leaving me alone with that damn nutcracker.

The Sounds Of Summers Past

1.- Croaking frogs beneath my bedroom window.

2.- Alvin-Audrey-Paul - Mrs. Otto's call for dinner.

3.- The echoing clackety-clack of kick the can under a dim street light.

4.- Creaking rocking chairs on the front porch.

5.- The iceman's tongs cracking chunks and slivers.

6.- Women in white aprons snapping green beans dropping into a metal colander.

7.- Squealing children running through a rubber garden hose.

8.- The rag man's horse clopping slowly up the street.

9.- Slippery salamanders splashing in a stagnant pond.

10.- The ice cream man's bells - "wait up - wait up."

These are the sounds of summers past.

QUIET ON THE SET

Until recently, I've never been able to produce a good belly laugh. I never understood why, as I certainly have the necessary equipment. It must be my odd sense of humor. I cannot laugh at the obvious or expected.

I have never laughed at the three stooges banging heads or gouging eyes. When Buster Keaton slipped on a banana peel others roared while funny bone fell asleep. And when Soupy Sales got a pie in the face I was more concerned about the mess.

Maybe I'm just too serious. Isn't it ironic that we have to learn to be serious while we are born with the gift of laughter?

If laughter is the best medicine, and I believe this true, my husband Albert will live to be one hundred and ten. When Albert watches old Laurel and Hardy movies he doesn't just titter or teehee. He laughs a deep belly laugh. Is this what is keeping his blood pressure perfect? I'm beginning to think so, as I wonder if I have any sense of humor at all.

It is a fact that the average human laughs seventeen times a day. If this is true, I am way behind schedule today. Of course, it is early and I never laugh until after my second cup of coffee.

Every morning Albert sings and laughs all the way to the kitchen where he finds me grumbling. At times his good nature gets on my nerves. How can he be so happy, day after day, after day? Does he know something I don't?

This morning he entered tap dancing in his stocking feet and sang two verses of "Good Morning To You".

His cheerful voice closed my left eye while the right one bulged raising my eyebrow above its boundary. My tangled hair fell to one side and my lower lip to the other.

At this sight, Albert chuckled, made a picture frame with his hands and said, "I'm ready for my close up, Mr. Demille."

I felt my insides getting giddy. Toxins and stress released. I hung on as my knees caved. There it was-my first real belly laugh and it felt so good. Through streaming tears I thought, "only sixteen more insults to go." This could be a great day.

And now if you will excuse me, I must get ready for my close up.

Cancer (June 21- July 22) *****

It is unusual for the moody, moon child, better know as Cancer the Crab to arise in a good spirits. This morning was no different but I knew a cup of coffee would change the crab's disposition.

The caffeine began working while reading the morning paper and seeing five stars next to my zodiac sign.

I used my first star at the grocery store noticing my favorite brand of coffee on sale for the unbelievable price of one dollar per can. I purchased twenty-two cans, only because I couldn't fit thirty cans in my cabinet.

The second star appeared two hours later. My ceramic instructor presented me with a blue ribbon. My entry had won first place at the Nutmeg Ceramic Competition Show.

The third star came in the afternoon. A magazine with a story I had written and was waiting for months to see in print had finally arrived.

My forth star walked through the door after work. He complimented me, the table setting and the dinner awaiting him. He is really my first star but that one was used at the coffee sale.

Waiting anxiously for the fifth star, I decided to wash the floor on my hands and knees. Getting up I whacked my head on the island counter and sure enough, I saw the fifth star.

It's great to be Cancer the Crab!

MIRACLE – GRO

Unlocking the door, she entered the dismal apartment she called home.

Sifting through her mail, an envelope from the electric company was stamped, Miss Sally Foster – Final Notice.

Soon she would be sitting in the dark along with her only house plant, a distressed philodendron.

She noticed its leaves were turning brown but had no money to buy more Miracle-Gro. It didn't seem to be working anyhow.

She sighed, "Maybe I should have splashed some on myself. We could both use a miracle."

Watering the sickly plant, she asked, "How was your day, Phil?"

Phil answered by dropping one shriveled leaf.

"Well, my day wasn't much better. The bills are piling up and the rent is due. So I hope you understand I can't waste money on plant food that doesn't work."

Sally bent to pick up the fallen leaf. In its place tie twenty dollar bill. Astonished, she stared at Andrew Jackson as the plant dropped another leaf. Once again a twenty dollar bill appeared.

She quickly grabbed Phil and shook him until twenty dollar bills covered the floor.

Looking at the naked plant, she said, "Now I can pay the rent and the electric bill. But don't worry Phil, first I will buy you a case of Miracle -Gro."

My Favorite Place in the Whole World

I have traveled the United States, Canada and Europe but my favorite place in the world is 22 Vermont Avenue Milford, Connecticut. It is home. It is where my husband is. It is where my heart finds comfort.

One needs to suffer a bit when traveling. Hopping in and out of cars, trains, buses, boats and planes to get to one's destination while dragging luggage is not at all restful. But of course, to site-see one must get there. Sometimes the "there" is disappointing. That's one thing about Vermont Avenue, it's never disappointing. The Colosseum may crumble and fall but I will maintain my Milford homestead where the sights comfort me.

~~~~

4 of Diamonds

My Family would describe as...

The only family I have is my husband. I asked him, "If you had to describe me, what would you say?"

Without hesitation he answered, "Practically perfect."

I lit up for a second, then questioned, "practically'?

Oh well, I guess no one is perfect. I'll have to work harder. My work is never done. Of course, when it is I'll be perfect.

~~~~

The Thing That Makes Me Happiest

The thing that makes me happiest is when all my pegs are in place. I find peace knowing my husband is home safely after a hectic day. I find comfort knowing my friends are enjoying a lovely home together. I am relieved when another calls to say a medical report came back good after a long illness. Calmness comes when I talk to my elderly mother-in-law and she tells me all is well with her and Papa.

My day ends after many phone calls. It's OK now to go to bed - all my pegs are in place. This makes me happy.

~~~~

I Am Saddest When...

Grief is the strongest of all emotions. It goes deeper than love or hate.

Sadness fills the emptiness that grief has left.

I am saddest when grief rears its ugly head. Sadness can be pushed aside but grief lives forever.

~~~~

The Thing That Really Stresses Me Out

I get stressed out when there are too many men in my life. Oh no-it's not what you think. The men are home repair workers.

I've had days, when there's a plumber under my kitchen sink fixing a pipe while an electrician asks me to hold a flashlight while he rips out the old electrical box.

The wall paper hanger tells me we need another double roll and hopes it is stock. The exterior painter asks the landscaper to stop kicking up dirt. An argument breaks out. The neighbors begin to call. The driveway guy is measuring footage for asphalt and stops to talk to the tree surgeon who is estimating removal of an old oak.

I call all the men by first names. They have been to my home several times throughout the years. They all call me ma'am.

The workmen do their best to put up with me while I am stressed. Then they say, "Here's the bill ma'am."

~~~~

My Idea Of A Perfect Day

My goal is to get things accomplished. Shakespeare said, "All's well that ends well."

If by the end of the day, my family and friends are well and all chores are accomplished, my day is complete and it has been the perfect day.

~~~~

10 of Diamonds

My Favorite Dream

My best friend lost her battle with cancer at the age of thirty six. Her suffering had ended where mine began. My life felt empty without her.

One night she visited me in a dream. The heaviness of grief lifted. I knew she was at peace and free from pain. We laughed together-one last time. We held hands and said good-bye.

~~~~

Jack of Diamonds

My Scariest Dream

My dream took me into a dark concrete tunnel. The farther I walked, the colder it became. Icicles hung low and spooky stalagmites rose from the frigid ground.

My heart ached at the sight of a ragged woman crouched against the wall. I reached for her thin, cold hand.

I spoke with clouded breath. "I have come to get you out of here."

I turned her decrepit body toward the light coming from the entrance of the tunnel.

Her large sunken eyes asked, "Where am I?"

I pointed to blood written graffiti. It read, "Welcome to Hell."

~~~~

My Friends Describe Me As...

I don't know how to tie a sheep-shank or a granny knot but my friends compare me to a boy scout. They say I am honorable, faithful, loyal and trustworthy. All I need now are short pants and the urge to help an old lady cross the street.

~~~~

Queen of Clubs

The Most Important Things In My Life

Like a book, life has many chapters. At different times different things are important. My husband, family and friends are always important. This never changes.

Some things that seemed important at the time proved unimportant later in life.

The most important thing now is knowing what will remain forever important.

~~~~

2 of Hearts

The Person I Look Up To The Most

In 1961 the song 'Mother In law' was number one on the charts. The lyrics gave all mothers-in law a bad rap.

My mother-in law is my friend. She always understands and gives good advice. I respect her because I have learned she is wiser than I. Wisdom usually comes with age. She is almost ninety. She takes good care of my father-in law - he is ninety four.

She raised two devoted children (one my husband). She will admit she loves him more than any other on earth. For this reason, I love her. I take good care of her son and for that reason she loves me.

She calls to tell me I give her peace of mind knowing her son is loved and well taken care of. She trusts me and I trust her. Trust goes hand in hand with love.

I look up to my mother-in law and I don't care what that ridiculous song says.

~~~~

3 of Hearts

I Really Should Stop...

I really should stop worrying about trivial things- like how does one repair a bongo?

I began worrying in kindergarten. The teacher handed out musical instruments. I hoped to get the triangle but Tommy pushed ahead. The wooden sticks were my next favorite. I watched Maryanne smugly click them together. I began to worry that I would be left with the empty oatmeal box. The teacher convinced me it was a bongo drum.

I worried I wouldn't be able to keep the tempo. Anxiety kept me one beat ahead of the triangle and wooden sticks.

The one-step ahead beat took me through life. Worrying brought on anxiety and tension. Tension put a hole in my oatmeal box. So now you know.

~~~~

The Most Beautiful Thing In Nature

Have you stopped to smell the roses lately? Look around-beauty is everywhere. Nature seems to know what it is doing, although some will disagree.

The planet Earth is about 12 billion years old-I rest my case.

At times we have a problem reasoning with nature. Nature holds seniority-it was here before man. Violent storms, tornadoes and earth quakes are frightening, it is natures way of turning over the soil.

Until we can figure out how to change the seasons, we must trust nature. I do. Isn't nature beautiful?

~~~~

I Have The Most Fun When I...

...attend Writer Unlimited meetings. I put the world on hold for a couple of hours.

I listen and learn from my gifted teacher and talented classmates. They make me laugh-they

make me cry.

Inspiration takes the place of tension. Oh, what fun.

~~~~

The People That Bring Out The Best In Me Are...

... friends who have seen me at my worst.

I feel comfortable with true friends. We can talk about anything and never worry about offending. We always find a common ground and tears turn into smiles.

Friends bring out the best in me and I hope I bring out the best in them.

~~~~

Write A Letter To Yourself

Dear Carol,

As your co-pilot, I think it time to warn you to check your fuel gauge. It's time to land honey-you are out of gas. Find a landing strip, lower your wheels and coast in. I know you can do it.

Forever your co-pilot,
Carol

~~~~

My Goals For Myself This Year

I took the goal post down long ago. I had to-it is easier to step over.

I take smaller steps now. It takes longer to arrive but better late than never. When I finally get to where I'm going, I feel like I have made a touch down. How many points do I get for that?

~~~~

I Could Be Great At

I could be great at acting. I would love to be in a play.

In high school I joined a drama class. The director set the scene-a dead body on the floor of a dark room. He said to enter the room and do anything except scream. I screamed and that was the end of my acting career.

It's too late now because I would never be able to remember my lines. Maybe they will bring back silent movies.

"I'm ready for my close up, Mr. DeMille."

~~~~

King of Spades

I Made Someone Smile

I told my friend the following story; My husband was with another teacher was-in a small room using a copying machine. His colleague, a Nigerian woman, who speaks with a thick accent, was also using a copier.

He bent to removed copies from the machine while she reached over his head to get her copies. When he stood, she accidentally touched his head. Thinking nothing of it, he continued to gather papers. The woman threw her arms up ranting and raving in her native tongue.

My husband said, "Calm down. What's the matter?"

She said, "In my country, if a woman touches a man's head she must give him-two goats."

She now avoids him in the halls. She knows he is waiting for the goats.

~~~~

7 of Diamonds

The Thing I Wish Other People Would Get About Me

Although I appear to be tough and at times sassy, I am really made of marshmallow fluff. I feel most comfortable with people I like and I like most people.

~~~~

Queen of Diamonds

People Misunderstand Me When...

Some people say "no" when they mean "maybe". When I say "no" I mean just that. No is no. I wonder what part of the word no they do not understand.

If I need time to think about it, I'll simply say, "I'll think about it." If I then say no, please accept it. Don't say, "well, maybe you will change your mind." Believe me, I won't.

At times there is a part two to the question. If I say "no", they ask, "Why not?"

My answer is always the same, "Because I said so." Capital 'N' small 'o' - No!!

~~~~

4 of Clubs

I Really Don't Like...

Brussel sprouts are cute little cabbages. They appear tasty but I don't like he smell or taste. Broccoli is also high on my list of things I don't like. It's just as well because my doctor has warned me to stay away from vegetables that are high in potassium. I have recently learned my kidneys are failing and can no longer tolerate potassium. Thank goodness it's not ice cream.

MYTHICAL CREATURE COMES TO LIFE

This morning started out like any other winter morning. Feeding the birds was an enjoyable duty. The crows always arrive first. The large, black, noisy birds let their feathered neighbors know, breakfast is being served. The starlings arrive next, only to be chased away by the sea gulls. They are definitely first in nature's pecking order. The crows put up a fight but their size is diminished by the gulls. As the birds swooped down to claim their morsel, I noticed a large shadow cast on the ground. Could it be a plane flying much too low? It was at that moment I saw the strange creature. It had the body of man and fierce, darting eyes. It's feathered head was cocked to one side as if listening. When it opened it's large beak, the pecking order was instantly changed. I held my breath. My eyes widened, not believing what I was seeing. I ran to get the camera trying to focus with shaking hands. "Say Cheese." I thought. It looked at me with frightened eyes. His ostrich-like legs began to crouch for takeoff. I lowered the camera without snapping the picture. I knew he had come a long way from the land of myth. I also knew he would return someday. I will wait.

The Interview

Today I had some business to do at the town hall. I arrived a little early and decided to sit on a bench and watch the ducks. Actually, they were watching me and honking. "Sorry guys, I didn't bring you anything to eat today." I continued to converse with them. "I drew the queen of clubs today. That means I have to interview someone. Where am I going to find someone to interview? Am I suppose to wait for a complete stranger to walk by and tell him I drew the queen of clubs? Shall I do this before or after he mugs me?"

I now noticed a little gray squirrel heading my way, getting closer with each hop. He was directly in front of me when he sat up putting his little hands together as if in prayer. His face looked like any rodent but his fluffy white bib and trusting nature made it seem like someone I could tell about drawing the queen of clubs.

"So you live around the town hall, do you?"

"I live in the town hall." He said with his tiny voice. My interview had begun. "That must be interesting." I said. "Tell me about it."

"Well, I used to live in that big tree and as the branches grew, I was able to reach the roof of the town hall. After days of hard work, I was able to gnaw through. It's cozy in there. When the employees leave at the end of the day, I'm able to go into the tax office. The cash drawers are locked but you're not keeping this little gray squirrel out! The paper money makes great insulation for my nest. I just shore it through the hole in the roof. So, now you know where your tax dollars are going. You won't tell anyone will you?"

"Oh sure, I'm going to say, I was talking to a squirrel about drawing the queen of clubs and in return he told me where our tax money is going! Your secret is safe with me and thanks for the interview."

Hot Drink

Don't talk to me or even look at me until I've had that first cup of coffee in the morning. One of the first things I do is grab the electric coffee pot and fill it with cold water. Scooping the dry coffee into the metal basket, arouses my first sense. It smells so good and I know it won't be long until the taste wakes my other senses. I love the blubbering sound of the perking pot. As the coffee becomes stronger, so does my craving. The first delicious swallow of the magic potion makes me almost human again. My eyes widen and the "caffeine jolt" gets the old brain going.

I'm not a big coffee drinker. Two or three cups during a long day is sufficient. Actually, I enjoy a cup of hot chocolate. It's a cozy drink and not as serious as coffee and you can feel it's warmth all the way down to your shoes.

Coffee has served me well to write this paper. Without it I wouldn't be able to stay on the lines...

WRITE FAIRY TALE FROM VILLAIN'S POINT OF VIEW RUMPELSTILTSKIN SPEAKS

I don't know why I'm considered to be the villain of the story. The real villain is the Miller. He's the one who lied to the king, telling him his daughter could spin straw into gold. How dumb was the king to believe this? The king could also be the villain. He's the one who locks the miller's daughter in a room with a spinning wheel and tells her he will cut off her head if she can't spin the straw into gold. And they have the nerve to call me the villain!

Another thing, I know how to spin straw into gold but do you expect me to do it for nothing? What would the Gold Spinner Union have to say about that?

I'm the one who felt sorry for the girl and let her give me her beads as payment. What am I going to do with these cheap beads? I'm a little old man and I can spin gold. Beads, Indeed! The next room the king put her in was larger and to fill that room, she gave me her ring. It looked like a cracker Jack prize but I still did the job for her didn't I?

The next room was so big I had to work my tail off filling it. Don't you think I was entitled to her promise of giving me her first born child? I can't work like this for nothing you know. I have overhead, between union dues and the price of straw – or do you think straw grows on trees? She didn't seem to mind the deal when we made it. Then she reneged! I was still kind enough to give her three days to guess my name. I didn't have to do that you know. I could have taken her to court.

She sends out all the kings men to find out my name and one of them happens to see me dancing around, singing my name. I know I shouldn't have done that but I was happy. I had it planned to pick up

Rumpelstiltskin Jr., take him to a ballgame and teach him my gold spinning trade.

Well anyway, I go to collect the promised child and she comes up with my name. She toys with me first asking, "Is it Bill? Is it Pete?"

Do I look like a Bill or Pete? Pardon the pun but this is the last straw and I stomp myself into the ground saying, "I'm not the villain. I'm not the villain."

King of Clubs

A Great Invention For The Future

As a child, I toured New York City with my parents. It was snowing but the sidewalks were clear. My father explained that under the concrete, electric coils heated and melted the snow. What a great invention.

I think of it every time my driveway and walks are deep with snow. The backbreaking job of shoveling continues throughout the snow storm only to have the city plow throw it back.

I always thought by now, all walks and roads would have electric coils. New York proved the cost too expensive for the luxury. The coils remain buried under the sidewalks of New York but the idea is always with me. Someday I will figure out a way to have underground rodents run around on wheels generating electricity to heat sidewalks and roads. Until that day I will keep the snow shovel nearby.

~~~

King of Hearts

The True Meaning Of Cool To Me Is...

The word cool has several meanings. If something is cool it is at a fairly low temperature. I often wonder how we ever survived the summers before air-conditioning. Our cooling system was called a fan and only used on the hottest of days.

The word cool also means calm and collected. I fondly remember a young Jai-Alai player named Lopetegui. I followed his career for over twenty years. He came to the United States from the Basque region. He was a front court man and wore the number twenty on his jersey. There was something cool about the way he played. He never tried to kill the ball (pelota). Instead he wore his opponent down with his calm and collected mannerism.

After years of playing, he was going for a record win. I was there to cheer him on. When he walked onto the court I shouted, "Come on Lope. You can do it."

Hearing a pet name from a fan encouraged him to win. He broke all records. I stood and applauded. He raised his cesta (Jai-Alai basket) to me as he calmly walked off the court.

I asked Churruka a retired player and now in public relations if I could meet and congratulate Lopetgui.

Lopetegui handed me the winning cesta. I still have it. How cool is that?

~~~

Queen of Hearts

If Money Were No Object And I Could Do Something For A Loved One

Money isn't everything. How much is a loved one's smile worth?

If money were no object, I would buy my husband a big smile. I would move him near the beach where he could swim everyday. He could retire and never worry about paying taxes, insurance or monthly bills.

On rainy days he could write a book or attend lectures. He would go to classical concerts at night.

I think about 40 million should cover expenses-but his smile is worth it.

THE BEGGAR'S WISH

Barney the beggar stood on a busy street corner rattling two pebbles in a tin cup. People lowered heads and rushed by.

"Get a job," one man snarled.

"Disgraceful," said the lady walking her dog.

Tom O'Malley, the cop on the beat, felt sorry for Barney but used his authority.

"Move on Barney or I'll have to run you in."

Barney pleaded, "I wish – just this one time, you would look the other way."

Officer O'Malley placed his hand on Barney's shoulder.

"I have a wish too. I wish I never had to walk this beat again. I'm sorry, Barney. I know times are tough but they are for me too. The baby needs shoes and the rent is overdue. A cop doesn't make enough to make ends meet these days."

He wondered why he was telling Barney his problems. He knew Barney had enough of his own. He reached into his uniform pocket and placed a dollar bill in Barney's cup.

Barney dragged his oversized shoes down the street. He entered the express store and read the sign, "Sandwiches $3.00." The next sign read, "Lottery tickets $1.00."

The next morning Barney sat on a bench next to a man reading the newspaper. The man left the paper when his bus arrived. Barney turned to page two and checked his lottery numbers.

"Make the check out to Officer Tom O'Malley," he told the lottery agent.

Barney the beggar stood on a busy street corner rattling two pebbles in a tin cup. Officer O'Malley was not on his beat.

TIE IT UP

By Helen Chapin Williams

Grudges drain away happy living
Swim through bitterness
Let your heart be giving

Don't allow anger to ruin a day
Take time to replay and repeat it
Sift through anger, toss it away

Search for the mystery of life
Run naked in the rain
Trust what the days bring, banish strife

Inhale fragrances of lovely flowers
Wear a colorful scarf and a sexy bra
Tie anger up in a box, have happy hours

LIFE IN ANOTHER TIME PERIOD

If I had to chose any time period to live, I guess I would have to consider what part of the world I would be living in. My thoughts would quickly bring me back to America because I don't believe there is a more beautiful place to live than the Hudson Valley from Tarrytown to Rhinebeck.

Oh, to be Henry Hudson as he first saw the breathtaking valley in 1609. That time period would be a little early for me. I would choose to live in the early 1800's, long before the Vanderbilt's and Roosevelts settled there. A simple piece of farmland would make <u>me</u> feel like a millionaire!

Is it any wonder writers such as Washington Irving or Herman Melville were stimulated? I had the occasion to stand behind the desk that Melville was at as he imagined the rolling hills were a huge whale. From his window he saw Moby Dick before his eyes.

I would live on a small farm where hard work and the feeling of accomplishment at the end of each day would bring me content.

The Hudson River has been called, "King of the rivers" and I would visit the King on Sundays. I would hitch my horse to the buggy and after church services, a picnic lunch along the river bank would be my well deserved reward after farming all week.

The beautiful scenery would inspire me to write and the river would whisper wonderful stories in my ear. I would be able to write a classic and my name would be on the spine of a wonderful book. To Hell with the farm! It's a writers life for me.

P.S.

It just dawned on me – I was in the Berkshires in Massachusetts when I said Herman Mervilles view. So I guess I've changed my mind!

I AM INNOCENT

Living in the land of fairy tales is not easy when one is a wolf. Let me tell you how I ended up in this courtroom today pleading innocent and begging for mercy.

My name is Big-Bad and I am a fine looking wolf with pointed ears, beady eyes, wiry gray fur, a long nose and oh, yes sharp white teeth.

The trial begins with raising my right paw and swearing to tell the truth. The judge is a muskrat, my favorite meal and to make ˢ matters worse, he knows it. My attorney is Foxy Loxi, not exactly a credit to his profession. He lost his last case. Tom, the piper's son was sent to prison for stealing a pig. Speaking of pigs, the jury consists of three little ones. They sent my brother up the river for blowing on their houses. He was not carrying a weapon but they proved his huffing and puffing lethal. The pigs hired Chicken Lickin to represent them. He's the Johnnie Cochrane of fairy tale land. It was Chicken Lickin' who convinced everyone the sky was falling. I'm doomed.

I'm finally allowed to tell my side of the story. It began the day my long nose picked up the scent of corned beef on rye. I was starving. The woodcutter was diminishing the forest, taking away my food supply. I saw the little hooded girl skipping along, carrying a basket of goodies. I knew she was headed to her grandmother's house at the edge of the woods. I decided to run ahead and ask Grandma to find kindness in her heart and share the food basket with a hungry, good-looking wolf. When she saw me, she jumped out of bed and ran out the door. I needed another plan. I hopped into bed and pulled the covers to my chin. Little Red Skipping Hood said,

"Grandmother, what big eyes you have."

I harmlessly answered, "Better to see you with, my dear."

I had no intention of harming Little Red. I only wanted the corned beef sandwich and a maybe a pickle.

As our conversation went on, my hunger pains grew. It was then the woodsman broke down the door and came at me with an axe. Why wasn't he on trial for breaking and entering not to mention terrorizing with intent to murder an innocent wolf? The verdict was read by the first little pig, "Guilty without a shadow of doubt."

The muskrat judge gave a life sentence with no parole. Flashbulbs went off. The fairy tale court room oinked and cackled as I growled, "I am innocent."

****

OLD CROW AND THE NEST EGG

A pretty young crow sat in a tree.
On her nest, happy was she.
A dashing young crow flew by one day,
Caught her eye and cawed, "Let's play."
"Oh, no, oh no, I cannot go.
I need to watch my nest egg grow."
The other crows went to the dance
But she could never take the chance
To leave her egg up in the tree
This could not - would not - ever be.
Through the rain and through the snow
For years and years she watched it grow.
Her raven feathers now ashen gray
Her old crow eyes had feet.
Still she sat upon the egg
And would not leave her seat.
The egg grew heavy and very round
It snapped the bough and hit the ground
And that was where Old Crow was found

THWACK

Slamming it against the tabletop, the newspaper echoed, "Thwack."

"Why has the world become so violent?" I asked, while washing black print from my hands, watching robbery, war, rape and murder swirl down the drain.

I again picked up the paper before throwing it into the trash, where it belonged. I read the large print, 'Children Abducted.' "Oh no, the children- not the children." THWACK!"

Maybe this planet we call Earth, the most beautiful in the solar system, should have been placed closer to the sun as it seems half-baked.

Headlines: Astronomer, Carol Ruggiero discovers new planet beyond Pluto, naming it "Thwack."

At a news conference she is quoted, "I found it and I own it. You know, finders-keepers. I have big plans for Thwack. I will rid the world of vermin and plant trees where penitentiaries cast dark shadows. I will transfer violent human criminals from the prisons of Earth, never to return as they have given up all rights to humanity. The former Earthlings will be called "Thwacklings.' Human beings will never again fear them as Thwacklings only fear each other each other on their dark, cold, loveless planet."

The majestic Earth will not share heaven with the evil Thwack. In the event, an Earthling chooses violence over peace, he should be prepared to board a shuttle. Upon landing, he will read the electrified sign, "Welcome to Thwack. One way in - no way out."

The Sky Is Falling

On a cold October night I was preheating the oven and trying to decide what to prepare for dinner when the door bell rang.

When I opened the door I was surprised to see a chicken standing on the porch.

Assuming it was someone dressed in a costume, I said, "Go away chicken. Halloween isn't until next week."

The shivering chicken cackled, "I'm not trick-or-treating. My name is Chicken Lickin and Pm here to warn you the sky is falling. May I come in? It's cold out here."

I answered, "Well, I usually don't entertain poultry, but you may come and warm yourself near the stove."

I opened the oven door allowing the heat to circulate. "Now tell me, what makes you think the sky is falling?"

The chicken ruffled its feathers. "I felt a piece of sky hit me on the head."

I laughed, "Are you sure it wasn't just an acom falling from an oak tree?"

The chicken began to cry. "No no, you must believe me, 'the sky is falling."

Trying to console, I tenderly patted the plump chicken. "Oh, you poor thing. I can feel that you are still cold. Maybe you should get into the oven where it is warmer." The chicken agreed, "Oh thank you. You are so kind."

When the chicken hopped in, I closed die oven door and raised the baking temperature.

My dinner was chicken lickin' good on that cold October night.... and then the sky fell.

ENGLAND'S GOING TO THE DOGS

Entering the dimly lit bedroom, Penelope carried a tray of tea and crumpets placing it on a serving table.

The queen stirred.

"Sorry to wake you, your Majesty. We must leave the palace early this morning. We are traveling to the United States where we shall visit the lovely town of Milford, Connecticut."

"The citizens of Milford are celebrating the opening of their new fire department today- complete with a shiny red truck."

Propped up against purple pillows, the queen began to practice her elegant wave.

"How absolutely marvelous. What have you chosen for me to wear?"

Penelope answered, "Not to clash with the fire truck, you will wear a white suit, high rubber boots and of course one of your goofy shaped hats. Under your hat will be a supply of dog treats."

Raising her lovely cheekbones, the queen almost giggled. "Why would that be?"

"Allow me to explain, your Majesty. The Milford Fire Department has named their pet Dalmation "Lizzie" in your honor. They say she is the queen of the firehouse. In addition, the firefighters claim, when they are bored, they connect Lizzie's black dots and an image of you appears on her shiny coat."

As a dog lover, the queen was delighted to meet Lizzie and gave an immediate order to fly the dog to England to live with her in Buckingham Palace.

Everyone scrambled to comply. Somehow during the commotion of boarding the dog, the good queen was left behind.

The next morning Penelope entered the queen's bedroom.

"Good morning, your majesty – your kibble and bits are on your serving tray."

EX LIBRIS

Carol Ruggiero sends her regrets. She is unable to attend the Writers Unlimited meeting this morning. I have come in her place.

Allow me to introduce myself. I am from a galaxy called "Libris" where Librians are in desperate need of writers. We have no essays, poems, short stories or books. What we do have though, is the ability to replicate earthling writers.

Carol was not exactly my first choice and of course you must agree. Go ahead. Remember she is not here. She has been transported to Libris.

Our goal is simple; Each of you will be replaced by a Librian before your instructor returns from her hiatus. She will never know the difference except at times we glow a little. She will think we are having an amber moment and continue to teach.

Since your instructor will be returning shortly, you may believe there is not enough time to accomplish our goal. If you believe this, then you must believe that is Maij sitting at the end of the table.

The Scarlet Neighbor

Squinting through the slats of the blinds I watched the new neighbor move in. I noticed she was very pregnant and struggling with some old wooden, straight-back chairs. I wondered why her child's father was not there to help her. She looked so familiar, but I couldn't place her and hoped she would be friendly. It would be nice to have someone to talk with about gardening, while sharing neighborhood news.

I noticed a monogram on her gray dress and was curious about the initial "A". I love the name Ann. Of course, her name could be Alice or Alexandria, but I hoped it was Ann.

The next morning I was surprised by a knock and wondered if the doorbell was out of order.

"Hello," I greeted the "A" on my porch holding a wooden bucket. "Is my doorbell not working?"

"What dost thou mean?" she asked.

"How charming," I thought. "I can't wait to ask what country she is from."

Oddly I still sensed that we had met before.

She lowered her eyes asking, "Wouldst thou be so kind as to give me some water? I can not find the well."

"We don't have wells in this neighborhood. Come into the kitchen and take as much as you need," I obliged.

She stared at the sink and seemed confused.

"Push the chrome lever and the water will come out. Are you from another country or another planet?" I joked.

The "A" did not laugh.

"I better be gentler," I thought and pointed to the initial. "Did you embroider that yourself?" It certainly is a fine piece of work." I complimented. "What is your name?"

"Hester," she said. "Surely thou hast heard of me."

"Oh my goodness, you're Hester Prynne! Well, so much for Ann. I knew, I knew you from somewhere. I have not thought of you since freshman high school. I remember how the Puritans of colonial Boston forced you to wear a red A on your bosom as punishment for your sin. Hester, after all these years, is it really you?"

She placed her hand on the A and said, "I will bear the illegitimate child and if it is a girl I will name her Pearl as she will be my only treasure."

"Just keep her out of my flower bed." I warned. "And what do you mean if it is a girl? Haven't you had an ultra sound? Don't you know the sex of the child? And speaking of sex, why did you never tell who the father is? The Reverend Dimmesdale needs to pay child support and take care of your needs. We have enough mothers on welfare." I raised my voice a little more than intended. Once again, after all this time I felt sorry for poor Hester Prynne.

"Sit down. I'll make some tea and you can tell me all about it now that we are neighbors."

She began, "I refuseth to speak because the Reverend Dimmeadale takes it very grievously to heart that such scandal should come upon his congregation. I must protect his good name. People look to him as a saint. Please, you must not tell what thou knows. If thou promises, I will teach thou to embroider fancy letters. We can start with the letter "A".

"I have known you for many years Hester and I know how well you can keep a secret. I think that is important in case I have some juicy neighborhood gossip."

I watched her wonderment as she pulled the tea bag up and down.

"It is making thy and thou tea," she giggled.

"Yes it is Hester and thy hast much, much, more to show thee."

A Dramatized Obsession With Groucho

It seemed the phone would never ring and when it did I cut it short, grabbing the receiver. Breathlessly I answered, "Hello Johnny? Is it you?"

My heart sank hearing my friend Susan's consoling voice. "You have to get on with your life," she said." He's not going to call."

"Oh Sue, why did I have to bring him home that night to meet Mother?" I cried.

"You knew he had to meet her sooner or later," she said. Your mom is a nice person. She loves to make people laugh. Johnny had no right to judge her by her appearance."

"But couldn't Mom just have said, "It's nice to meet you Johnny, instead of singing, "My name is Captain Spalding. Hello, I must be going...." You should have seen Johnny's face drain when Mom said, "last night I shot an elephant in my pajamas. How he got in my pajamas I'll never know."

"After noticing Mom's mustache he started feeling my upper lip. He also insinuated that my eyebrows are getting bushy and wished I would stop raising them above my glasses. My mother was still acting like a silly goose when the duck dropped out of the ceiling and announced Johnny had said the secret word."

"It was right after the duck incident that Dad came into the room dragging his harp and tooting his horn. When Johnny reached out to shake his hand, Dad lifted his leg and dropped it into Johnny palm."

Dad said, "honk-honk" as Johnny ran out the door tripping over Uncle Chico.

I reached for one of Mom's cigars asking Susan, "Why, oh why doesn't Johnny call?"

She answered, "He must be obsessed with the fact that your mother genuinely resembles Groucho Marx."

Writers Unlimited Assignment

Strange circumstances found Jennifer driving in a snow storm. She had received a call from Thomas, her grandmother's care taker. After many years Thomas had become more of a friend and companion to Gran.

The snow was getting deeper as Jen traveled the winding road leading to the old Victorian house where she found Thomas clearing the driveway. He dropped his shovel and waved. Helping Jen from the car he said, "Your Grandmother will be delighted to see you. She has been waiting since she saw the first snow flake falling.

"How's she doing?" Jennifer asked.

Thomas answered, "Well you know, she has her good days and her bad days. Today is one of her good days because she knows you are coming."

Entering the foyer, Jen caught a glimpse of herself in the large, ornate oval mirror. Brushing snow from her woolen hat she laughed, "I look like a snowman."

Thomas returned the laugh. "No, no, you look like a snow lady. Remember how you and your grandmother used to build snow ladies on the front lawn? She's been talking about that for days - since she heard the weatherman's snow forecast.

Jen quietly opened her Grandmother's bedroom door, wrinkling her nose at the musty odor.

"Stop tip-toeing. I'm not sleeping - only resting my eyes. Come in. Let me see you."

"Hi Gran. How ya doing?"

"How could I be doing? The nurses come and say, 'Give us a blood sample' then they smile at Thomas and leave. But I figured out what's talcing me so long to die. There's something I want to do one more time before I leave. That's why I had you come today in the snow."

Jen lowered her tear filled eyes. "What is it Gran?"

"I want us to build a snow lady together - one last time."

"You'll catch your death Gran. You can't go out there."

"I can and I will Jennifer. Bundle me up and get Thomas to put me in the wheelchair. I'm going to build a snow lady. Then I can die happy."

Putting the finishing touches on the snow lady, Gran ordered, "Give her big eyes Jen."

Jennifer pushed large black nuggets of coal into the face.

Now the snow lady stared, frozen in place - as did Gran.

Detective Sam Spoon was not the sharpest cop on the Sterling City police force but he was polished enough to recognize his own address.

He arrived at the crime scene finding his wife Crock-Pot Carol on the kitchen floor. Standing over Crock-Pot with a smoldering utensil was Dora.

Spoon held a special place in his stainless-steel heart for Dora. She was a "real dish."

"Just think, Spoon," Dora smiled, exposing chipped enamel, "she can't sink her pronged tines into you anymore."

Spoon gleamed as he reached the point of conclusion. "Fork over the weapon Dish, and let's grab a gravy boat to China. When we get there we can order take-out and eat in. What do you say, Dish? Do you like Chinese food?"

Her Dresden head spinning with excitement answered, "I prefer French, Mon Cher, but I'm sure my fortune cookie will read 'bon appetite'."

And so....

The dish ran away with the spoon.

CAROL IN WONDERLAND

Driving to the Senior Center, I hit a pot hole on New Haven Avenue. The hole was deeper than I thought-I spun down, down, down until I landed in an oval room filled with the strangest people.

At the head of the table sat a mad hatter named Anne-Marie who pulled quick-writes from her whacky hat. The man next to her resembled a caterpillar and blew smoke rings into my face. He introduced himself as Edgar and asked, in smoke shaped letters, "Who R U ?"

Before I could answer, Shirley the tipsy dormouse popped out of a tea pot and began reciting "Twinkle, twinkle little star." Boy, that was enough for me. I wanted out of there.

Across the table, a regal looking woman wearing a tiara and red hearts on her dress smiled. I thought I found comfort, until Queen Dorothy suddenly yelled, "Off with her head."

Helen the Cheshire Cat, agreed with the queen and grinned from ear to ear. Then she disappeared leaving her bushy tail and smile behind.

I bolted towar d the door but was blocked by Jim who was just arriving. In a dither he shouted, "I'm late, I'm late. Of course he was-all white rabbits are late.

The windows were now the only way out but the sills were lined with flowers and to make matters worse, they had faces and were singing, "You could learn a lot of things from the flowers." I was sure I could, but the harmonizing voices were a little too sweet for me. I just wanted to leave.

It was then Brian the doo-wop buttercup dressed in a white sport coat and a pink carnation woke me up with golden oldies along with his golden voice.

I now wanted to stay, took a seat and wished everyone a very happy un-birthday.

Plagiarism

I am sure you are all familiar with the picture of Snoopy sitting on the rooftop of his dog house clicking his typewriter keys.

I have a couple of things in common with Snoopy – first of all, we are both writers.

In 1950, cartoonist Charles Shultz introduced Charlie Brown's pet beagle to his Peanuts comic strip. Sadly, the talented Mr. Shulz has passed – but Snoopy still looks pretty good for his age – considering dog years.

The droopy- eared beagle taps the space bar and begins his opening chapter - "It was a dark and stormy night."

I shouted, "Good grief, I thought beagles were smarter than that. Don't you know it is a serious offense to steal someone's written words? You have committed plagiarism."

Snoopy's paw pointed to his license.

"Silly beagle, that's a dog license. It doesn't give special permission to steal from another author."

At this point Snoopy whimpered and shed big cartoon tears.

I immediately tried to comfort the wet nosed puppy. "Come with me to Writers Unlimited at the wonderful Milford Senior Center. This entertaining group will make your tail wag in no time. I should know – mine never stops."

Snoopy and I wish you all a tail wagging day.

It Depends

The lead singer tilts the microphone towards her and asks the audience, "Did you ever wonder what happened to the beautiful and talented Mandrell sisters? Well, you can keep on wondering because we are not them.

Allow me to introduce my guitar playing sister Josephine who insists on being called Jo. She looks like a guy because she recently decided to change her gender. She chopped off her long hair and seems to have no problem growing a beard, but she is having difficulty parting with her favorite pleated skirt. Be careful Jo – your walker is kind of close to the edge of the stage. Don't fall off.

Behind me on drums is my little sister Gertrude. Gert wasn't always little. She forgot to take her calcium pills, developed osteo problems and shrunk. Now she can barely reach the cymbals, but she can still click those drum sticks better than Gene Krupa or Ringo Starr.

As for me, I'm concerned about the wires running across the stage. You see, I forgot to wear my Depends and if I step into a puddle of piddle I will surely get electrocuted.

Oh where are the Mandrell sisters when you need them?"

What If Humans Could Fly?

Would if be so wonderful to be able to fly like birds? Would we, as humans be satisfied to sit in a tree on eggs in a nest made of a couple of prickly twigs? Or would our human nature strive for more and not thrive at all?

Remember the story of Icarus and his genius father the inventor Daedalus? The Athenian and his son were imprisoned by the king of Crete for murdering his apprentice, whose skill was greater than his master. The inventor refused to suffer in captivity and built two pairs of wings adhering feathers and wax to a wooden frame. Giving one pair to his son, he cautioned him that flying to close to the sun would cause the wax to melt. But Icarus became ecstatic with the ability to fly and forgot his father's warning. Icarus plunged to his death.

The idea of humans flying did not end with Icarus. Leonardo Da Vinci's plan looked logical on paper. But even the great Da Vinci couldn't get his plan off the ground.

But now, would we dare tell the following humans they can not fly?

Orville and Wilbur Wright

Eddie Rickenbacker

Charles Lindberg

Amelia Earhart

Igor Sikorsky

John Glen

And let's not forget the remarkable Mary Martin singing in every performance of Peter Pan, "I can fly. I can fly."

Here A Duck – There A Duck

When I checked my seat number I noticed it was occupied.

"Excuse me madam, is that your duck?"

"Yes," she answered. "Her name is Daphne."

"Well, please tell Daphne to move her beak and big webbed feet. I paid for this seat and I intend to sit here."

"Tell her yourself. Daphne doesn't have to pay for a seat. She is a service animal and can sit wherever she may please. I guess you just don't like animals."

"You are so wrong. I love animals, but what kind of service can a duck give?"

"She keeps passengers calm during take off and throughout the flight."

The duck squawked when the overhead lights began to flicker.

I tightened my seat belt and listened to the announcement.

"Attention all passengers. This is your Captain speaking. I regret to inform you we have lost an engine. I will try to land in a com field – that is, if I can find a com field."

The duck loudly quacked and fluttered her white feathers.

"Daphne is delighted. It's her favorite kind of field. She loves corn."

I screamed, "Oh my God, don't you understand we're going to die?"

I climbed on the duck's back and threw my arms around her skinny neck.

"What are you doing to that poor duck?"

I answered, "Daphne doesn't need an engine. She has wings."

I felt safe for a moment until I saw the mountain and forgot to duck.

Meow And Then

"You've got to be kidding Ralph. Can't you see I'm trying to read' A Tale of Two Kitties'? I'm just not in the mood to play fetch with you. It always ends with you rolling over begging for a belly rub."

"If you have nothing better to do. Stop panting and work on your hygiene. You have doggie breath – not to mention fleas. You get those things from your side of the family."

"I'm a cat Ralph – a cat – which means I don't drool. I'm classsier than you – not to mention smarter."

"I think I've outgrown you. I knew this marriage would never work. I don't know what I ever saw in you. It must have been that catnip during my kittenish years. Or... maybe it was your soft brown eyes, cute waggily tail and adorable floppy ears. Remember how your wet nose always made my whiskers tingle?"

"Oh Ralphie, I'm beginning to purr."

"I'll put my book away and throw the ball for you to fetch. It's good to play together meow and then."

I The Stowaway

Everyone knows the Lord commanded Noah to build a massive ship and board two of every land animal.

But did you know, Noah did not like animals? And to make matters worse they did not like him.

While loading the ark, he was spit in the face by a llama, kicked in the crotch by a mule and laughed at by a hyena.

He pleaded, "Lord, I am too old for this job."

"Of course you are Noah. Everyone in the bible is old. Just obey my command. It's the only way I can save the world from evil. And Noah, you better hurry up, it's starting to rain."

It was about this time I realized I must also take cover.

While Noah was distracted by a feisty ferret I got on board and hid under the hay. Hoping the elephants would not trample me, I listened to the heavy rain for forty days and forty nights.

When the sky cleared and a rainbow appeared Noah was sure the flood had killed evil and the world was pure and ready to begin again.

But when cleaning out the stalls, Noah found me hidden under the hay.

His eyes widened. "Who are you? What is your name?"

I smirked, "I am a stowaway. I have survived the flood and will always be on Earth. My name is Evil."

Spaceship Stumbles Onto
Planet Of Alien Flowers

Zu-Zu and Zack Zong were celebrating their 40th anniversary. Zack had finally retired and promised Zu-Zu the trip of her dreams. They rented a spaceship and left the planet Zaelp.

Looking out the ship's window Zu Zu said, "Oh Zack, look at that blue and green planet. It must be lovely. Let's stop there for lunch.

Zack opened the atlas. "Let's see, third planet from the sun. Here it is. It's called Earth. I am hungry but I'm not so sure about stopping on Earth. I've heard the inhabitants don't get along well with each other. It could be dangerous."

Zu-Zu saddened. "Oh Zack, don't be afraid. Remember I speak a little Earthling from my 101 language class.

"O.K, hang on," Zack said landing the spaceship.

Zu-Zu held Zack's hand. "Well, they look harmless enough. If they are as sweet as they smell we'll be fine."

Zu-Zu spoke first to the beautiful red creature. "Hello, we're the Zong's from Zaelp. She reached out her hand. "Ouch. She stuck me with a weapon. Maybe the yellow one will be kinder. Hello, allow me to introduce ourselves. I'm Zu-Zu and this is my husband Zack."

"We're the Zongs. Nice to meet you." Zack said. "Ouch," Zack yelled watching green ooze run from his skinny finger.

Zu-Zu pointed her nose toward the sky. "Well, of all the nerve. Let's eat lunch and get out of here."

Putting on his thick dining gloves, Jack agreed handing Zu-Zu a pair. They pulled all the petals from the Earthlings and ate them.

"What does that sign say Zu-Zu?" He asked his wife.

She answered, 'White House rose garden-Visiting hours 10-3.' "It's time to go Zack."

New Home Owner Discovers Old Photo In Attic

David carried Darlene over the threshold. The house was old but David was handy and Darlene was looking forward to malting new curtains.

"It will be fun fixing it up." Darlene said to her husband.

"Where shall we begin?" David asked.

Tying on an apron, Darlene answered, "From the top down."

The attic held only a few boxes of old Christmas decorations and a couple of odd curtain rods. Darlene wondered if she could use the rods and bent to pick them up.

"Oh David, look- an old photograph was stuck between the floor boards."

She gazed at a boy standing next to a small tree with a dog. She turned the photo over and read, "Jack-1939".

"How old do you think Jack is in this picture?" she asked David.

"About eight or nine." he guessed.

Darlene stuck the photo into her apron pocket and carried the curtain rods downstairs. She measured the rods against the kitchen window. "They fit," she said. "Let's do the kitchen next."

David stirred the sunny yellow paint while Darlene washed the window over the sink. They agreed that the faded brown walls were once yellow. Darlene beamed when David rolled out the first hope of sunshine.

Looking toward the back yard, Darlene admired the huge Maple tree. She was grateful for the shade and privacy it gave.

"David, isn't the tree..... David-there's an old man in our yard."

David climbed down from the ladder. "Where?"

"Standing under the tree." Darlene pointed.

"Stay here." David ordered.

"No I'm coming with you."

Darlene spoke first. "Excuse us. May we help you?"

Startled, the old man said, "I'm sorry, I didn't realize someone bought the old house. I grew up here and visit Jack whenever I can. He was my best friend."

"Jack?" Darlene questioned.

The old man patted the tree. "Jack and I planted this tree many years ago. I buried him under the tree."

Darlene shuddered and clung to David.

The old man laughed. "Oh no, it's not what you think. You see, Jack was my dog."

Relieved, Darlene took the photo from her pocket and handed it to the man.

His eyes glistened. "I still miss him. We spent many fine days in this house. Most of all I remember the sunny yellow kitchen. This picture hung in the kitchen for a long time. I am all alone now."

David and Darlene spoke together. "You may visit Jack whenever you like. Please come in and see what we are doing. We will hang the picture of you and Jack near the window. You are both family now."

BEAUTY AND THE PROMPT

I never realized how much I depended on a writing prompt until I opened my assignment book and read, 'write anything'. Oh-oh - I was in trouble. I needed an idea. I just finished watching 'The Music Man' starring Robert Preston and the beautiful, talented Shirley Jones. I decided to read her biography on the computer. I found it ironic after all the wholesome parts she played she won her academy award for her role as a prostitute in Elmer Gantry. I also found it strange she would marry Marty Ingels. What was she thinking? She once said he made her laugh. I think Marty laughed all the way to the bank. But who am I to judge? After 30 years they are still together. I decided to write about Shirley Jones. Then I read it, said "so what" and tore it up. Still, there will never be anyone as beautiful as Shirley Jones.

I was waiting for inspiration when I heard Madeline's voice – "open a book, turn to page whatever and use the third complete sentence for a prompt." I reached for a book and read, "DE LITTLE RABBITS DEY RUN DOWN TO DE SPRING EN TRY TER DIP UP DE WATER."

I placed Uncle Remus by Joel Chandler Harris back on the shelf but not before smiling and smoothing out its cover. My copy of Uncle Remus is almost 100 yrs old. I love it but who has the patience to read it? Although I never tire of the illustrations.

"No prompt here" I said and reached for the next book. What the bible was doing next to Brer Rabbit was beyond me but maybe I could find a prompt. I turned to proverbs. I found a couple of beauts but sadly – no prompt.

As a last resort I called my friend Dorothy Close.

"Hi Dorth. I need a prompt. Time is running out. Can you think of something I can write about?"

She answered in her sing-song voice – the one she uses when she finds me anxious or frustrated.

Fairy Tale Villain

Living in the land of fairy tales is not easy when one is a wolf.

Let me tell you how I ended up in this courtroom today pleading innocent and begging for mercy.

My name is Big-Bad and I'm a fine looking wolf with pointed ears, beady eyes, wiry gray fur, a long nose and oh yes, sharp white teeth.

The trial begins with raising my right paw and swearing to tell the truth. The judge is a muskrat, my favorite meal and to make matters worse he knows it. My attorney is Foxy Loxy, not exactly a credit to his profession. He lost his last case. Tom, the piper's son was sent to prison for stealing a pig. Speaking of pigs, the juiy consists of three little ones. They sent my brother up the river for blowing on their houses. He was not carrying a weapon but they proved his huffing and puffing lethal. The pigs hired Chicken Licken to represent them. He's the Johnny Cochran of fairy tale land. It was Chicken Licken who convinced everyone the sky was falling. I'm doomed!

I'm finally allowed to tell my story. It began the day my long nose picked up the scent of comed-beef on rye. I was starving. The woodcutter was diminishing the forest, taking away my food supply. I saw the little hooded girl skipping along, carrying a basket of goodies. I knew she was headed to her grandmother's house located at the edge of the woods. I decided to run ahead and ask grandma to find kindness in her heart and share the food basket with a hungry, good- looking wolf. When she saw me, she jumped out of bed and ran out the door. I needed another plan. I hopped into bed and pulled the covers to my chin. Little Red Skipping Hood said, "Grandmother, what big eyes you have."

I harmlessly answered, "better to see you with my dear."

I had no intention of harming Little Red. I only wanted the comed-beef sandwich and maybe a pickle.

As our conversation went on, my hunger pains grew. It was then the woodsman broke down the door and came at me with an axe. Why wasn't he on trial for breaking and entering and terrorizing not to mention swinging an axe with intent to murder an innocent wolf.

The verdict was read by the first little pig. "Guilty, without a shadow of a doubt."

The muskrat judge gave a life sentence with no parole. Flashbulbs went off and the fairy tale courtroom oinked and cackled.

When a child is handed his first box of crayons more than likely he will reach for the red crayon. Some children will take the brown crayonand immediately put in their mouth hoping it will taste like chocolate. Not me, I chose the blue crayon and it remained my favorite color through the years.

Poets like to mention the color blue in their work, maybe because purple is impossible to rhyme. Songwriters also use the color blue more than any other in their song titles. Do you remember Elvis' "Blue Christmas" not to mention his "Blue Suede Shoes?" Fats Domino broke records with his "Blue Monday" and how can anyone forget "Sweet Little Alice Blue Gown?"

It's the Blue Ribbon that takes first prize and the Blue Plate Special that gives you more for your money.

I came across an art gallery in the Hudson Valley. In a room of its own hung an abstract painting in different shades of blue. I sat with the painting until the director tiptoed into the room. "Your admiration is overwhelming. The artist has titled the painting "Blue." I guess that does not come as a surprise." He said.

"I love the color blue more than I ever have." I answered thinking of my first blue crayon.

I wish I could say I purchased the painting and "Blue" hangs in my home but it does not and yet, in some way I feel it belongs to me.

I hope I feel blue all day!

Dililah's Diner

Joe came into the kitchen carrying the morning paper. "Good morning Dee. What smells so good,?"

"Blueberry pancakes and hot maple syrup."

"Wow. You haven't made those in years. Not since your brother took over Dililah's Diner. I'll never understand why Charlie took that diner away from you. He knew how much you loved it."

"Don't go there Joe. I told you I never wanted to talk about that again."

"Well, it just isn't fair Dee. You were the one who helped run the diner everyday after school-not your brother. Charlie knew your father always wanted you to have it. He even gave you the deed as a graduation gift. It was his most prized possession."

Dee's eyes welled with tears. "Yeah Joe, but when Dad died I couldn't find it-so Dad's estate along with the diner went to the oldest. My selfish brother never changed. As a kid Charlie never shared his toys with me so I didn't expect him to share the diner. Please Joe, let's change the subject. I hope you haven't forgotten you promised to help me box up books for the library's used book sale."

"How could I? You reminded me all week. Now how about some pancakes."

Joe opened the newspaper. "Well I'll be darned. Look at this Dee. Diliah's Diner is celebrating twenty-five years in business. Let's go have a look at the old place."

"I told you I would never step foot in that dinner again. I'm afraid of the memories and how about Charlie? What would I say to Charlie?"

"Well, we won't find out unless we go. Then you can put your fears to rest. Come on Dee, let's do it."

"Ok Joe, ok-but not before we pack the books. We can drop them on the way."

Sorting through the books Joe said, "I think we can part with your high school Latin books now don't you? And here's your old year book."

While passing the book to Dee a paper fell out.

"Oh my God Joe-it's the original deed to Diliah's."

The diner door squeaked as always, bringing back precious memories of a teenager and her dad working behind the counter. But today was different. Charlie looked up from the counter.

"Well, well, if it isn't my long lost sister. I haven't seen you in so long I've almost forgotten your name."

Slamming the deed against the cold Formica counter Dee shouted, "My name is Diliah. It's time to pack up your toys Charlie. Diliah's Diner is legally mine."

Superstition

Superstitious Aloysius, got out of bed, looked back and wondered if he got out on the right side. He knew today was Friday the thirteenth. He jumped back in bed and got out on the other side, just to play safe.

Pulling on his trousers, left leg first, he strung his lucky rabbit's foot through the belt loop giving it a pat. He checked his billfold to be sure his four-leaf clover was there before stuffing it into his pocket. He wished he could stay in bed all day but he had to get groceries if he wanted to eat dinner tonight.

His breakfast of fried eggs needed salt but he decided not to take the chance of spilling the shaker. He ate the eggs, not enjoying them without seasoning but it was better than having bad luck today.

Over his kitchen door hung a horseshoe, prongs facing up to keep the luck from falling out. He winked at it before he left to go to the store.

Walking down the sidewalk to the car, being extra careful not to step on any cracks, he saw a black cat heading his way. His throat tightened and he could hardly breathe from fright. He decided walking to the store would be better than taking a chance of the black cat crossing his path. He turned around and headed away from the car and the black cat.

Exhausted from the two- mile walk he approached the entrance of the store noticing a man on a ladder painting the door trim. "Just go under." The man said. "It's okay." But it wasn't okay for Aloysius. His superstitions left him no choice but to walk to the next store three more miles away.

Panting, he pulled on the handle of the door before he saw the note. "Closed due to death in family."

"This is an omen." He thought. "I'd better get home as fast as my aching legs will carry me."

Breathless and in pain, he pushed hard against the kitchen door jarring the frame. The horseshoe fell, hitting him just above his forehead swelling to the size of a grapefruit.

Crumpled, beaten, accomplishing nothing, he crawled into bed hungry but wondered if he had gotten in on the right side!

Wouldn't it be strange if...

Wouldn't it be strange if we had no thumbs? The short thick digit of the hand that separates us from the animal kingdom is taken for granted. How would we cope without our thumbs?

I'm not in the habit of picking up hitchers. Not only is it illegal but too scary these days. It would be scarier to see a hitchhiker sticking out any other finger in lack of a thumb.

What would Little Jack Homer use to pull out his plum? How about ancient Roman times at the coliseum where the thumb is of the utmost importance? Waiting for the thumbs up sign or the dreaded thumbs down could change history.

How could a gardener have a green thumb, if he didn't have a thumb at all?

What would P.T. Barnum have named his famous midget? General Thom Index Finger, just doesn't sound right.

Looking on the brighter side, children would not be able to suck their thumb, but I feel they would find a replacement to distort their teeth.

Worst of all, how could writers write? They would not be able to hold a pen. Not being able to use the space bar, all typed work would run together.

Something tells me, thumbs or not, the writer will always find a way!

IS IT DRU?

In my garden, nestled among Lilies of the Valley, a Jack-in-the- Pulpit thrives. His short visit brings to mind the Druid I came upon while walking in the woods.

I was astonished when I first saw him and ducked behind a large oak tree. He was dancing around a ring of neatly placed stones. Had I discovered the barefooted Rumplestiltskin or merely a hippie alienated from society?

He romped in a knee-length tunic and hooded cloak while tucking plant clippings into a burlap bag that hung from his belt.

He chanted, looking toward the oak. "Shadows warn me you are here."

Frightened, I found enough voice to whimper, "I'm sorry to disturb you sir. I live in the neighborhood and often follow this path through the woods."

I gathered up enough courage, placed my hand on my hip and said, "Wait a minute. Who are you? Where are you from and what are you doing here?"

The chest of his tunic rose as his pride answered, "I am of the Celtic people. I date back to the second century B.C. I am from an intellectual class comprised of philosophers, judges, educators, historians, doctors, astronomers and astrologers. I am a Druid. Who are you and what do you do?"

"Me? Oh, I just take walks and hide behind trees, I guess. How shall I address you, sir? May I call you Dru?"

Dru shrugged, pointed to the tree and said, "The oak is sacred. The Roman writer, Pliny the Elder believed the word Druid came from 'dru' meaning oak and 'wid' meaning 'to know' or 'see'. I know and see all. I live close to nature to survive. By firelight I play the harp and dream magic for my people. My spirit is emerged from the light of the sun, the wind in the oak and the cry of the deer. I live in an inspired and uplifted world. I am the religious intelligentsia of my culture. Mythologies describe me as having magical powers able to heal, control weather, levitate and change my form into plant or animal. Some call me a priest but I am reluctant because I do not minister a congregation. What else do you do besides hide behind trees?"

"I am a writer." I said.

Dru looked skyward. "My Celtic spirit is written about by William Yeats and James Joyce, among others. Maybe you will write about me," he said, lowering his eyes.

"I would like to, but no one would believe of our meeting. On second thought Dru, I do know of some who may. I promise you, I will tell them."

Dru untied his bag, offered the contents and vanished. I carried the wilted Jack-in-the Pulpit home and planted it among the lilies.

Every summer I greet the little pod arising in the hooded cloak and I know- it is Dru.

Do We August?

I heard quarreling voices coming from the kitchen. Had I left the radio on or was my imagination working over time?

I looked around, no longer hearing the commotion. Everything seemed to be in order, except the calendar pages were rumpled. Smoothing out the top page I realized it was close to the end of July.

Through the years anxiety always kept me ahead of myself and today was no different. I drew an X through July and turned the page. To my surprise September appeared.

"What happened to August?" I said aloud,

A little voice answered, "I'm down here. Please help me."

I slid a yardstick in the narrow space between the refrigerator and a cabinet. I dragged August out along with some fuzzy dust. "Get up," I ordered, "we have 31 days to get through. How did you fall on the floor?"

"I didn't fall." His hot temper yelled. He pointed to the remaining eleven and said, "I was pushed. They threw me out just because I do not have a holiday. At least I have thirty-one days which is more than I can say for some." He looked at February's chilling twenty-eight.

February frosted and started to speak but January cut in. "Excuse me. I believe I am first. He's got to go. Leave him on the floor. He's good for nothing and I'm sure my Martin Luther King would agree."

March butted in. "Top o' the mornin' to ya. I agree with the others. No parades, no need for him."

So it went, as the feminine voices of April, May and June were heard, all showing off their holidays. Then July took the stand. "I feel I'm being stalked. He's always following me. Get rid of him."

Poor August began to weep as I defended. "You can't have an eleven month year. People will get older much faster. They won't like that."

The ghoulish voice of October announced, "We received an application from a younger month. He is willing to be placed at the end of the year. His name is Remember."

I groaned, "Oh great, November, December and Remember."

"Sounds good to me," November said. "We'll have an election and vote him in."

August pleaded, looking back at February. "Use your presidential powers and convince them to let me stay. Your fourteenth tells me you have a heart."

It was at that moment I remembered, on August 7th 1782 the Purple Heart medal was established. What greater honor could a month carry? A day set aside for heroes.

I rifled through my junk-drawer and found a broken purple crayon. I drew a large purple heart on the seventh, taped August back on the calendar and watched his page expand with pride.

This August, let us remember our men and women in uniform fighting the war on terrorism. They are our true heroes.

GOING DOWN?

After visiting a patient on the tenth floor of Saint Vincent's hospital, I felt uneasy entering the elevator. Descending turns my butterflies into ferocious bats.

I stepped to the rear, allowing room for a priest and a young intern dressed in green scrubs.

My anxious heart thumped as I watched the floor indicator move to nine – then eight. I silently talked to myself, "Stay calm. Soon we'll be on the ground floor."

Between the sixth and seventh floor, a loud snap and a grinding screech jolted the elevator. When the car stopped the lights went out. It was quiet until I screamed- "Son of a bitch!"

When a dim auxiliary light blinked on I apologized, "Sorry, Father."

"Oh, was that you? he answered. I thought it was me."

The intern laughed. "Don't worry – this happens a lot here. These elevators are almost as old as Elisha Otis. Good thing he was clever enough to invent an elevator that would immediately stop if a cable snapped."

He pushed the emergency button and activated the alarm. "A couple of guys from the firehouse will come and get us out of here."

The priest opened his prayer book. "Dear Lord, please have mercy on Mrs. O'Reilly's soul. I think I'll be too late to administer the last rights."

I lowered my head. "Keep that page open, Father. I'm going to need it."

About an hour and a half later, I was thanking a firefighter and his crowbar as he escorted me to the next elevator.

The intern was on his assigned floor and I tearfully said good-bye and wished him luck with his medical career.

Not wanting to get in the elevator first, I said, "After you, Father."

I pushed the ground floor button and counted down – "five- four – Snap- Grind- Screech."

"Son of a bitch!"

The Scarlet Neighbor

Squinting through the slats of the blinds I watched the new neighbor move in. I noticed she was very pregnant and struggling with some old wooden, straight-back chairs. I wondered why her child's father was not there to help her. She looked so familiar, but I couldn't place her and hoped she would be friendly. It would be nice to have someone to talk with about gardening, while sharing neighborhood news.

I noticed a monogram on her gray dress and was curious about the initial "A". I love the name Ann. Of course, her name could be Alice or Alexandria, but I hoped it was Ann.

The next morning I was surprised by a knock and wondered if the doorbell was out of order.

"Hello," I greeted the "A" on my porch holding a wooden bucket. "Is my doorbell not working?"

"What dost thou mean?" she asked.

"How charming," I thought. "I can't wait to ask what country she is from."

Oddly I still sensed that we had met before.

She lowered her eyes asking, "Wouldst thou be so kind as to give me some water? I can not find the well."

"We don't have wells in this neighborhood. Come into the kitchen and take as much as you need," I obliged.

She stared at the sink and seemed confused.

"Push the chrome lever and the water will come out. Are you from another country or another planet?" I joked.

The "A" did not laugh.

"I better be gentler," I thought and pointed to the initial. "Did you embroider that yourself?" It certainly is a fine piece of work." I complimented. "What is your name?"

"Hester," she said. "Surely thou hast heard of me."

"Oh my goodness, you're Hester Prynne! Well, so much for Ann. I knew, I knew you from somewhere. I have not thought of you since freshman high school. I remember how the Puritans of colonial Boston forced you to wear a red A on your bosom as punishment for your sin. Hester, after all these years, is it really you?"

She placed her hand on the A and said, "I will bear the illegitimate child and if it is a girl I will name her Pearl as she will be my only treasure."

"Just keep her out of my flower bed." I warned. "And what do you mean if it is a girl? Haven't you had an ultra sound? Don't you know the sex of the child? And speaking of sex, why did you never tell who the father is? The Reverend Dimmesdale needs to pay child support and take care of your needs. We have enough mothers on welfare." I raised my voice a little more than intended. Once again, after all this time I felt sorry for poor Hester Prynne.

"Sit down. I'll make some tea and you can tell me all about it now that we are neighbors."

She began, "I refuseth to speak because the Reverend Dimmeadale takes it very grievously to heart that such scandal should come upon his congregation. I must protect his good name. People look to him as a saint. Please, you must not tell what thou knows. If thou promises, I will teach thou to embroider fancy letters. We can start with the letter "A".

"I have known you for many years Hester and I know how well you can keep a secret. I think that is important in case I have some juicy neighborhood gossip."

I watched her wonderment as she pulled the tea bag up and down.

"It is making thy and thou tea," she giggled.

"Yes it is Hester and thy hast much, much, more to show thee."

The Life of a Mosquito

Hi, It's nice to meet you. We're the Mosquito's. I'm Rita. This is my husband Roy.

We need to talk fast because we don't live too long. No time for idle chit-chat, you know. Roy will live about a week and I about a month.

We have a large family tree. There are 2,500 species of mosquitoes-150 live in the United States. We are born in water. Roy was born in a crotch of a lovely maple tree. I floated through my early stages in sewerage. But Roy always treated me kindly.

Our life cycle begins as eggs turning into larva, then pupa and finally adulthood. This takes about ten days.

Our feeding habits are unique. Roy feeds on flower nectar. He's so sweet. I, the female feed on animal and human blood. I need the blood to reproduce. So you see, I only need Roy for a short time.

Tomorrow I will say good-bye to Roy as I stay on to hatch our eggs. I hope you have neglected to clean your drain spouts or have left stagnant water nearby.

Well, I gotta go get a bite. I'm sure I'll see you soon.

~~~

If I Were A Super Hero

The hardest thing about being a super hero is pulling on the tights. My shirt is spangled with the letter 'C' and my white cape is trimmed with sequins.

Tonight snow is falling in the city of Milford. Snow plow drivers look toward the sky. A streak of glitter catches a driver's eye. "Is it a bird? Is it a plane?"

Another driver answers, "No it's Crusader Carol."

They begin singing, "Here she comes to save the day. Crusader Carol is on her way."

The mayor has asked all citizens to remove vehicles from streets but chooses not to enforce the law. Snow plow drivers must maneuver around them leaving streets a mess.

Crusader Carol stays ahead of the plows, lifting automobiles until the plows clear to the curb. She wonders why people are so inconsiderate. Are they uncaring or just plain lazy? Or do they leave the vehicles just because they can? Warnings should be issued.

Crusader Carol continues to help the hard working snow plow drivers. She returns home after a job well done. Now to remove the damn tights.

~~~

The Most Beautiful Thing In Nature

Have you stopped to smell the roses lately? Look around-beauty is everywhere. Nature seems to know what it is doing, although some will disagree.

The planet Earth is about 12 billion years old-I rest my case.

At times we have a problem reasoning with nature. Nature holds seniority-it was here before man. Violent storms, tornadoes and earth quakes are frightening, it is natures way of turning over the soil.

Until we can figure out how to change the seasons, we must trust nature. I do. Isn't nature beautiful?

Beverly's Birthday Bash

Beverly's thoughts began racing before her eyes flew open. She was sure he would come today. He had to come. It was her birthday and she planned to make it very special.

She mailed herself several birthday cards tucked into pastel envelopes. She was careful to address them with different color inks and wrote some with her left hand. Now she was sure he would come.

Mr. Sidney will arrive at one o'clock, give or take a few minutes. He will park the white truck on the hill and walk down the steep embankment to the front door where she will be waiting in her frilly party dress.

"Lot's of mail for you today ma'am," he will smile. That is when she will invite him in for pink lemonade and birthday cake she made herself. He will probably refuse at first, saying he has a schedule to keep but she will coax him with, "Please Mr. Sidney, it's my birthday."

She thought of birthdays past, the cottage full of music, laughter, good friends, Mother and Daddy. All were gone now. Her only friend was Theda and she seemed to be missing the last few days.

A noise at the back door startled her. "It couldn't be Mr. Sidney this early," she said aloud. "He would come to the front door as usual."

She opened the squeaking screen door. It was Theda! "Where have you been? I suppose down at the lake with that Tom. Look at your beautiful coat, full of briar, thicket and thorn."

Theda's amber eyes widened to Beverly's shouting voice. The orange cat weaved her body around Beverly's ankles and all was forgiven. "Theda the Vamp – that's you", she laughed and bent to pet her friend. She was happy to know Theda will be at her party.

Beverly went back to planning the festivities. She placed Mother's heavy silver candlestick in the center of the table. She had polished it until it shone blue. "It will be like having Mother here."

She looked toward Father's caned chair where she had placed a coil of hemp. It was the same rope Father used to tie the row boat each night to the pier. "Father will be at my party," she giggled. "Now let's see, Mother, Father, Theda and of course, Mr. Sidney. What a wonderful birthday this will be."

She checked the arrangements one more time. "Oh, the poetry book. I almost forgot the poetry book," she said placing it on the table.

The clock chimed once as Mr. Sidney approached the front door. "Lot's of mail for you today, ma'am," he smiled. Beverly smiled back batting her black mascara lashes.

"Come in, Mr. Sidney and join me in a cold glass of lemonade and a piece of birthday cake.

"I would love to ma'am but I have a mail route to complete. I can't' be late getting the truck back to the terminal."

Beverly's voice rose, "I won't take no for an answer today. It's my birthday." She sweetened as she tried again. "Come meet Theda and let me tell you about Mother and Daddy."

"Sorry ma'am, I have to go. Here's your mail."

Her voice now trembled, "Step in and place it on the table."

The pastel colored envelopes flew into the air as Beverly bashed Mr. Sidney on the head with Mother's silver candlestick. She then tied him with Father's rope as Theda arched her back and hissed.

She reached for the poetry book, recited to Mr. Sidney and reminded him, "It's my birthday."

DIALOGUE TWO CHARACTERS

Books are like old friends to me. They are very hard to part with and some I have kept since I was a teenager. I know I'll never read them again but it gives me comfort to know they are there.

One day I heard a conversation between two of my favorite novels and I couldn't help eavesdropping.

"Mrs. Hanson, Mrs. Hanson, are you home?"

"I can hear you Mrs. Nolan. Where else would a fine Norwegian mother of four be? Lars will be home soon and I'm getting dinner ready. How are things in Brooklyn?"

"Not as wonderful as your life in San Francisco I'm afraid. I'm having a problem with Francie. She just stares out the window at a tree and is dreaming her life away while I scrub floors trying to make ends meet. She needs to understand what life really is like. My husband Johnny, puts such foolish dreams in her head. She adores him and stiffens to me."

"Your alcholic husband is no help. Singing in Irish taverns is no way to put money in the bank. Children need to feel secure. Lie to them. Tell them you have a bank account like I do. Teach them that they must never use this money so it will always be there for security. By the way, Mrs. Nolan, why did you name your son that ridiculous name? I never heard the name, Nealy."

"Do you think Dagmar, Katrin and Nels are such great names? I can't even remember your other daughter's name. She is so insignificant to the story."

"Her name is Christina and she's named after my Uncle Chris who taught me to lie to my children if it would make them feel secure. Don't tell me you have an Uncle Nealy!"

"What is your first name Mrs. Hanson?"

"I really can't remember Mrs. Nolan, because I've been called

"Mama" for so long. I won't easily forget that name. I can remember Mama. Now back to your problem. I think your author should kill off your husband so you can marry that nice cop on the beat. Then you can have a baby and name her Annie Laurie. That was Johnnys favorite song. I know this because I'm placed so close to your novel on the shelf I couldn't help but hear him staggering in after hours, singing "Annie Laurie." Yes, Francie will miss him but you will be able to move out of that cold water flat with your children and new husband. I was sorry to hear they are taking Francie's tree down. Another one will grow in it's place and so will the bank account. I have to go now Mrs. Nolan. I can hear Lars coming and I need to get his sweater and pipe. Thanks for sharing the bookshelf with me. Maybe your author will write a sequel, "Another Tree Grows in Brooklyn."

"Goodbye Mama, I'll always remember you."

What Happens To A Dream
Deferred ... Raisin In The Sun

Does a dream ever completely dry up? It may be suppressed. You may face the reality of the dream never to come true.

You remember why this dream was unfulfilled. You say, "if only" or "why didn't I" or "it just wasn't meant to be."

A dream is like a living plant. If not given water it will dry up. Water, in this case being encouragement, support and drive. Sprinkle a little luck with the right timing and a dream will come true.

If life has taken you down another path and you find it impossible for your dream to come true, you will visit the dream from time to time in your mind. These visits will be the rain fall to unshrivel the raisin in the sun.

The Fall Of A Sparrow - W. Shakespeare

Well Mr. Shakespeare, we meet again. What did you mean when you said, "There is a special providence in the fall of a sparrow?"

One day while out walking, I saw a dead sparrow on the sidewalk. Had it been a cat or was it just his time to leave God's earth. What had he accomplished in his short lived life?

The next day I hung four bird houses in his memory from the tree branches. I watched as a male sparrow checked out the real estate. I and a few days all of his relatives joined him. The happy chirping made the trees seem much fuller now. The chirping had turn to shrieking, the morning the crow invaded the bird houses. I ran out with the broom chasing him away. I picked up lint, straw, string and even cellophane from the ground and stuffed it back into the nest hoping I was not too late. Two baby sparrows with their mouths wide open were happy to see me. Something about them reminded me of Al Jolson!

Mother bird flew in the house, checking her kids and then poked her head out to look at me. "Your welcome" I said "Just keep the mosquito population down for me O.K?"

Now I wonder, is there a special providence in the fall of a mosquito?

Wouldn't It Be Strange If...

Isaac Newton was sitting under the apple tree and he noticed the apple fell up? If gravity pulled up, the tides would certainly be affected and a day at the beach would probably be a night at the beach.

Snow shovel sales would decrease because the snow would be falling up and the autumn leaves wouldn't have to be raked. It sounds great to me! Just think how happy barbers would be when they realized they didn't have to sweep their shops. We would never have to bend down to pick anything up. No one would ever need a face lift and all other body parts would be facing up too. After you have read this story and throw up, you really will!

Walk With Note Pad - Write Down Things With Letter "C"

Almost everyday I take a walk through the neighborhood. I've seen the same houses hundreds of times but today was different. I brought a note pad with me and wrote down everything I saw beginning with the letter "C". I'm sure the neighbors thought I was crazy, while I looked at their homes and made notes. I also believe I was talking to myself saying, "Chimney, That's a good one!" A CAT was sitting on a porch waiting to be let in. I also saw my neighbors go by. Carol waved and her son Chris tooted the horn. Their last name is Corbett and I noticed the license plate reads "CORBS". I saw a Christmas tree cut in half and placed at the curb for pick up. Around the corner I saw the huge Cedar with the double trunk and wondered how old it is. I was hoping to see the cardinal that lives in the tree as I have in the past. I saw someone peeking from behind their curtains wondering what I was up to. What are the chances I would see a camel? I did see a cigarette but in the gutter. It could have been a Camel!

When I got home I started to wonder where the next assignment will lead me and what other crazy things I'm expected to do!

MAKE A LIST - IF YOU WON THE LOTTERY

1.- SMELLING SALTS

2.- SMELLING SALTS

3.- MORE SMELLING SALTS

I can't imagine winning the lottery. I have never bought a lottery ticket. Do I like to gamble? Yes, I do but I like the odds to be in my favor. Two million to one are not good odds!

Ella Grasso introduced gambling to "the nutmeg state." Besides the lottery, daily numbers and rub off tickets are sold. There are off-track betting parlors in almost every town and the Jai-Alai Fronton is in Milford. At the Jai-Alai you can also bet on horse racing and the dogs. I think it will only be a matter of time before Bridgeport opens a casino.

Has gambling helped the state? Where is the money going? When you see the lines at the pari-mutual windows, our street should be paved with gold.

Are the elderly using their Social Security to gamble? Are welfare checks being cashed and used for gambling? Of course!

I like to gamble but I will not part with that dollar to buy a lottery ticket so I guess I'll never be a millionaire but look at all the money I'm saving on smelling salts!

Watch A Movie-Rewrite Ending.

Last night I watched "Twelve Angry Men," for the tenth time. It was an excellent story with incredible acting. Henry Fonda tries to convince the other eleven jurors, a shadow of a doubt may save a young boys life. Maybe he did commit the murder, but what if he didn't? That is the dilemma they are faced with while locked in the juror's room on a hot summer day. What better way to get to know each other? An old man is the first to side with Henry Fonda. The count stands 10-2. Eventually they all agree that there very well maybe, a shadow of a doubt.

The last scence shows them leaving the courthouse. The old man walks up to Henry Fonda, introduces himself and they look at each other with respect. Then they walk away in separate directions. Awesome!

I would have ended it a little differently. The old man would walk up to Henry Fonda and say, "He did it, didn't he?" Fonda would look into the old man's eyes and say, "I'm afraid so." Very Awesome!!

"I WOULD HAVE WRITTEN ON MY STONE: I had a Lover's Quarrel with the World." Robert Frost

Well Bob, since your writing on your stone, I guess it's too late for you to send candy and flowers. Too bad you didn't apologize sooner or did you not want to?

In order to have a lover's quarrel with the world, you must have been in love with the world at some point in time. What caused your dispute? Did you get bored with your faithful world? Did you grow apart from it or did it disappoint you in some way? Maybe you felt YOU were the one who had disappointed the world and that started the spat. Were you quarreling with yourself?

To quarrel with the world, would be a losing battle. Every stone proves this to be true!

Ann Landers has such an easy job. It seems to me her readers do all the work. One reader writes to her about something ridiculous and another reader will send in a ridiculous solution! She must be doing something right. She has been writing her column for eons and she doesn't age. Her picture stays the same. Her hairdo stays the same, her earrings stay the same and her perfect smile never changes.

In today's column, a man writes in about a rooster. Is this real, everyday life? Well, in my life it is. My next door neighbor raises chickens. They are a special breed. They make a soft clucking sound that is almost comforting. They are big, white and fluffy. When they walk they remind me of muppets. Well, where there are chickens there is always a rooster. He's a good looking fowl but very fresk. He does his job well, taking care of "the girls" as he guards the hen house. He always looks like he's expecting a visit from the Colonel. His most important duty is to wake the neighborhood at the crack of dawn. I certainly have outsmarted him, as I get up before the sun and turn the tables on him. When I turn on the bed room light at 4 A.M. he starts to "COCK-A-DOODEE DOO." Actually, I like the sound as it makes me feel I'm out in the country. He cockles and doodles a few times before he settles down and goes about his chicken business. Tomorrow will be the same, as he starts his newsreel, as though in a movie theater.

I would never write Ann Landers about this wonderful rooster but I am getting the urge to get out the Shake and Bake. That should cockle his doodle!

SENTIMENTAL ME

Through the years I have saved worthless items for sentimental reasons.

A handkerchief I carried on my first day of kindergarten is folded in a drawer. A hairpin my grandmother clipped in my hair as we danced the Tarrantella to the sound of the Victrola. A diaper pin with a little yellow duck brings tears but I will always keep it.

Cards and love notes from my husband are tucked away. I read them now and then.

Recently I discovered how sentimentally attached I've become to my old car. We have been together for twenty-two years. She is periwinkle in color but I call her Blue.

I've never had a problem with Blue until one day she began to shimmy and shake. Somehow she got me home to the safety of the garage. I cried watching her towed away to a repair shop.

The next day the mechanic called saying, "I can make this car like new for a thousand dollars."

I now had a decision to make. Should I buy a new car or fix old Blue?"

I was not ready to part with my old friend just because she developed a bit of palsy.

Needless to say, Blue and I are still together thanks to sentimental me.

ROLLING ON THE RIVER

I was recently hired by 'Rolling on the River Magazine' to write an advice column for fishermen.

My name is Tina Tima – not to be confused with Tina Turner, although she did roll on the river – boy did she ever!

The first fisherman writes in-

Bear Tina Tuna,

What type of pole is best used for fresh water fishing?

Signed,
Bobby Bass

Dear Bob,

A clear fiber glass fishing rod is best because it leaves no shadow on the water to warn the fish. But don't underestimate die fish. They are smart – after all they do travel in schools.

The only other letter I received, was also from Bobby Bass.

Dear Tina Tuna,

What are morays and are they hard to catch?

Dear Bob,

It is nice to hear from you again. You seem to be the only angler I have reeled in. To answer your question, yes, eels also known as morays are difficult to catch. You must attach several lead sinkers to your line, cast out far and go deep.

These creatures hang out at the darkest and deepest pari of the lake. When the moray takes the bait you will feel a sharp tug. At this point slowly reel in until you see a long snake-like fish wriggling like – Tina Turner at the end of your line.

And as Dean Martin said, "That's a moray!"

HAPPILY EVER AFTER

Returning from their honeymoon, Mark carried Sally over the threshold of their small apartment.

"Well Sal, this is home for now, but my wish is to someday buy you a beautiful home with a large yard for children where we will live happily ever after.

Sally looked lovingly at her husband. "That is my wish too, but in the meantime we still have wedding gifts to open."

On a small table three gifts were waiting to be unwrapped. The first was from Aunt Ida.

"Oh, what a lovely tea pot," Sally said, "but since we don't drink tea I'll have to find somewhere to store it."

Surprisingly, the second gift was also a tea pot. Together Mark and Sally laughed.

The last gift was from Uncle Billy along with an apology. He was sorry he could not attend the wedding because he was traveling the world. While in Baghdad, he thought of us when he saw this unique gift.

"Oh, no." Sally frowned, "another tea pot."

"I don't think it's a tea pot at all," Mark said. "It looks more like Aladdin's lamp to me." Mark jokingly rubbed the lamp. A smoky-blue mist escaped from the spout and took the form of a genie wearing a turban.

Frightened, Sally held on to Mark.

Folding his arms across his chest, the genie spoke. "What's the matter? Were you expecting Barbara Eden? I am here to grant you one wish and make it snappy. I was in the middle of a poker game when you summoned me."

Mark carried Sally over the threshold of their new home complete with a large yard where they would live happily ever after.

GOOD LUCK JIM

This morning I was shocked to find a man standing in my kitchen.

"Who are you?" I asked.

Tire incredibly handsome man answered, "Bond - James Bond."

Although frightened, I was impressed with his suave manner and wanted to know more about him.

I lowered my eyes and blushed. "Shall I call you Jim?"

His charming English accent answered, "Never Madam – I am James Bond also known as 007. Surely you have heard of fen Fleming's British spy."

"I have, but I don't know much about you. I do know how much you Englishmen enjoy tea. Let me fix you a cup."

When I opened the cupboard The magnificent voice of Shirley Bassie began singing, "Gold Finger' - the man with the rnidas touch..."

"Forget the tea dear' lady- just shut Shirley up and fix me a martini and please shake don't stir."

Since my body was already shaking from head to foot I found this an easy task.

My courage asked, "What brings you here?"

"I am here because your writing instructor has used me for an assignment. I need to know who she is. I believe she is trying to expose me. Tell me her name."

I snapped, "I'll never tell you. I consider her a friend and I am loyal and devoted to my friends. Please finish your drink and leave. I will never, ever tell."

It was then he drew his gun and aimed it at me. So much for loyalty - "Her name is Anne- Marie. Devotion also caved- Sutton, Anne-Marie Sutton."

Bond raised one eyebrow. "Where can I find her?"

I sassed, "That's for you to find out."

When he tightened his trigger finger I spilled my guts. "She's in the oval room at the senior center handing out assignments. She strained my brain with this one and she deserves what she gets. Good luck Jim."

THE LOOK

Remember "The Look"? Of course you do - it's the one your mother gave when you misbehaved in public. One eyebrow raised slightly as a glazed glare scolded unspoken words.

Mother had power. She was Wonder Woman without the jeweled tiara or the magical rope of truth.

With one look, my hands folded immediately and a halo surrounded my saintly head.

As a super senior I have inherited the look.

Nearly knocking me over, a young man with a bunch of keys dangling from his belt pushed ahead of me in the grocery store. I teetered like a bowling pin.

When he looked back to see if had scored a strike I used my super power.

The look made him quiver until his keys jangled. He sheepishly apologized and walked me to my car where he unloaded my grocery cart.

It's great to be Super Senior and have the power of the look.

The Inheritance

The phone rang and a man claiming to be a lawyer introduced himself as Ernest...something or other.

Thinking it was a crank call I answered, "Yeah sure-I get it, you're Ernie the attorney."

"Please listen," he continued. "Your Great Aunt Emily has left you a key. I have no idea what it is for but you may pick it up at my office."

I was about four years old the last time Mother took me to visit my great aunt. She gave me ginger cookies and warm milk.

To keep me occupied she handed me an ornate lacquered box trimmed with opal inlay.

She said she had two keys but misplaced both and could no longer open the box.

"You can keep it dear, and if I ever find the key I will send it to you. Then the contents will be yours."

I shook the box. There was definitely something inside. I didn't know what the word contents meant but hoped it was a diamond ring or a ruby brooch.

Through the years I was tempted to pry open the box but decided I might ruin the beautiful finish.

I tucked the box away and hoped someday Great Aunt Emily would send a key. Leaving Ernie's office I could hardly wait to get home and try my inheritance. Sure enough- the key fit the lock and one quick turn to the right opened the box.

In the box was the other key.

Call Me Irresponsible

Never a responsible person, Harry once again lost his job due to constant tardyness.

This meant Monday morning he would be in the unemployment line where he would be granted a small check. Most would go toward alimony.

The only thing Harry did well was fail. Not only did he do it well - he did it often.

This morning while reading the newspaper he turned to the horse racing page and laughed when he saw the name 'Call Me Irresponsible' entered in the fifth at Aqueduct.

He decided to go to the track and placed the last of his money across the board on Call Me Irresponsible.

The odds on the nag were so long, all the other horses would have to fall down.

Of course, Call Me Irresponsible did not win – in fact, he may still be running.

As Harry tore up his para-mutual ticket he noticed a help wanted sign on a concession stand where he was hired with the promise to be on time the next morning.

And of course, like Call Me Irresponsible, Harry did not show.

I Hope Its Goulash

"Please remain seated and you can loosen your grip on your pocketbook. I am Madam Zambolvia. I have been called a gypsy, but I am not a thief. I run a legitimate business. When the candle behind me bums out, your session is over. At that point you may leave forty-two dollars and fifty cents on the table."

"It's nice to meet you Madam, but you don't understand. I am not here for a reading. I ran over some nails in front of your establishment and all four tires on my car are flat. I don't have a cell phone and I need to call a tow truck. I was fioping I could use your phone."

The disturbed psychic snapped, "I can not earn a living letting strangers use my phone. Allow me to read your fortune and then you may call for help."

I seemed to have no choice. She looked deeply into the crystal ball and said, "I see a tall, handsome man in uniform coming into your life very soon?'

Although I did not believe in fortune tellers, it sounded pretty good to me and I laid out forty-two dollars and fifty cents next to the crystal ball.

As Madam Zambolvia scooped up the cash, a tall good looking police officer entered and looked directly at me.

"Oh my – she was right." I was beginning to believe.

The handsome cop raised one eyebrow like Clark Gable in Gone With The Wind. "Is that your vehicle outside with the flat tires? You can't leave it there. It must be moved at once."

"I'm sorry officer. I ran over some nails. I have no phone. Can you help me?"

"Yes, ma'am. I have already called a tow truck. You can wait outside for the driver."

I said good bye to Madam Zambolvia and scooted out the door still wondering about the nails. Through the thin panned window I saw the fortune teller hug the cop. I also could hear their conversation.

"Thank you son – the nails were a good idea. Business is booming and your brother is also doing well with his tow truck."

"Any time Ma. I'll see you for supper. I hope it's goulash."

MY BEST FIEND

I wish I hadn't been in such a hurry when the teacher gave her students their assignment to be handed in at the next gathering of their "Writer's Unlimited" class. I was having great difficulty tryong to read my own handwriting as I looked at the scribble in my assignment book. It read, "Write a paper and title it- My Best Fiend!" it only made sense to me when I realized that Halloween was only weeks away. But still, how can one have a best fiend? Does this mean Bela Lugosi is better than Boris Karloff or Lon Chaney is superior to Vincent Price? Peter Lorre was an excellent fiend compared to Michael Landon. Michael was just too cute to be a teenage werewolf. He looked more like a Disney puppy.

Once again I wondered how anyone could have a best fiend. This would mean I would have to know and also, be very fond of an evil, inhumanly, wicked person.

Dr. Jeckle's wife had Mr. Hyde for a best fiend. I'm just not that lucky to have a best fiend! Or am I? Maybe I'm my own best fiend because I am so addicted to cigarettes.

I looked at my assignment book again. There was a second part to the assignment. The teacher will try to match the paper to the student. I am sure she will know because she is very familiar with each writers work. She will never guess mine though! I am not a face in the classroom. Only my fiendish spirit is there sitting next to my best friend.

Oh, Best Friend!!

THE BLUE MASK

I read about it in the paper, on the bus, on my way to work.

The blue dust has been falling forty days now. Frightened nations share scientists giving the dust an official name, Blue Masceradicator now commonly known as "blue mask." The male population has been eradicated. There are no bodies. Disintegrated traces of bone are swept along with blue mask into the storm drains.

This morning the bus driver squarely hit a pothole jarring the passengers. "Aren't they ever going to fix these damn holes?" she swears while checking her manicure. I begin to wonder if this tiny woman has control of this huge public vehicle as my newspaper scatters across the leather seat into the aisle. A fellow passenger leans to pick it up. Strange I should think of her as a "fellow" passenger. Thanking her I say, "Why are we so concerned about a pot hole? Doesn't anyone care that blue dust is falling from the sky and any breathing male is instantly eradicated?" The woman turns away and stares out the window at the buildings covered with blue mask.

Five more blocks to watch women carry dusty blue umbrellas held over their small daughters heads as they window shop. I notice two muscular women on scaffolding removing a sign that reads, "Thompson & Sons." "One of them should be driving this bus," I think aloud as the dainty driver jerks and jams the brakes hitting another pothole. Two others are hoisting the pretty pink and gold replacement sign. It reads, "Lillian & Daughters."

My high-rise office comes into view as I gather my belongings and teeter up the aisle. The door opens with a loud "swoosh" as I step onto the blue dust covered concrete sidewalk. I lift my sleeve slightly to check my watch. Blowing the blue dust away, I see I have time to run into Frieda's Flower Shop and buy fresh cut peonies. Frieda is very busy this morning but is happy to see me. "Business is better than even- Women are buying fresh flowers every day," she says, as Susie her little toy poodle runs to greet me. I squat, giving me eye contact with Susie. "Do you miss your little buddy, Sammy?" I ask her expecting to see puddles in her eyes. Instead, she scampers away grateful to have the whole place to herself.

Entering the office building I see the maintenance woman removing the sign from the men's room door. "What will we use that room for now?" I ask her over the jangle of tools hanging from her belt. She raises one eyebrow answering, "Two ladies rooms will be wonderful." Ashamed I bow head and agree.

At my desk I fuss with the flowers and toss my newspaper into the wastebasket. With no male bees to pollinate, soon there will be no flowers. A soprano voice pages from the adjoining office. "Come in here," I poke my head in. Mr. Crowley's seat is filled with Mrs. Crowley. The room has been redecorated and the new T. V. set is on. Mrs. Crowley points at the screen. "Look, they're showing the blue cliffs of Dover from England. You missed France. They have changed the name of Mont Blanc to Mont Bleu." She clicks the set off and begins giving orders. "Open the drapes and let's get down to today's business."

Slowly, I open the drapes hoping to see a clear sky. Blue mask is still falling. "What's that large building under construction a few blocks away?" I ask Mrs. Crowley.

"That's the new cloning building I'm thinking of buying into. It wouldn't be a bad idea for you to invest. Women need to plan ahead and that cloning building would be just the place to start." She advises.

"Cloning building?" I shudder and think of the bees. Of course, there will always be flowers. I look back at the building as my eyes widen to the sight of a violet color hue. "Look, Mrs. Crowley! The color is changing. After forty days of blue dust, its turning pink, bright pink."

I watch the pink femmeradicator fall for forty days.

There is a Tide ..... Wm. Shakespeare

It sounds like Will was at the beach, the day he said, "There is a tide in the affairs of men." He never explained if he meant high tide or low tide. He goes on, "which taken at the flood." I guess that means high tide! He finishes, "leads on to fortune."

I think fortune would be easier to find at low tide. I notice people with metal detectors hoping to find their fortune at low tide. Maybe high tide would wash a fortune in. A note in a bottle could lead to a fortune if it were signed by William Shakespeare. The note could read, "Oh Carol, oh Carol, wherefore art thou Carol?"

"I'm on the beach Will. I'm on the beach!"

P.S.

Dear Mr. Shakespeare,

I'm so sorry, but I drew the darn Queen of Spades and since I never understood you, I just let my pen ramble on. May you rest in peace and not be disturbed by me again.

AM I BLUE?

On the optical spectrum, blue is located between violet and green. Green is my least favorite color - unless, of course, it has a president's face.

I don't know why blue is associated with sadness. I never feel sad when I see blue. From powder blue to my favorite, cobalt blue - any shade of blue makes me happy.

Through the years I have collected Mary Gregory glass. The American artist painted with white enamel, applying it to cobalt. Her charming illustrations were of children flying kites, blowing bubbles or simply playing.

When medical science discovered the chemical element for the treatment of cancer, cobalt was no longer used to color glass.

I enjoy my collection of bells, cruets, candle holders, candy jars and vases. The only problem is, the dark blue glass must be dusted every day. Sometimes I cheat and just blow the dust away - but lately I have less wind - so I'll end here and save my breath for the cobalt blue.

MYTHICAL CREATURE COMES TO LIFE

This morning started out like any other winter morning. Feeding the birds was an enjoyable duty. The crows always arrive first. The large, black, noisy birds let their feathered neighbors know, breakfast is being served. The starlings arrive next, only to be chased away by the sea gulls. They are definitely first in nature's pecking order. The crows put up a fight but their size is diminished by the gulls. As the birds swooped down to claim their morsel, I noticed a large shadow cast on the ground. Could it be a plane flying much too low? It was at that moment I saw the strange creature. It had the body of man and fierce, darting eyes. It's feathered head was cocked to one side as if listening. When it opened it's large beak, the pecking order was instantly changed. I held my breath. My eyes widened, not believing what I was seeing. I ran to get the camera trying to focus with shaking hands. "Say Cheese." I thought. It looked at me with frightened eyes. His ostrich-like legs began to crouch for takeoff. I lowered the camera without snapping the picture. I knew he had come a long way from the land of myth. I also knew he would return someday. I will wait.

WRITE FAIRY TALE FROM VILLAIN'S POINT OF VIEW RUMPELSTILSKIN SPEAKS

I don't know why I'm considered to be the villain of the story. The real villain is the Miller. He's the one who lied to the king, telling him his daughter could spin straw into gold. How dumb was the king to believe this? The king could also be the villain. He's the one who locks the miller's daughter in a room with a spinning wheel and tells her he will cut off her head if she can't spin the straw into gold. And they have the nerve to call me the villain!

Another thing, I know how to spin straw into gold but do you expect me to do it for nothing? What would the Gold Spinner Union have to say about that?

I'm the one who felt sorry for the girl and let her give me her beads as payment. What am I going to do with these cheap beads? I'm a little old man and I can spin gold. Beads, Indeed! The next room the king put her in was larger and to fill that room, she gave me her ring. It looked like a cracker Jack prize but I still did the job for her didn't I?

The next room was so big I had to work my tail off filling it. Don't you think

WORDS THAT COME TO MIND THIS MONTH

FEBRUARY	SHOVELING	MARCH	SCARES	GAS BILL
WINTER	PLOW	WICKED	GLOVES	WEATHER
COLD TEMPS.	DRIVING	OLD MAN WINTER	BOOTS	
SNOW	ICE	COATS	CONNECTICUT	

I no longer love the winter as I did when I was a kid. The cold temperatures make my bones ache. Even with aching bones, the snow needs to be shoveled. When I'm done, the plow comes and throws it back at me. I can't drive in bad weather because I really don't drive well on dry land, let alone ice and snow. February has only twenty-eight days and it does seem to be staying light a little longer. March is a wicked month with old man winter wearing out his welcome. If he stays around we sometimes have snow for Easter. I'll be glad to shed the coats, scarfs, gloves and boots as I wait to see the first Robin. Well, this is the price one pays living in Connecticut. Speaking of price, how about the price of gas? I can hardly lift the bill from the gas company. I've got to go - here comes the damn plow again. No sense crying over spilt snow. It's better than raking leaves!

G is for Groundhog
(Run Walter Run)

I miss Walter during the winter. Walter is a woodchuck better known as a groundhog. My husband and I adopted him four years ago or I should say he adopted us.

I was startled the first time I saw him. I never saw a groundhog before. Fascinated, I watched him lick an icicle hanging from the deck. Although groundhogs hibernate during the winter they do come out for water; unlike bears who are in a deeper state of hibernation.

Walter is the color of honey. He has soft brown eyes and long dark lashes. This timid creature would have melted Walt Disney's heart as it did mine. After considering many names, we named Walter after Mr. Disney. I'm sure they both like the idea.

Every spring Walter appears and flirts with sleepy eyes. I flirt back by offering peanut butter and jelly sandwiches. He sits up, holds the sandwich in his little hands and manages to get jelly all over his whiskers. Why would anyone want to harm this adorable animal? But oh, they do. You see Walter is a nuisance to my neighbors. They all plant vegetable gardens and Walter loves to raid them. He never eats the vegetables though. Why should he? He is well fed with whatever we are having for dinner. He eats everything from spaghetti to pot roast. His meal is always topped off with a large slice of watermelon or vanilla ice cream. So why is he raiding the vegetable gardens?

Not only is it his natural instinct like a cat bringing his prized catch home to his owner, Walter showers us with egg plant, tomatoes, zucchini and yellow squash.

I am grateful it is against the law in Milford to trap and kill wild life. Instead, 'have- a-heart' traps may be purchased at any veterinary hospital. The trapped animal is then to be escorted to a wooded area.

I've explained to Walter the danger of the traps and I guess he understands. In fact, why would he enter a baited contraption when the garden is plentiful? He did have one close call. He must have bumped against the trap door. When I heard it slam I yelled, "Run, Walter run."

Walter put Forest Gump to shame. After all Forest wasn't dragging a large purple eggplant.

Today is Groundhog Day. I looked for Walter in his tunnels under the foundation.

He did not appear. My house may collapse but Walter is warm and safe.

On Groundhog Day, Feb. 2nd.

The Unsinkable Suit

"You don't really expect me to wear this do you?" Essie asked her father hoping it was all a big joke, like the time he called to say he was bringing her home a big doll. It turned out to be a display mannequin with legs only to the knees. It served as a model for bras and girdles in the window of a lingerie shop. While delivering freight, he noticed it's head sticking out of a dumpster and brought the legless wonder home for Essie.

She looked at the new treasure he brought home today. This was not something he had found in a dumpster. In fact he had gone out of his way to get it for her. It came in a brown and black striped box with a ribbon tied around it. In large letters the box read, "The Unsinkable Swimsuit created for Buoyant Bathers."

Essie could not swim and somehow this ugly brown and black monstrosity was going to put her father's mind at ease. "Isn't it classy?" he beamed. "Did you notice it matches the box?" She definitely noticed it was in a class of it's own and scowled, "I'm not going to wear it." His voice rose, "Esther! Put it on now. Let's see how it fits."

"I feel like I'm inside a mattress. You don't understand. I can't wear this thing in front of my friends. You're punishing me for not be able to swim."

"Then stay home until you learn how to swim and the only thing I don't understand is why you can't swim. Your mother and I are strong swimmers and to make matters worse you were named after Esther Williams. Even Ginger can dog paddle." He said while giving the dog a pat on the head.

Essie knew her father was very serious but she sassed, "Let Ginger wear your wonderful swimsuit." She pictured the dog in the striped suit bobbing up and down in the waves.

She was now thinking of all the hard work she did earning credit to go on the beach trip with the playground recreational group. One point for attendance, two points for making a potholder and three points for each stupid wallet she laced together. When she reached the required forty-seven points, she was very excited to know a seat was reserved for her on the beach bus. What she didn't know was, in the morning she would have to wear the unsinkable suit. She went to her room and closed the door hard. She laid the swimsuit on the bed and reached for the scissors. Clipping the threads along the seam, she pulled the foam rubber out. She sewed the seam back together using the same whipstitch she learned while making wallets.

In the morning she put on the suit and pulled her clothes on over the entire mess. Her father was at the breakfast table. "Well, well, here comes the unsinkable Molly Brown. Do you have your suit on?"

"I sure do." She said holding her beach bag close to her. She was hoping he wouldn't notice how much the bag was bulging from it's contents of one towel and tons of foam rubber which she would watch float away as soon as she arrived at the beach.

BAA- BAA BLACK SHEEP

From my bedroom window I watched my new neighbor straggle with a few pieces of outdated furniture as he unload a small moving van.

Oddly, the decrepit old man seemed familiar but I couldn't place him. I only hoped he would be friendly and maintain his property.

"Bah," he loudly grumbled lifting the last piece. "Baa-baa" came an echo from inside the track. To my surprise, two curly black sheep jumped from the tail gate.

"Oh no," I gasped. "It's definitely time to go out and introduce myself."

I cut across the yard and began, "Excuse me neighbor..."

He reached out a bony hand. "I'm Ebeneezer Scrooge."

"Right," I replied. "And I'm Christmas Carol."

"Bah," he sputtered.

"Baa-baa," the sheep agreed.

"You know, Mr. Scrooge, this street is not zoned for livestock. Why do you have these sheep.?"

He answered, "You don't expect me to pay someone to mow the lawn do you? The sheep will keep the grass down and also fertilize. How much does your fancy landscaper charge for that?"

It suddenly dawned on me- this old codger came from the brilliant mind of Charles Dickens. He was indeed- the miserly Ebeneezer Scrooge.

"You belong in the year 1843. What are you doing here?" I asked.

"Bah" he began. "Baa-baa" die sheep bleated.

"The ghost of the futur e placed me here. He wept, "I want to go back."

"Well, good luck with that. It can't be soon enough for me."

The next morning in place of my missing newspaper, I found a note.. It read- "The ghost of Christmas past has taken me back. I know as a good neighbor you will tend to the sheep. I leave them in your care. Signed- Ebeneezer Scrooge.

I have since canceled my landscaper. "Baa-baa."

Why Oh Why Delilah

I never met a dog I didn't like – until I met Delilah.

My neighbor's little Shih-Tsu spent most of her summer days in my backyard and always left her business card before returning home.

Shih-Tsu means "little lion" in Japanese but I gave it a whole new meaning as I chased this three-pound, poor excuse for a dog out of my yard.

Delilah had a scrappy, defiant attitude. She yapped and kicked dirt at me with her skinny hind legs.

The war was on. "I'll fix you," I stormed. "I'll put up a fence."

It didn't take long for Delilah to win the first battle. She tunneled under the fence, looked me right in the eye and trampled on my begonias.

I shook a fist and did my best impression of General Douglas MacCarther. "You may have won the battle Shih-Tsu, but you haven't won the war."

I tried to stuff her back under the fence but she somehow puffed up and would not fit. I grabbed some rope and a bushel basket. I threw her in the basket and lowered her over the fence. By the time I put the ladder away – she was back.

I now ran one hundred and fifty feet of concrete edging along the bottom of the fence. It was back-breaking work, not to mention the expense in addition to the cost of the fence but I was determined to outsmart the pathetic mutt.

Then the unexpected happened – Delilah's family swimming pool collapsed. Thousands of gallons of rushing water took my entire fence down. I heard someone scream. It was me. Then I heard Delilah whimpering trying to dog paddle upstream against the current.

I watched her go under and evilly laughed, "Sayonara Shih-Tsu."

Her tiny head popped up, she looked at me with frieght and went under for the second time.

I waded through the raging river and pulled her out by the scruff of her scrawny neck. She held on to me like a child clinging to its mother.

Many years have passed since that day and I still wonder why, oh why, do I miss Delilah?

Not Even For Brenda Lee

I remember Brenda Lee singing, "I'm sorry – so sorry – please accept my apology."

Because of Brenda's exceptional voice, whatever she was sorry about, I immediately forgave her.

At a young age we are taught to forgive those who trespass against us. This of course, is not always easy. We have trouble letting go because it is hard to forget. Once burned we are afraid to step back into the fire. That seems logical to me, but in order to forgive we must let go.

This brings to mind the story of the monkey who put his hand in a narrow necked jar to get a walnut. His clenched fist tightened around the nut and he could not get his hand out. His frustration and suffering could have easily ended if he had just let go.

When I feel a deed is unforgivable, I _am_ that monkey. I can not accept an apology- not even for Brenda Lee.

The Circle In The Snow

It began with the sea gulls. Feeding them through the winter somehow felt rewarding.

I heard their eerie shrieks as they circled the house. I reached for the old, dented aluminum pot filling it with stale bread, leftover chopped meat, bananas, cereal and anything I could muster for the morning menu.

Bitterly cold, I draped a coat over my shoulders and headed toward the circle. I had as usual, shoveled a large round landing area for the gulls. It was soon to be filled with white fluttery wings and high- pitched voices as each gull battled for its share.

Through the frenzy I heard the unique sound of the brown gull perched on the roof. Many years had passed since his first visit to the circle in the snow and he had lost his place in the pecking order. Brownie knew I would feed him separately after the others flew back to the beach. My head tilted back, I smiled at him as he impatiently showed me his magnificent wingspan.

"You've still got it, Brownie old bird. I'll get you your breakfast now."

Heading back toward the house, a dark, frightening shadow cast over me. Brownie screeched a warning and swooped over my head. Was he trying to protect me or did he think there may be a morsel left in the pot? The shadow loomed lower as I pulled my neck into my shoulders and hunched putting the pot over my head. Was it a low flying plane? Were we being attacked? There was no engine sound, just an uncanny, leathery whispering from overhead.

I peeked from under the pot seeing an unbelievable creature standing in the circle. His enormous feathered body stood on muscular scaly legs twitching down to his massive talons. His jagged beak opened as he looked at me with reptilian eyes. He cocked his head and I cocked back sucking in my breath. I guess word had gotten around about the circle in the snow and I knew he had traveled from another dimension to reach it. I looked around for neighbors. I felt very alone. Where was everyone? I needed witnesses. No one would ever believe this.

I ran to the house knowing the creature's long strides could overtake me if he wished or was hungry enough and I was sure he was.

Shall I call the newspapers? I imagined them saying, "Sure lady, have a little more eggnog."

No sense calling the Peabody Museum. They would not believe me if I told them the ostrich is no longer the largest living bird on earth.

The only thing left to do was feed him and hope he would leave after his fill. I opened the refrigerator and saw two sirloin steaks waiting to be smothered in mushrooms for dinner. I watched the creature devour the meat He looked at me with gratitude before flying off into the unknown. From the rooftop, I heard Brownie screech and realized I indeed had a witness to what I saw in the circle in the snow.

CLANG-CLANG

This morning I awoke to a loud "Clang-Clang". "What the heck was that and why is it so cold in here?"

I had no idea what time it was. The digital clock was gone from my night stand. Shivering, I rushed to turn up the thermostat but found it also missing. Confused, I told myself I wasn't really awake yet and needed a strong cup of coffee. "Clang-Clang." Oh no, there it was again.

While searching for the electric coffee maker, a woman suddenly appeared in my kitchen carrying a galvanized bucket of coal. She shoveled scoops into a black-top stove then strained lifting a blue speckled cauldron. I realized my much needed coffee was going to take a while and asked, "Who are you?"

She did not answer and continued her work as if I wasn't there. I watched her slice bread and place it on a heated grate. "Where's my toaster?" I asked, while she reached for a stiff broom sweeping soot from the wooden floor.

"Why don't you use the vacuum cleaner?" Again no answer. "Clang-Clang."

"Well two can play this game," I said. "I have no time for you this morning. I must get to my writing class. I need to get dressed and warm the car."

I left her scrubbing laundry on a washboard with one hand and churning butter with the other. I noticed the water on the stove was boiling but no longer had time for coffee.

"I'll grab a cup at the Senior Center," I thought and hurried to get dressed.

My closet held only one long gray dress. I couldn't find my steam iron and tried to smooth it out with my hands. It was no use. I slipped the ugly dress on. At this point, I just didn't care and decided at least I was coordinated. The wrinkled dress seemed to match my face. "Clang-Clang."

I couldn't find the garage but an automobile was waiting. I hopped in noticing an extra pedal on the floor board. I never operated a standard shift or clutch before and knew I needed to find other means of transportation to the center. The way things were going maybe Paul Revere would come galloping down the road and I could hitch a ride with him. "Clang-Clang."

You will be glad to know, this is where my story ends and so does the "Clang-Clang". It's the end of the line for the trolley and it's obvious I am off of mine. "Clang-Clang."

PATIENCE OR PRISON

Returning home from writing class I pulled into the driveway and saw a woman with a small child sitting on my porch.

Although I had not seen her in nearly fifty years I recognized her unforgettable blue eyes.

Rushing from the car I squealed, "Patty, is it really you?"

"It sure is – but I haven't been called Patty since I was twenty-five years old. I'm Patricia now."

"Yes, I noticed that every year on your Christmas card but you'll always be Patty to me."

Dangling from her leg, a frowning little boy stuck out his tongue when I asked, "Who is this sweet child?"

Swelling with pride, Patty answered. "This is my great-grandson. Max, say hello to Grammy's friend."

Instead Max chose to kick me in the shins. Limping, I reached out to keep him at a distance only to be bitten on my right index finger. Mad Max had struck again.

"Maybe he should work for Quest" I suggested. "He's good at drawing blood."

Grammy defended. "Oh, he's only going through a stage. I'm sure he'll out-grow it. We need to have patience."

Patience has never been my strongest virtue but for some unknown reason I felt sorry for the boy.

I patted Max on the head to be sure there were no horns growing before leading him to my flower garden.

"Look at the pretty pansies I planted yesterday. Do you see their little faces?"

In fifteen seconds or less, Max pulled every plant out by the roots and threw them to the ground. Then, just to make sure they were no longer breathing, he jumped on their faces. So much for patience. I had to get rid of Max.

I numbly looked at Patty. "I'd like to invite you and Max in but my bed-ridden husband has a rare decease. The doctors are still not sure if it is contagious."

My only fear now was that my perfectly healthy husband would pull into the driveway at any moment.

"Well PATRICIA, I guess I'll see you in another fifty years and don't forget to bring Max – if he's not in prison."

Where To Ma'am?

I was born in the wrong century. I would be quite content to ride a horse and use the word "whoa" instead of the brake pedal. But Henry Ford had other plans and produced an affordable automobile scaring skittish horses from cobbled streets.

Unlike other teenagers, I never wanted to drive. Approaching the age of sixteen, my parents offered to buy me a new 1958 Oldsmobile. I immediately declined because I never felt comfortable in a car- let alone driving one. I was satisfied to ride the city bus or walk.

At the age of twenty-seven, I found it necessary to apply for a drivers license. To this day I don't know how I passed the test. And oh yes, after all these years, I still hate driving.

When I saw a driverless car on the market I decided to check it out. This ugly robotic vehicle looked like a bread box with headlights- not at all like the classy chromed Oldsmobile from the 50's.

I programmed the brainless wonder to take me around the block for a test drive. I shouted, "You're going too fast. Watch out for the child on the sidewalk. Do you see the pedestrian on the corner? Use your signal light. Do you have signal lights?"

By the time the bread box pulled back into the showroom, I was a total wreck.

The car salesman beamed, "Well, what do you think? Shall I wrap it up?"

I snapped, "Call me a taxi."

I soon realized the courteous cab driver was all I needed when he asked, "Where to ma'am?"

Mystery Solved

It was a mystery to me why Agatha Christie said, "When you see people looking ridiculous you realize just how much you love them."

Then, one day my husband walked into the kitchen where he found me chopping red peppers, celery and potatoes.

"Oh great," he said. "It's nice to see your famous potato salad is in my future."

I took a quick look at him. "Aren't those pants you're wearing a little large?"

He answered, "I'm only going to be working in the back yard. No one will see me."

He went out the door and I went back to the potato salad. It was time to add the mayonnaise but I couldn't get the lid off I whacked it and smacked it but it would not budge.

I opened the door and held the jar out "Can you put the rake down for a minute? I can't get the lid off this mayo."

He came running while holding up his pants. He gave the jar one turn and it popped open.

At that exact same moment his pants fell down around his ankles.

It was like watching a Buster Keaton movie. And as for Agatha Christie- mystery solved.

Measure Twice

Hector was the kind of guy who never measured twice. He claimed to always be right the first time.

The braggart boasted he knew everything from finances to politics to plant and animal life. He even knew who put the ram in the rama – lama – ding – dong.

Yes, Hector knew it all – until the day he saw a ferocious brown bear in his back yard clawing a cedar tree.

Hector made a fist and waved his arm. "Get away from there stupid bear. I'm not afraid of you. I know everything about bears. You are only searching for honey and will not harm me and I am never wrong.

Of course, there is a first time for everything.

Hector now has one arm and measures everything twice.

Passionate Passings

At the age of ten, I had a passion for beavers – yes beavers. I spent most of my time along the river bank near the marsh where busy beavers built dams and tunnels connected to their homes called lodges.

Every morning as I approached, the largest beaver slapped his wide tail against the muddy ground and warned others of my intrusion.

It seemed he was in charge and I always greeted him with, "No need for alarm Mayor – it's only me."

Then, one day he sat up and showed me his large teeth – not as a threat, but as a welcome. He waddled out of the water and placed a twig at my feet. I believed he passed his position on to me. Indeed, I was now the mayor of Beaver Town.

With teenage years quickly approaching my passion for beavers diminished.

Like most teenagers of the fifties, my new passion was dancing to rock and roll music. My favorite entertainer was Chuck Berry – and that is where it ended as my newest and strongest passion in life for homemaking and motherhood took over.

Today I have a passion for writing and congregating with other writers who understand that special passion.

And who knows – maybe someday I will tell them about my passion for beavers.

Where Are You Alexander Graham Bell

Remember the days when you dialed a phone number and someone said, "Hello".

Today push button phones have replaced the dial. A recording says, "If you want such and such, push this or if you need this push that."

I recently was without phone service for seventeen days. I could hear the party calling in, but they could not hear me. I called telephone repair service and listened to instructions. "If your problem is this, push that. If that is your problem, push this."

There was no button for my problem so I stayed on the line listening to music until a voice said, "This is Marcie. What is your problem?"

I tried to explain while wondering if Marcie was a real person. Then she said, "I can not hear you. What is your problem?"

My vocal cords strained. "That is my problem."

She gave orders not to hang up and she would fix it over the line. Then I heard "click" and was sure Marcie was out to lunch. I redialed repair service.

"This is Gregory. What is the problem? I cannot hear you. What is the problem?"

Immediately I knew Gregory was out to lunch with Marcie.

The next three calls introduced me to Harold, Grace and Joanne. Believe me, they were at the same buffet. It was Sharma who said she would send out a pole man. He went up the pole in a bucket, did his thing and left. The phone problem remained the same. Once again I called telephone repair.

"This is Thomas. What is your problem?"

Thomas told me his records showed a pole man was there and fixed it.

I sputtered, "Good grief. I must be in the twilight zone. Can you hear me?"

"Barely," he answered.

I pleaded. "Send him back. Please send him back."

The next day I watched him ascend in the bucket. When he left I made another call to repair service. When he pulled up for the third time I wanted to climb the pole myself. Instead I scolded. "Don't you dare leave until this phone is fixed. Come in when you're done playing with the wires."

He did and told me to call someone to see if they could hear me. I shouted to my friend. "Can you hear me?"

"Not any better than the last two weeks," she answered.

Surprised, the pole man said, "I think you must need a new jack."

"Well," I answered. "Now we're getting somewhere. Go ahead, put one in."

"Oh I don't carry parts on the truck. I'm a pole man."

He pointed to his shirt. It read Louis. Pole man.

Desperate, I said, "listen Lou, please look in your truck for a jack. I'll give you something nice if you come back with one. He did. I handed him a shiny apple and said, "nice, huh?"

He replaced the jack. I uncrossed my fingers when he said, "Well, I did all I could. It's not the jack. I think you need a new phone. You'll have to buy one and install it yourself. The phone company no longer installs phones."

I choked. "You don't understand. The phone company owns this phone."

"No way," he said and bit into the apple.

I pictured tomorrow's headlines. 'Senior citizen murders pole man.' Beaten, I handed Lou a banana and said, "If I were you I'd go now."

Back at square one, I called telephone repair.

"This is Rose. What is your problem?"

"Ah hah. They ran out of people. Flowers are answering now." I threw myself at the mercy of the flower. "Please Rose help me."

She answered. "It sounds like you need a new phone. No problem. The phone company owns the phone. I will send you a new one with a postage free mailing bag to return the old one."

I now had a new phone and it worked. But there was no mailing bag, so I put the old phone in a box and applied the mailing sticker. The postal clerk said, "We don't mail phones. You have to take it to United

Parcel. They charged me $4.50 for free mailing to the phone company. I just didn't care and here's where my story should end. But oh no, I am now being charged for two phones. The phone company claims they never received the old one. They told me to call the postal service complaint department.

I picked up the receiver of my new phone. A recording said, "Push this if you want that or push that if you want this."

I followed instructions until a real person said, "You have reached postal service complaints. What is your problem?"

POETRY

WHY I'M LATE

There was an elephant in my driveway
and I couldn't back out the car.
When I looked in my side view mirror, it warned,
"elephants appear closer than they are."

I backed out nice easy hoping the elephant
had shrunk.
We now were at a standoff
facing trunk to trunk.

With the beast I tried to reason,
telling him I would be late,
if he didn't move his tail
and all the rest of his weight.

He thought this quite funny, threw his head
back tusks to sky.
T'was then we made a deal,
the elephant and I.

"If you could just inhale and get a
little thinner,
when I get home tonight,
I'll have you in for dinner."

He flapped his ears from side to side agreeing
he would wait.
There was an elephant in my driveway
And that is why I'm late!

Protest Protest Every Villanelle

Protest, protest every villanelle
Frustration singes raw nerve ending
Indentations on the skin of Hell

Eardrums pounding trapped inside bell
Rigid bones snapping, breaking, unbending
Protest, protest every villanelle

Locked inside a frigid cell
Frosty fire rages still stoking, tending
Indentations on the skin of Hell

Fiery icicles never sell
Dizzy, floating, always pending
Protest, protest every villanelle

Flowing blood begins to gel
Broken heart in need of mending
Indentations on the skin of Hell

Floating, gasping in a well
Borrowing patience never lending
Protest, protest every villanelle
Indentations on the skin of Hell

WHERE'S THERE'S SMOKE

"Disgraceful" I yelled when I opened the door
Unbuttoned blouse falls to the floor
An orgy of arms entangled-hugging
Legs bent askew twisted-tugging
Trousers stiffen-unzipped yet warm
Clinging argyles mate through whirling storm
Vibration now quiets-noise seems to die
Relieved I am happy
My laundry is dry

INDEPENDENCE DAY

Where did my independence go?
Have they changed the bill of rights?
My children tell me what to do
And keep me in their sights

Hired strangers take care of me
They go through all my things
My children who are cabbages
Believe they now are kings

I still can make a cup of tea
And play a game of gin
But they're always fussing over me
And seem to let me win

They treat me like a child
And tuck me in at night
With all my pillows piled
They won't shut off the light

I listen to the footsteps
I count them one to ten
Then I kick off all the covers
Now I'm in charge again.

SONNET NUMBER ONE

Shall I pretend that you are near?
I search for signs of wisdom's eyes
I listen for words to unbind fear,
And taste the sweet until it dies.
Sometimes the cold of hell does bite.
I pull you back to keep me warm.
I reach for you 'til all seems right
Safe from brown bees deadly swarm.
No need pretense to claim a place
Each day the steps are growing less
Soon I will see your gentle face
A joyous heart beats without stress
So long as I can hope for this
Life is just a passing kiss.

SALEMA BEARS IT ALL

A haggard old witch named Salema,
lived in a very old cave.
She shared her dark and dingy abode
with a big brown bear named Dave.

When Salema was a young witchlet
and Davey just a cub,
they went gathering roots and lots of newts
and put them in a tub.

Back at the cave they boiled and mixed
and blended and stirred them up.
Then they poured the potion
and drank two or three from a cup.

Now, when Salema looked at Davey
she threw him a big wink.
The bear was so embarrassed,
his big brown nose turned pink!

When Salema's beautiful child was born,
she named her Briar Rose.
She had fuzzy brown ears, a stubby tail,
and oh yes, a large pink nose!

I'M REALLY NOT MYSELF TODAY

I'm really not myself today.
I can't imagine why.
I smile at all who pass my way and never sulk or sigh.

I don't feel old,
don't feel the cold,
no aches and pains I bear.
No one needs to shout at me,
now that I can hear.

My vision has returned to me.
And I can even bend my knee.
And, oh, I'm not so crotchety.
Can't you see? Could it be?

I'm really not myself today.
Today's the day, I passed away!

WHO'S DRIVING?

She's on the phone
just calling home.
Who's driving?

A comb through the hair
mascara repair
waving wet nails
to dry in the air.
But who's driving?

A reach for the bagels
then she finagles
some cream cheese,
squeezing hot strofoam
between naked knees.

Oh please-oh please
Who's driving?

MASTERS OF PEACE

Artist, man your palette!
Hold your brushes high in hand.
Paint for us a world of peace.
Make us understand.

Poet, write your rhyming words
and take away our breath.
Write of total harmony,
not battlefields and death.

Sculptor, mold your cakes of clay.
Unarm the man and let him play,
With smiling children by his side
in a world of peace and pride.

Composer, write your symphony
with flutes and violin.
The instruments will tell the world
war is the greatest sin.

Writer, write your story.
Take your pen and make it clear,
that heaven is a distance,
but hell is very near.

Masters, use your expertise
And help the world to find
a human race, full of peace
with unity of mind.

NEWS ARTICLE

Pushing science to the brink
Making monkeys green and pink
I guess they tired of cloning sheep
Their baas put scientists to sleep

Jelly fish and kangaroos
Kitty cats and cockatoos
Put them in a jar an shake
Out will come a feathered snake

I pray the Lord will intervene
Before our souls are glowing green

WHERE IS YOUR TWIN?

In my mirror lives my twin
She smiles back when I look in.
We are twelve and full of fun
When I look back we're twenty-one.
I'm jealous of the face I see
She's much prettier than me.
I look again, now thirty-three
A serious face is what I see.
Then again at forty two
Where's the twin that I once knew?
I never noticed she had gray hair.
Being twins just isn't fair.
She looks quite old at fifty-six
A face a surgeon-couldn't fix
In my mirror lives my twin
Glad I'm not her when I look in!

TEN THING IN A CLOSET

1.- Coats
2.- Flashlight
3.- Spare Batteries
4.- Hat
5.- Scarf
6.- Gloves
7.- Umbrella
8.- Pocket Book
9.- Light Bulbs
10.- Sweater

My winter closet is such a sight
Not only coats, a big flashlight.
The batteries are probably dead.
A fedora hat for husband's head.
A leather glove without a mate
To find it's match will have to wait
Until the spring when I will clean
Oh, a scarf I haven't seen.
Umbrella hanging on a hook.
And yes, there is my pocket book
A box of light bulbs on the shelf above
And the old blue sweater that I love.

SELECT TWO WORDS FROM DICTIONARY AT RANDOM USE THESE WORDS FIRST AND LAST

I was hoping to draw a heart from the deck today as it is Valentine Day. I drew the fire of clubs which means I have to write a piece with CHENILLE as my first word and RUST as my last word. This is going to be tough!

CHENILLE was a type of spread
That laid across my tiny bed.
It kept me warm through pox and mumps.
I loved to feel its nubs and bumps.
Many washings made it worn,
So into pieces it was torn.
The rags were used to clean and dust
On metal things, it took off <u>rust</u>!

Tis the first week of January
And all through my mind
Dance themes of my lifetimes
In genres of every kind.

ROCK-A-BYE-BABY

As I lay in my bassinet
Goodman plays his clarinet
My crib begins to swing and sway
With Glenn Miler and Sammy Kaye

Crib gone-a child size bed
Big band music now is dead
Bee-bop fills the empty space
Dizzy Gillespie takes its place

And on vibes Hampton rocks
Nylon stockings - gone bobby socks

Hip-hop and Bubblegum take the place
Of every cool musician's face
Then it happens-Rock and Roll
Creeps into my heart and soul

Elvis, king on my queen size bed
Love me tender is what he said

Rockin' and reelin' teen years fly
Then I knew the reason why
Double bed not far away
Still rock and roll is here to stay

Everly brothers put on hold
Bye-bye love I was told

Radio playing while making bed
New sound they call Rap
Over the pillows I smooth the spread
And call this music crap

My final bed still full of hope
They'll bring back some day
The music loved in my crib
The songs of yesterday
Carol Ruggiero

THE BEASTLY BAND

An African Antelope on Alto sax
Baboons Banging Bongos Bound to Bare Backs

Chimpanzees and Cheetahs Click Castanets
Drumming Dogs Dancing, Drooling Duets

Eels Electrify Elegant stage
Four Foolish Frogs Fiddle in rage

Gangly Giraffes, Giddy Geese, carps
Hysterical Hyenas Haul Heavy Harps

Inchworms measure Instrumental feet
Joyous Jackals Jitterbug Jumping to beat

Kangaroos Kick Keeping up with the rest
Llama spits Lyrics Leaving a mess

Monkeys Make Mandolin Melodies go ape
Nestlings in nightshirts tweet as they wake

Owl hoot-hoots holding a stick
Penguins Parade while Piccolos Pick

Quivering Quail-Quills float in the air
Rhythmic Raccoons bring up the Rear

Scampering Skunk Sings Stinking Song
Tiger's Tubas oom-pahs Too long

Under Unfailing Uproarious moon
Vigilant Vixen Veils Violin's tune

Wolves Waving Wands When Woodwinds blow
Xylophone played by a cat named Joe

Yellow Yaks Yield giving the way
To Zealous Zebra and the Zither he plays.

If I HAD A BROTHER

If I had a brother
I'd knit him warm sweaters
And argyle socks
I'd keep all his letters
Tucked away in a box
At my holiday table
His seat next to mine
I'd toast him and clink
Crystal glasses of wine
I'd fuss with his hair
I'd pet his cheek
And recall the day he fell in the creek
We'd laugh 'til we cry
My brother and I
Remembering childhood days
Gone by.
I'd hug him tightly
When he had to go
Just one second more
I'd love him so
My friend-my hero
Never another
He'd always be near
Oh, if I had a brother

FRIENDSHIP

It was the wooden bucket
Filled with water from the well
That pulled Maria to the ground
For that is where she fell

Hanging laundry in the next yard
Junie saw her fall
And ran to help Maria
Understanding after all

I am just a woman too
Your burden's much too weighted
Together we can lift the load
And other chores we've hated

Each held the bucket's handle
It lifted now with ease
Then together hung the laundry
Blowing in the breeze

They worked, laughed and talked
Of mates and kids and things
And problems seemed to fade
It's just what friendship brings

The bucket's never heavy
With a friend who understands
She reaches for the handle
In turn you hold her hand

HELLO – HELLO

She lives in a corner of my room
And never disagrees.
If I say blue is red or red is blue
She concurs this is true.

She sounds like me when I am mad
Cries like me when I am sad
Laughs like me when I am glad
Best dam friend I ever had.

I say, "hello"
"Hello" she greets
If I lie
She will repeat.

She never fails- thinks the way I do.
When I have nothing to say
She is silent too
My echo.

THE REVENGE OF THE LLAMAS

A neighbor by the name of Grace
Complained about my llama
So I brought two more home
To aggravate her drama
If the trio neared her property
She'd whack them with her broom
Frightened eyes filled with fear
Knowing Grace meant doom
She'd jab them with her pitch fork
She'd twist the small one's ear
They quickly learned to run away
Whenever Grace was near
Then one day a great wind storm
Flatten Grace's shed
Burying her 'neath the wooden wreck
She was all but dead
The llamas seemed to titter
As I tried to set Grace free
'Cuz the lumber was too heavy
And would not budge for me
Spying a thick coil of rope
I called the llamas near
Tied it to the wooly beasts
And whacked them on the rear
"Pull" I ordered "Pull again."
And that is what they did
'Til Grace was free from all debris
With only a bump on her head
She reached to hug the llamas
"Thank you so" said Grace
The gentle llamas puckered up
And spit right in her face.

The little red house on the hill
Oh yes - I remember it still
Where the child at play
In my room learned to pray
In the little red house on the hill
Where my Mom and Dad made me happy
then sad
As the years swiftly took them away
But I think of it still
The red house on the hill
And the wonderful times
that I had.

A PIECE OF LINT

A little bird with a speckled head
flew into my dryer vent,
And when she came out, in her tiny beak,
she was holding a piece of lint.
While looking around for the enemy,
she twitched and checked the scene.
If she could make it to the tree,
her nest would soon begin.
All day she built with twigs and string
and pieces of thatch and just anything.
A little dirt, a drop of dew
would hold the grout and make the glue.
The final touch was a piece of a sock,
was then she screamed,
"Crow! Crow, at two o'clock."
She puffed herself up,
her wing to her heart.
Too late, alas,
Crow had pulled the nest apart.
She flew to the nearest telephone wire
and made a call to her home owners insuranc.
Some vulcher answered and squawked,
"Oh no, oh no, you're not covered for crow.
It's really nature's way, you know.
I'm very sorry about that,
maybe if it were the family cat..."
But crow oh no!
The little bird with the speckled head,
flew into my dryer vent,
and in her beak, when she came out,
she was holding a piece of lint.

SPAGHETTI - CHAIR - BATHTUB

Gather 'round the table
Pull up your favorite <u>chair</u>
I'll try if I am able
To make this fable clear
A lad named Eddie <u>Spaghetti</u>
Loved a maiden young and fair
His dreams were full of Betty
Visions saw her everywhere
In his closet - under his bed
and in his <u>bathtub</u> too
His hope – get Betty to the altar
Where she would say "I do".
After years of courting Betty
He watched his dream come true
And Eddie and Betty Spaghetti
built a little house for two.
Then Betty smiled at Eddie
That's when Eddie knows
It's time for pattering footsteps
With tiny little toes
Now Betty and Eddie Spaghetti
Are raising Spaghetti???

THE HEARTLESS ROBOT

I built him from some scraps of metal
A dented hubcap and a tarnished kettle.

Welded washers to his chest
Bent chicken wire to make his vest.

His arms were made from a toothless rake
And a garden hose hung like a snake.

Rolling casters served as feet
My robot now was really neat.

He began to coo like a mourning dove
That was when I fell in love.

But of me - he'd have no part
Because my robot had no heart.

To Helen Chapin Williams
on her birthday

THEN SHE HEARS THE MUSIC PLAY

She leans back in her easy chair
To rest her tired eyes
On her brow a wisp of hair
Flutters when she sighs
Then she hears the music play

Dangling from her ears
Prisms all aglow
Icy chandeliers
And sequins head to toe
Then she hears the music play

The band begins to swing
Her skirt begins to rise
She wears a diamond ring
And sparkles in her eyes
Then she hears the music play

Some Johnnie dances her to the floor
She smiles at handsome him
He seems to know she wants more
As the lights go very dim
Then she hears the music play

She sits up in her easy chair
Not a dream- like once before
There is glitter everywhere
And one earring on the floor
Then she hears the music play

Writers Unlimited

No School Today

Go back to bed
My mother said
There is no school today

With drifting snow
I knew by noon
I could go out and play

I'd build a fort
With blocks of snow
And a snowman standing guard

Then I'll pull my sled
Up hill
And sleigh across the yard

My cheeks turned red
To match my nose
And soon my mitten fingers froze

The sun went down
Much too soon
A bright outline around the moon

An omen – tomorrow more snow on the way
I could only hope and pray
That once again
I'd hear Mom say

Go back to bed
No school today

A Stinking Poem

Grubs and bugs
Bugs and grubs
That is what I eat
I rout them with my pointed nose
And grab them with my feet

Some say I am quite pretty
Resembling a cat
But I am not a kitty
I never will be that

When I walk I seem to be
Just a little drunk
And so the old cliché
He's drunker than a skunk

I have a famous uncle
His name – Pepe La Pew
And when it comes to amour
Oooh – la- la – He knows just what to do

So when I lift my tail
Run – don't stop to think
'cuz like this reeking poem
You will also stink.

THE TALE OF HENRÍ LA COUZ

This is the tale of Henrí La Couz
Who lived in a loft
With holes in his shoes

With palette and easel
And brushes and such
His stipend meager
He didn't sell much

Some called him crazy
Others a jerk
He paints 'cuz he's lazy
Knows nothing of work

Seascapes - landscapes
And nature 'tho crude
A cow in a pasture
And even a nude

Still he sold nothing
Starvationjset in
And Henrí La Couz
Grew bony and thin

Every penny he had
He used to buy paint
And while at his easel
Fell fatally faint

His artwork was stored
In rafters above
'Til a curious boarder
Gave it a shove

All called his work genius
Worth lots of bread
But what good now
Poor Henri is dead

If I Were Born An Animal

If I were born a tiger
I'd wear stripes upon my chest
I'd growl and stalk
and strut my stuff
showing off to all the rest

If I were a monkey
I'd swing high up in a tree
I'd do my monkey business
While others laughed at me

If I were a dog
I'd learn to shake a paw
Or I'd like to be a shiny crow
Just sit around and caw

When I am feeling lazy
I long to be a sloth
Or maybe I'd flit around
like a hungry moth

I guess when all is said and done
I'd like to be a cat
and just curl up purr-fectly
on some kitty lover's lap

Carol Ruggiero
Ace of Clubs

I Love...

Little gray burros
Timid and shy
Jacks and Jennies
With dark lashed eyes

At a county fair
I read a sign
"One burro for sale"
He could be mine

With long ears he listened
As I told him the plan
He'd live in my backyard
I'd name him Dan

I with a shovel
The burro just played
He chewed on the house
Hee-hawed and brayed

An angry neighbor called to say
"Get rid of that donkey now-today
He knocked down the fence
And ate all my grass."

I love my burro
But he's a pain in the ass.

MASTERS OF PEACE

Artist, man your palette!
Hold your brushes high in hand.
Paint for us a world of peace.
Make us understand.

Poet, write your rhyming words
and take away our breath.
Write of total harmony,
not battlefields and death.

Sculptor, mold your cakes of clay.
Unarm the man and let him play,
With smiling children by his side
in a world of peace and pride.

Composer, write your symphony
with flutes and violin.
The instruments will tell the world
war is the greatest sin.

Writer, write your story.
Take your pen and make it clear,
that heaven is a distance,
but hell is very near.

Masters, use your expertise
And help the world to find
a human race, full of peace
with unity of mind.

MAMA PUT A FIVE INSIDE MY MITTEN

Mama put a five inside my mitten,
on a cold and snowy night so long ago.
"Dad is running late tonight,
and I must tend the stew.
If we're to have a Christmas tree,
I need to count on you."

"Go down the hill and take two rights.
You'll see the man with the Christmas lights,
strung all around the trees.
Get the best a five will bring.
Don't let him sell you some skimpy thing.
Not too big but not too small.
Be sure the top is nice and tall,
so we can place our shiny star."

I took my sled.
I took some rope.
My young heart was full of hope,
that I would buy the perfect tree,
for my Mama, Dad and me.

The five inside my mitten
seemed to cut into my hand,
as I pulled the empty sled
across the snowy land.

I saw the lights.
I saw the trees.
And then I saw - the man!
Thick woolen cap,
a heavy coat,
a ragged glove, on just one hand.

"Business not so good this year," he bellowed to another.
The fear inside me rose,
but then I thought of Mother.
"Pick the best a five will bring.
Don't let him sell you some skimpy thing."

The smell of spruce, the smell of pine,
made me want them all.
Just then, I saw the perfect tree.
Not too short and not too tall.

I squeezed the five and then I knew,
I must be very thrifty.
"How much Is this one?" I asked the man.
T'was then he growled, "Six- fifty."
I looked at his dark beard
with the snow upon It,
as he yelled, "Well, do ya wan' it?"

"Too much," said I "for such a tree.
It's not that nice," I lied.
"I'll take six and not a penny less.
That was when he sighed.

"I've a five inside my mitten,
My Mama put it there.
I think this tree is worth no more.
I hope you will be fair."

"Take this nice one." He grabbed a tree,
as it's yellow needles fell.
Now his turn, to lie to me.
But really, I could tell.

I slipped the warm five from my mitten.
"Give me the five." He snarled. "Take the tree."

He reached for his box on the shelf.
Stuck in the five and said to me,
"Tie it on yourself!"

So, home I trudged,
with my fine tree.
Mama would be so proud of me.
And that she was, as Dad came trough the door.

"Where did you get such a perfect tree?"
He looked at her.
She smiled at me.
"I'll tell you Dad,
of the night I've had."
I stood therey, oh so smitten.
"It all began tonight, dear Dad.
When Mama put a five inside my mitten."

RUINED FEATHERS – FLOATED LIKE PRAYERS - DIAMOND STRUNG

A lonely loved - starved spinster
Saved a lifetime for a trip
Now tucked into a cabin
Aboard a sailing ship

When flowers were delivered
She thought it a mistake
The attached note read - please meet me
On the upper deck - I'll wait.

The note was signed - Henry
With an ink blot from the pen
Her shaky hands now steadied
As she read the note again

She wore a feathered boa
Strung diamonds through her hair
She wondered what he looked like
Or did she really care?

She grabbed the note signed Henry
And stuffed it in her purse
Then waited on the upper deck
And guessed that she was first

The wind - it started kicking
The rain - its pellets threw
Her feathered boa ruined
Her diamonds feel askew

She tore the note signed Henry
And threw it in the wake
Then watched it float like hopeless prayers
As her heart began to ache

Tomorrow she will play again
How well she knew the game
She'll cry herself to sleep tonight
'Cuz Henry never came.

In My Day

A simple black dress
and a strand of pearls
Separated the boys from the girls
Today's styles are such
that I just don't think much
of the combat boots girls wear
Boys prancing in clogs
while girls look like hogs
exposing their derriéré
Navels peek out to flirt
from under a shirt
where a silver ring hands from some skin
with tattoos galore
need I say more
piercings indeed are a sin
This new generation
leaves no imagination
except is it a boy or a girl
Give me the simple black dress
and oh yes - oh yes
a little strand of pearls.

A FOOLS PRAYER

I prayed someday to marry a king
But a jester turned my head
He made me laugh and want to sing
So I married him instead.

The king warned - You'll be sorry
for the jester is a fool
He'll rouse at night - leaving you alone
while he breaks each vow and rule.

You'll listen for the silver bells
he wears upon his shoes
Their jingle tells he's home at last
breath reeking from the booze

Yes, I prayed someday to marry a king
with a castle and a pool
But alas - too late I clearly see
It's not the jester who's the fool..

TRAVELLER

Atop of me sits Bobby Lee
A finer man will never be
I'm so proud he's chosen me
of all in his fine cavalry.

Both our coats confederate gray
we share the battles day by day
He talks to me, I hear him pray
On to Gettysburg today

The war is done
The North has won
Though sad, he mounts with pride
We rode to Appomattox
The day the General cried

Behind the casket my gait now slow
I hear his voice, I miss him so
There is a resting place for me
I will soon be next to he
That is where I long to stay
In my coat confederate gray
With my Robert E. Lee

POLITICS OR POETRY

Long before Mother Goose, Longfellow or Dr. Seuss
A caveman chiseled into stone
Near a cave he called his own

"Ug-Ug" he wrote upon a rock
"Og-Og" was his next line
These grunting words were all he knew
But he expressed them fine

Others gathered 'round the stone
To read and point with sticks
"Ug-Ug, Og-Og" the words went on
Now known as politics

LET'S MAKE SOUP

Writing is like making soup. Writers' Unlimited workshops supply the finest ingredients beginning with a hearty stock. The instructor stirs and stimulates with a clever 'quick-write'.

The pot begins to boil and is lowered to simmer as students add a dash of creativity along with a large spoonful of friendship. They listen, learn and blend their unique voices.

Like all good soup, the results are always warm and comforting.

Carol Ruggiero

An overweight lady named Jane
Boarded a passenger plane
She squeezed into her seat
And dangled her feet
While her flabby tighs
Screamed in pain

She wiggled - She giggled
'Til the seat fell apart
She fell to the floor
holding her heart

"What shall I do?" she cried to the bunch.
They answered, "Just stay there.
Soon they'll serve lunch.

She ate from two trays
Meat loaf and peas
She sprinkled on pepper
Which made her sneeze
She caused great commotion
flying over the ocean
The plane went into a dive
But don't worry - they're still all alive
'Cuz overweight Jane proved to be nice
And offered her body
As a floatation device.

ABOUT THE AUTHOR

CAROL ANN RUGGIERO, MY WIFE OF 35 YEARS, CAME TO THE WORLD OF WRITING ALMOST BY ACCIDENT.

ONE DAY, HER BEST FRIEND, DORTHY, ASKED HER IF SHE WOULD LIKE TO JOIN A WRITING GROUP IN THE LOCAL SENIOR CENTER.

AT THAT TIME, CAROL'S INTEREST WAS IN CERAMICS. IN THIS PURSUIT, SHE WON SEVERAL AWARDS.

AFTER SEVERAL REFUSALS, CAROL JOINED THE WRITING GROUP AND THERE SHE STAYED FOR THE NEXT 20 YEARS.

CAROL'S WRITING STYLE IMMEDIATELY DREW PRAISE IN THE GROUP. SHE ENJOYED TELLING A STORY OR TURNING A SERIOUS TOPIC ON ITS HEAD WITH A SURPRISE ENDING. CAROL USUALLY REFUSED TO WRITE ABOUT HER PERSONAL LIFE EXCEPT IN "HEART WARMING" CASES.

TRUTH BE TOLD, SHE SUFFERED MANY TRAGIC EVENTS SUCH AS THE LOST OF CHILDREN AND YET SHE WAS ALWAYS READY

AND PLEASED TO SMILE AT A GREETING AND LISTEN TO ANY CALL FOR HELP.

SHE WAS PETITE (FOUR FT 10 INCHES), PITHY IN HER SPEECH AND POSSESSED A HUGE AMOUNT OF COMMON SENSE.

WE PLAYED SCRABBLE AT LEAST TWICE DAILY AND JEOPARDY! BECAME A NIGHTLY AFFAIR. SHE WAS CONSTANTLY WORKING ON CROSSWORDS AND LOGIC PROBLEMS.

I LOVED HER DEEPLY. SHE WAS THE BEST WIFE ANY MAN COULD HOPE FOR. ETERNITY WITH HER WOULD BE HEAVEN.

"Carol Ann, I will be home soon."

CPSIA information can be obtained
at www.ICGtesting.com
Printed in the USA
JSHW020917150822
29156JS00005B/17